The Economics, Law, and Public Policy of Market Power Manipulation

THE ECONOMICS, LAW, AND PUBLIC POLICY OF MARKET POWER MANIPULATION

Stephen Craig Pirrong
John M. Olin School of Business
Washington University

Kluwer Academic Publishers
Boston/London/Dordrecht

Distributors for North America:
Kluwer Academic Publishers
101 Philip Drive
Assinippi Park
Norwell, Massachusetts 02061 USA

Distributors for all other countries:
Kluwer Academic Publishers Group
Distribution Centre
Post Office Box 322
3300 AH Dordrecht, THE NETHERLANDS

Library of Congress Cataloging-in-Publication Data

Pirrong, Stephen Craig, 1959 -
The economics, law, and public policy of market power manipulation / by Craig Pirrong.
p. cm.
Includes bibliographical references and index.
ISBN 0-7923-9762-2
1. Commodity futures--United States. 2. Speculation--United States. 3. Restraint of trade--United States. I. Title.
HG6049.P57 1996
332.63'28--dc20 96-26901
CIP

Printed on acid-free paper.

Printed in the United States of America

To Terry, Renee, and Genevieve, who have supported me in my work. In memory of Beauregard, my loyal companion during the years I labored on this project.

Table of Contents

CHAPTER 1
INTRODUCTION

1.1. From Black Friday to the Sumitomo Squeeze: An Overview of Market Manipulation and Its Importance

On Friday, September 24, 1869, United States Secretary of the Treasury George S. Bouton ordered the sale of $4 million in gold from the vaults of the Sub-treasury in New York City. As news of this seemingly inconsequential action[1] reached Wall Street's "gold room" at the New York Gold Exchange--a lavishly decorated edifice that anticipated the dawning Gilded Age--the teeming traders there burst into a frenzy of activity. The price of gold in terms of United States paper currency--"greenbacks"--which just before the news of Bouton's order had hovered at $160 per ounce, plummeted as a wave of panic selling inundated the stunned gold bull speculators.[2] Within minutes, the price had fallen to $133 per ounce, and would never again reach the heady heights that it had attained on Friday morning.[3] The first of the "Black" days of American finance--Black Friday--had occurred.

The effects of the Treasury Secretary's announcement were so spectacular because the sale of gold (even in such a trivial quantity; the total amount of gold in circulation at the time equaled $142 million) came at the peak of one of the most audacious commodity manipulations ever attempted: the Gould and Fisk gold deal. These two titans--made notorious by Henry Adams in Chapters of Erie--had attempted to corner the gold market in and around New York by accumulating claims on gold far in excess of the free stocks available in the city to satisfy these claims. Only Bouton's sale of government gold (and the implicit threat to sell more) ended this brazen raid.

The Fisk-Gould corner heralded an entire era of manipulation. For the next fifty odd years the financial history of major American commodity markets--the Chicago Board of Trade (CBT), the New York Cotton Exchange (NYCE), the New Orleans Cotton Exchange (NOCE), and the New York Produce Exchange (NYPE) prominent among them--is in large part a chronicle of corners and squeezes both spectacularly successful and doomed. I document 121 manipulations (successful and failed) in grains and meats at the CBT and twenty-eight corners in cotton in the period 1868 through 1921.[4] Corners were also common on financial markets. Before 1900, financial operators frequently cornered railroad stocks traded on the New York Stock Exchange. The names of men like Armour, Leiter, Patten, Drew, Vanderbilt, and Gould, while obscure today, were well known to the financial sophisticate and the rustic farmer alike because their actions in the wheat pit on the CBT, the cotton ring in New York, or on the stock exchange had effects that extended from those hectic, cramped, and often inscrutable confines to the world beyond.

These manipulations were extremely disruptive. Their effect on prices was sometimes severe. The June 1868 wheat corner (1868 was termed "the year of corners") forced the price in Chicago 10 percent above prices in New York, even though the price at the latter point in nonmanipulated conditions was 10 to 15 percent above the Chicago price. Moreover, the price of #2 wheat (the deliverable grade) was 22 percent above the price of superior #1 wheat; immediately after the end of June (and the expiration of the corner) the price of wheat in Chicago fell 21 percent.[5] Nor was this particularly exceptional. To take two examples, a June 1872 oats corner caused a 28 percent inflation in the price of this grain while an 1876 barley corner forced the May contract price 45 percent above the June contract price, even though the June price should typically exceed the May due to the cost of carrying inventory.[6]

Unsurprisingly, these extreme price distortions caused a variety of acute economic dislocations. The documented effects include exceptionally large flows of stocks of grain into Chicago;[7] artificial shortages of rail cars and congestion in Chicago freight yards;[8] flows of grain and provisions from markets that Chicago typically shipped to;[9] the failure of banks that had extended credit to futures traders who were bankrupted in a corner;[10] the idling of grain carrying lake vessels (because stocks were hoarded in Chicago in anticipation of a squeeze);[11] excessive basis volatility and consequently poor hedging performance;[12] and the temporary idling of processing facilities due to the high prices.[13]

Squeezes made some rich, and bankrupted others. The more severe episodes placed enormous strains on the nation's financial system. For example, the Fisk and Gould corner caused the failure of the important Gold Exchange Bank and several other financial institutions and brokerage houses to whom it owed money. Indeed, the gold corner shook the administration of Ulysses S. Grant (who was indirectly linked to the scheme) to its core and largely foreshadowed its litany of scandal. Manipulations were, in sum, frequent and extremely disruptive.

Nor are they simply relics of the distant past. The past fifteen years have seen several major corners that have had important effects in a variety of markets. The billionaire Hunt family allegedly squeezed soybeans in 1977, and attempted a major play in the silver market in 1979 and 1980 that eventually was their undoing. In 1989, the CBT soybean market was rocked by the manipulation attempt of Ferruzzi S.A. and the fallout resulting from the exchange's actions designed to thwart this attempt. In 1991, the eminent investment bank and primary government securities dealer Salomon Brothers successfully cornered several issues of Treasury notes, thereby causing huge disruptions in the world's largest financial market and throwing a cloud of suspicion over it that has yet to dissipate completely. Moreover, Sumitomo, a large Japanese corporation, is widely believed to have manipulated the copper market in 1995 and 1996. And these are only the more spectacular attempts. Other, smaller manipulations have taken place in recent years.

In addition to their immediate effects, corners also have had a pronounced impact on how commodity markets operate and how they are regulated. Specifically, manipulation has largely shaped public attitude toward futures markets, and more important, it has motivated much of the extensive government involvement in these markets over the last seventy years.

Given their typically spectacular and public nature, it is unsurprising that manipulation has played a major role in shaping the popular perception of commodity futures markets. Readers of Chicago and New York newspapers were routinely regaled with detailed coverage of the many squeeze operations that prevailed during the last third of the nineteenth and first decade of the twentieth century. Popular magazines (such as *Munsey's* and *Everybody's*) carried muckraking morality tales of the accounts of the "plungers." About this reporting, a scholar of public attitudes and government policies regarding commodity and stock speculation writes

> Alert to human interest and the spectacular, newsmen played up the personalities of the marketplace, crafty 'Old Hutch,' the indomitable Pardridge, John Cudahy, Norman Ream, and other big traders. For weeks in succession financial pages told of 'Old Hutch' in control, or, later, Pardridge doing most of the trading

while the public looked on. The titans of LaSalle Street put the market up, they put it down . . . . If this drama of financial tangling in the trading pits sold newspapers, it also caused thoughtful readers to question the justice of half a dozen 'heavyweights' channeling the flow of commodities through their grasping figures. . . . Agrarians cited these lurid tales of exchange 'sluggers' to substantiate their charges.[14]

The interest in the doings of major market players was not limited to the readers of popular magazines and newspapers. The plots of serious fictional works, such as Frank Norris's *The Pit* and Dies's *The Plunger* centered on massive manipulation attempts. Famous muckraker Henry Demarest Lloyd's earliest populist crusade (in 1883) was against corners that "made bread dear"; Lloyd's article was published in the highbrow *North American Review.* Even a popular game--Milton Bradley's "Pit"--requires the winner to corner a commodity and squeeze the other players.

The frequency and severity of manipulation also contributed to the development of American commodity law. During the Populist Era, farm belt discontent with the manipulative operations of large futures traders in Chicago, New York, and New Orleans was a major impetus behind the numerous (but in the end abortive) attempts to ban futures trading or tax it out of existence.[15] In the period immediately preceding and immediately following World War I, however, distrust of futures markets motivated in large part by manipulative episodes resulted in the passage of the Cotton Futures Act (1916), the Futures Trading Act (passed in 1921 but declared unconstitutional) and the Grain Futures Act (1922). The last two Acts named explicitly banned manipulation, as did their New Deal successor, the Commodity Exchange Act (1936). Moreover, the fear of further regulatory intervention spurred the commodity exchanges to take more aggressive action against manipulation. For instance, in order to forestall the threats of the Agriculture Secretary to press for more restrictive regulation in the face of the frequent attempts of the speculator Arthur Cutter to corner the CBT's grain contracts, the exchange founded the Business Conduct Committee, which is a cornerstone of its self-regulatory structure to this day and which has provided a model that other exchanges have adopted.[16]

The fear of manipulation also affects the day-to-day operations of the regulators of commodity markets. The primary futures market regulatory authority in the United States, the Commodity Futures Trading Commission (CFTC), constantly monitors the positions and activities of large traders in order to detect any nascent manipulations; some 60 percent of the expenses of the CFTC are devoted to surveillance efforts. The individual exchanges also devote considerable resources to surveillance. Moreover, the exchanges and the government limit the size of the positions that some traders can hold in order to circumscribe their market power. Furthermore, before permitting the trading of any new futures contract the CFTC must determine that its terms and conditions materially reduce the likelihood of manipulation; a contract deemed vulnerable to manipulation cannot be approved. Finally, the CFTC sometimes exerts considerable pressure on exchanges with existing contracts to change the terms of contracts that the Commission considers unduly subject to manipulation. In sum, the prevention of manipulation is a primary objective of Federal commodity regulators. Indeed, it has been argued by responsible and independent authorities that the Commission's concern with manipulation overrides other important economic considerations about futures trading.[17]

It is clear, then, that the subject of manipulation is central to the study of commodity markets. Manipulation has exerted a decisive influence on the operations of these markets since the Civil War, on the public perception of these markets, and on the legal and regulatory environment in which they now operate. Despite its economic, legal, and historical importance, however, commodity manipulation is largely misunderstood. The economic analysis (such as it is) is often incomplete and conflicting. The legal analysis is full of contradiction and haphazard thinking. As I argue in Chapter 5 below, because of the incoherence of much of the existing case law on the subject, it is doubtful whether a regulatory or judicial intervention to stop a corner could survive a determined legal challenge.

The objective of this book is to fill this scholarly void. Specifically, I intend to provide a rigorous analysis of manipulation and its deterrence in order to provide a better understanding of its causes and effects, and therefore, to provide a firmer foundation for future academic, regulatory, legislative, and judicial treatments of the subject. The first step of this process is to define the term *manipulation* precisely.

1.2 Defining Manipulation

I have already used the term manipulation (and the related terms corner and squeeze) several times, but have yet to define it. This is not a straightforward task, given the varied ways in which the word has been used in the past. Virtually every sort of conduct in commodity and financial markets, real or imagined, has been labeled manipulative at some time. In their endeavors to specify the scope of the Commodity Exchange Act (which outlaws manipulation but does not define it) some students of these markets have resembled medieval Schoolmen constructing a taxonomy of sins. The list is large indeed: trading ahead of customers (*frontrunning*), repeated purchases at rising prices (*bulling the market*), repeated sales at falling prices (*bearing the market*), buying or selling to activate resting limit orders so as to touch-off technical rallies or declines (*gunning the stops*), rigged trading at the open or close, wash sales, and the spreading of rumors.[18] Indeed, any large price move in a commodity market is sure to result in allegations of manipulation. If the price of a good rises, those short cry foul; if it falls, those long take up the cry. At times it seems that if Ambrose Bierce had written the *Devil's Dictionary of American Finance*, he would have included the entry:

> **Manipulation**. n. A market has been manipulated when the price moves against you.[19]

These uses of the term manipulation are useful for polemical, but not analytical, purposes. In order to advance the analysis, I will use the term in a much more narrow fashion. Specifically:

> Manipulation is the exercise of monopoly or monopsony power in a futures market (or more generally a derivative securities market) and/or the cash market for the underlying commodity near the expiration date of the future (derivative security).

The potential for this "market power" in the commodity market exists, in turn, when a single trader or a small number of traders accumulates a large long position in a commodity and/or a contingent claim on that commodity (in the case of a monopoly power), or a large short position in the commodity and/or contingent claim (in the case of monopsony).[20]

The contingent claim (or derivative asset or security) is typically a futures or forward contract, although in theory it could be an option contract or a more complex claim.

Six considerations justify this limitation of the analysis of manipulation to corners and squeezes. First, the exercise of market power in a commodity market is universally recognized as a form of manipulation; there is no such agreement for other forms of conduct so labeled.[21] Indeed, the Commodity Exchange Act explicitly proscribes corners, although it also bans other, but unspecified, kinds of manipulative conduct. As a result, most of the important manipulation cases involve a corner.[22] Second, corners and squeezes are historically important. Numerous market power manipulations have occurred in the past, and these episodes have generated popular, legal, and legislative responses.[23] Third, theory implies that market power manipulations help make other sorts of conduct that are sometimes deemed manipulative possible. To take an important example, market power manipulation makes so-called bear raids (the sales of massive numbers of futures contracts in order to depress prices) profitable.[24] Fourth, the exercise of market power at contract expiration distorts market prices prior to contract expiration, and makes these prices more volatile and less informative than would be the case if no traders exercised market power.[25] Fifth, the exercise of market power at contract expiration distorts consumption and production decisions, thereby creating deadweight losses.[26] The combination of reduced price efficiency and distortions in economic decisions makes it desirable to reduce market power if this can be accomplished at low cost. Sixth, and finally, many of the other forms of conduct condemned as "manipulative" are of dubious practical importance. For example, some consider the trading activities of large traders prior to contract expiration as inherently manipulative. It is sometimes argued that speculators can drive prices below the competitive level by short selling in massive quantities. Similarly, speculators can allegedly raise the price above the competitive level (without squeezing the market during the delivery period) by buying in large quantities. The work of Jarrow demonstrates conclusively, however, that such strategies are viable if and only if other traders follow a "herd instinct" and buy after price rises, and sell after price declines.[27] There is no reliable evidence that such herding behavior is empirically important. It is therefore appropriate to disregard the other forms of allegedly "manipulative" conduct and focus on undeniably important forms of manipulation--corner and squeezes.

It is essential to distinguish the exercise of market power near expiration of a futures contract from the effect of large trades that move prices. That is, a hedger's or speculator's trading can cause prices to rise or fall without being manipulative. To see why, consider the case of a large speculator who purchases vast quantities of a commodity because he believes it to be undervalued. Prices increase in response to this trading activity because other traders recognize that the speculator may possess private information on the true value of the commodity. Thus, the price rises to reflect his bullish private information.

The speculator's trading moves the market, but in itself it is not an exercise of market power. Indeed, the speculator would prefer that his trading not move the market. As long as the large trader does not stand for deliveries with the purpose of raising the price during the delivery period, his trading is not manipulative. Thus, the concept of market power should not be equated with the ability to move prices. Instead, use of the term should be restricted to those instances in which a trader uses the power inherent in a large futures position to cause the price *at contract expiration* to rise above what she believes to be its fundamental value.[28]

The equation of manipulation and market power raises other issues. Most important this linkage immediately brings antitrust law to mind. The definition and measurement of market power in that context have proven illusive. Moreover, under antitrust law, the use of monopoly power to raise prices is not illegal. This raises the question: If the concept of market power is well nigh useless in antitrust analysis, why should it prove any more illuminating in a futures market context?

There are two answers to this question. First, it is undeniable that a corner or squeeze represents the exercise of market power. Thus, a failure to connect the concept of market power to the statutory prohibitions against corners is to ignore the essence of the offense. Put another way, the incorporation into commodity law of the antitrust view that it is legal to exercise market power in order to increase prices would represent a de facto legalization of corners. This would render the antimanipulation sections of federal commodity statutes meaningless.[29] Second, it is undeniably true that the concept of monopoly power is nebulous in many markets. In these cases, it is difficult, if not impossible, to define the relevant market and to determine whether a firm or individual artificially reduced output or raised price. Fortunately, this is not the case in futures markets, as the relevant market is very well defined: it is the market at the delivery point during the delivery period. Moreover, because economic theory demonstrates clearly the effects of a long futures market manipulation on prices and quantities, it is possible to collect and observe the relevant data to determine whether the predicted effects of the exercise of market power occurred in a particular instance.

1.3. Analyzing Manipulation: An Overview of the Remainder of the Book

Several important questions flow directly from the market power definition of manipulation. These include:

- How do traders who possess market power exercise it?
- What are the observable consequences of a market power manipulation?
- What are the welfare effects of manipulation?
- What structural conditions facilitate manipulation?
- How do traders obtain market power?
- How does manipulation affect the hedging performance of a futures market? Its value as a price discovery mechanism? Its liquidity?
- How is manipulation most efficiently deterred?

The remainder of this book employs a rigorous theoretical and empirical analysis in order to answer these seven questions in great detail. The investigation proceeds as follows.

Chapter 2 examines the economics of the *delivery end game*. That is, it considers how the holder of a large futures position can exercise market power when a contingent claim or derivative asset requiring delivery of some underlying commodity nears expiration. The chapter demonstrates that economic frictions (including transportation, storage, and search costs) which impede the transfer of the underlying commodity among different parties separated in space or time can create the conditions that the large trader can exploit in order to cause a supercompetitive price. Take, for example, a manipulation by the holder of a large long futures position (a *long manipulation*). As the futures contracts near expiration, those that have sold to the manipulator must either acquire the commodity to deliver to him or repurchase their contracts from him (that is, they *cover their shorts*). The price that shorts are willing to pay to cover is therefore bounded by the cost they incur to deliver. The analysis of Chapter 2 demonstrates that if the long's position is large enough, the frictions just mentioned may force the shorts to bear a very high cost to acquire supplies for delivery. Under these circumstances, they are willing to pay the long a large premium to escape the delivery obligation, and he can therefore liquidate his positions (that is, sell them) at a price that is higher than would prevail if he were to act competitively instead.

This analysis has many important implications. For example, it implies that long manipulation distorts spatial and intertemporal price relations. Prices in the market where delivery occurs rise relative to prices elsewhere. Prices for immediate delivery rise relative to prices for deferred delivery. Prices of deliverable grades rise relative to prices of nondeliverable ones. Long manipulation also distorts commodity flows and consumption patterns; too much of the commodity flows to the delivery market, and too little is consumed elsewhere. These distortions in consumption, transportation, and storage decisions are wasteful, and total income and wealth declines as a result. Moreover, wealth is redistributed from the shorts and consumers of the commodity to the manipulator, other longs, and those fortunate enough to own the commodity prior to the delivery period. The theory also predicts how the profitability of manipulation varies with certain structural variables, such as transportation costs, demand and supply elasticities, commodity flows, storage costs, and intertemporal consumption preferences.

These findings provide a firm foundation for an analysis of public policy toward manipulation. An effective antimanipulation policy requires the assignment of liability and the imposition of sanctions. The predictions concerning the price and quantity effects of manipulation allow a regulator to determine whether a manipulation is impending (so he can intervene if necessary to prevent it) and permit a judge to decide whether one has occurred (so he can determine guilt).

The predictions concerning the costs of manipulation also permit the calibration of damages and the calculation of the value of the resources efficiently devoted to the detection and deterrence of manipulation. Similarly, an understanding of the relation between structural factors the likelihood and cost of manipulation allows a more precise allocation of scarce deterrence resources to where they are most beneficial.

Chapter 2 examines other aspects of the delivery end game as well. Specifically, it shows that economic frictions of the sort that facilitate long manipulation can allow short traders to manipulate the market as well. It also demonstrates that only one form of manipulation should predominate in a particular market, since the structural conditions that enhance the profitability long manipulation reduce the profitability of short manipulation and vice versa. The analysis also shows that frictions are not necessary for manipulation to occur but that very strong conditions must be met for manipulation to occur in a market (such as the modern silver or gold markets, for instance) in which transportation and storage costs are trivial. Furthermore, the chapter examines the differences between manipulations by traders who own considerable amounts of the deliverable supply of a commodity underlying a futures or forward contract and by those that do not own the deliverable. This distinction has vexed many analysts of commodity market law.[30]

By focusing on the analysis of the end game, Chapter 2 begs an important question: how can a trader acquire market power? Note that there is a significant difference between how market power is acquired in a commodity market and how it is obtained in other contexts. Outside a commodity futures market, it is unnecessary for the possessor of market power to acquire it from those that will suffer from it. For example, a firm may acquire market power in the trucking industry as a result of the creation of a barrier to entry by the government. In this case, those who bear the burden of the higher prices of truck transport--shippers--are in no way responsible for the monopoly power of the trucker. In a commodity futures market, in contrast, the victims of market power create the means of their own downfall by trading with the manipulator; if they did not trade with him on a large scale, he could not accumulate the large position that allows him to exploit frictions in the delivery end game. Put another way, the victims of market power in a commodity futures market sell the executioner the rope by which they are hung. Since most futures traders are sophisticated enough to be aware of this possibility, why would they ever put themselves in this position?

Previous analyses of this problem have asserted that either inside information[31] or fraud[32] allows a large trader to acquire market power. These answers are unsatisfactory. It is unlikely that any trader possesses the sort of inside information necessary to acquire market power profitably. Moreover, simply to assert that acquiring monopoly or monopsony power in a commodity futures market requires a trader to defraud his counter-parties begs the questions of how such a fraud can occur and what conditions facilitate it.

Chapter 3 provides a model that surmounts these difficulties. There a trader who does not possess any informational advantage over his competitors and potential counterparties is able to acquire market power as long as the flow of the orders from other traders to the futures market is sufficiently volatile and large relative to the size of the deliverable supply. Given these conditions, traders in the futures market cannot reliably distinguish a large influx of orders from many other traders from a large order placed by a single trader. As a result, they sometimes unwittingly sell a large position to a single trader at a price that does not reflect the market power that he can exercise during the delivery end game. Put another way, the existence of "noise traders" makes fraud possible.

This analysis also makes significant positive and normative predictions. Specifically, it implies that the potential for manipulation causes precontract-expiration prices to vary idiosyncratically with trading volume when there would be no such relationship in its absence. That is, manipulation reduces market liquidity and depth and increases price volatility. Furthermore, the potential for manipulation makes the cash-futures basis excessively variable, thereby reducing the hedging performance of a futures contract. Finally, manipulation increases the costs and risks that informed traders incur and reduces the returns to discovering information about fundamental values. This induces these agents to trade less and collect less information. As a result, the futures price is a less reliable measure of fundamental supply and demand.

Together, Chapters 2 and 3 demonstrate that manipulation can cause severe dislocations in a commodity market. The effective deterrence of manipulation may therefore offer considerable welfare benefits. Chapter 4 identifies the three basic types of manipulation deterrence: *ex ante*, *ex post*, and contractual, and describes how these methods have been employed in the United States since 1921. Chapter 5 then proceeds to analyze *ex post* deterrence in detail. Specifically, the critical analysis of the existing manipulation case law found in that chapter implies that existing manipulation law is less a deterrent to squeezes than an invitation to commit them. This failure of the law stems largely from a failure to understand the economics of manipulation discussed in Chapters 2 and 3. Relying on the insights found in those chapters, Chapter 5 also demonstrates that manipulation is not inherently difficult to detect or prove. Indeed, I outline a set of tests that a court or other *ex post* adjudicator can employ to determine liability and assign damages for a manipulation. The chapter also includes an examination of a particular episode of alleged manipulation to illustrate the applicability and validity of these tests.

Chapter 6 considers the other two forms of manipulation deterrence, *ex ante* and contractual mechanisms, and compares them to *ex post* deterrence. *Ex ante* deterrence is found to be potentially less effective than *ex post* deterrence under plausible conditions because it is predicated on less information and because the government and exchange regulators that carry it out are more vulnerable to political pressure. The chapter also shows that the effectiveness of *ex ante* deterrence relative to the *ex post* variety depends crucially on who is responsible for detecting and preventing manipulations. Specifically, the existence of sizable externalities and internal conflicts may induce self-regulating exchanges to take too few precautions against manipulation; the historical record strongly suggests that these problems were important during the heyday of laissez faire in commodity markets.

In addition, Chapter 6 demonstrates that contractual changes that reduce the likelihood of manipulation (such as, the expansion of delivery locations) also affects a futures contract's utility as a hedging, price discovery, and commodity marketing mechanism. In general, many of the resulting changes are highly beneficial; they tend to make the contract both more liquid and a better hedging instrument. In contrast, other contractual modifications, including position limits and entry barriers may reduce the frequency of manipulation, but only at a substantial cost in the form of greater than necessary price volatility and reduced levels of innovation.

Finally, Chapter 6 compares and contrasts the three forms of manipulation deterrence. The analysis concludes that when properly utilized, *ex post* deterrence is most appealing because *ex post* adjudicators possess superior information; are less vulnerable to pressures to intervene in markets for the benefits of particular parties in the name of manipulation prevention; and can compensate the victims of manipulation and thereby reduce the adverse effects of this conduct on prices prior to contract expiration.

The foregoing demonstrates that this book will cover all of the features of market manipulation listed by Anderson in his overview of the industrial organization of futures markets. Moreover, it answers all of the questions concerning manipulation that Anderson raises.[33] Thus, it undertakes an exhaustive examination of the economics and law of market power manipulation. It is intended to contribute to the understanding of these issues among academic economics and to provide guidance to commodity futures market policy makers in the United States and abroad. Given the dramatic increase in futures trading throughout the world in the past decade, and the prospect for the creation of even more new markets in Asia and the old Soviet bloc, the hunting grounds for would-be manipulators have expanded considerably and should continue to expand for years to come. Thus, I hope that the analysis contained in this work will help ensure that these markets achieve their full potential.

Endnotes

[1] The Treasury routinely bought and sold gold in order to carry out open market operations similar to those currently performed by the Federal Reserve.

[2] During the Civil War the United States government abandoned the gold standard and adopted a paper currency as legal tender. Immediately after this change, traders began to speculate on the price of gold in paper dollars. This practice continued until the nation returned to the gold standard after the "Crime of 1873." The New York Gold Exchange was not a futures market per se. Since traders could borrow and lend gold, however, they could effectively short sell the commodity and create positions with payoffs that duplicated those of an exchange traded futures contract. For a discussion of the isometry between a commodity loan and a futures contract, see Jeffrey Williams, The Economic Function of Futures Markets (1986).

[3] Kenneth Ackerman, The Gold Ring 186-188 (1988).

[4] Stephen Craig Pirrong, The Self-Regulation of Commodity Exchanges: The Case of Market Manipulation, 38 J. of Law & Econ. 141 (1995).

[5] Charles Taylor, 1 A History of the Chicago Board of Trade 370-372 (1917).

[6] Id. at 454, 535.

[7] Id. at 457-459.

[8] Id.

[9] Id. at 472; and William Ferris, The Grain Traders (1988).

[10] Ferris, supra note 9, at 79.

[11] 1 Taylor, supra note 5, at 426.

[12] Leon Kendall, The Chicago Board of Trade and the Federal Government 45 (Ph.D. dissertation, University of Chicago, 1956).

[13] 1 Taylor, supra note 5, at 465, 426; 2 Taylor, supra note 5, at 675. During the wheat corner of 1879, 75 percent of the nation's wheat milling capacity was idled for two months due to the price distortions.

[14] Cedric Cowing, Populists, Plungers, and Progressives 17 (1965).

[15] Id., passim.

[16] Ferris, supra note 9.

[17] United States General Accounting Office, Chicago Futures Markets: Selecting Agricultural Delivery Points Involves Trade-offs (report to the Chairman, House Committee on Agriculture, 1991). The GAO argues that conflicts between the CFTC and the various exchanges are sometimes due to the Commission's emphasis on deterring manipulation, to the exclusion of attaining other desirable objectives of futures markets, such as hedging effectiveness and price discovery.

[18] I obtained the items in this list from Jerry Markham, Manipulation: The Unprosecutable Crime, 87 Yale J. on Regulation 281 (1991).

[19] During a 1928 congressional investigation into cotton prices, one trader stated: "The word 'manipulation' . . . in its use is so broad as to include any operation in the cotton market that does not suit the gentleman who is speaking at the moment." Federal Trade Commission, 2 The Cotton Trade 20 (Senate Document 100, 68th Cong., 1st Sess., 1924).

[20] One of the objectives of the study is to determine what constitutes a "large" position.

[21] Dan Fischel and David Ross, Should the Law Prohibit "Manipulation" in Financial Markets?,105 Harvard L. Rev. 503 (1991), consider, but reject, the possibility that the exercise of market power is the essence of manipulation. At footnote 182 they argue that "the possibility of market power provides incentives for traders who believe prices will rise to go long and incentives for shorts to obtain deliverable supplies to alleviate possible shortages." This reasoning that market power has beneficial effects is specious because the possibility of market power gives too strong an incentive to go long and leads to excessive efforts to obtain deliverable supplies. They also claim that "market power can arise from legitimate trades." Id. at 546. By this they apparently mean that a trader can acquire a position (for hedging purposes, for instance) with no manipulative intent but exercise market power at contract expiration due to a fortuitous change in circumstances between the time she buys and contract expiration. This reasoning closely parallels that of several cases criticized heavily below. Thus, whereas Fischel and Ross appear to distinguish manipulative trading from the exercise of market power at contract expiration, I consider market power to be a particular type of manipulative conduct. My usage is more typical than Fishel's and Ross's. For example, Linda Edwards and Franklin Edwards, A Legal and Economic Analysis of Manipulation, 4 J. of Futures Markets 333 (1984), and Frank Easterbrook, Monopoly, Manipulation, and the Regulation of Futures Markets, 59 J. of Bus. S103 (1986), also identify manipulation with the exercise of market power. This list of works stating that the exercise of market power is the sine qua non of manipulation could be extended substantially with little effort.

[22] Markham, supra note 18, at 380-389 presents a list of manipulation cases brought under the CEA. Of the 44 cases, 37 (84 percent) are market power manipulation cases.

[23] Jerry Markham, The History of Commodity Futures Trading and Its Regulation 1-34 (1987); Julius Baer and George Woodruff, Commodity Exchanges and Futures Trading 182-195 (1929); Cowing, supra note 14, at 3-25.

[24] See the analysis in Section 3.3 of Chapter 3.

[25] Id.

[26] See the analysis in Chapter 2.

[27] Robert Jarrow, Market Manipulation, Bubbles, Corners, and Short Squeezes, 27 J. of Fin. & Quant. Anal. 311 (1992).

[28] At first blush, this test seems inherently subjective and thus impossible to implement in practice. This is incorrect. A true manipulator's actions reveal whether she indeed believes whether she caused the price to exceed fundamental value. For details of this argument, please refer to the discussion of discerning speculative from manipulative motives in the analysis titled "Answering Question 3" in Section 5.4.2 of Chapter 5.

[29] Section 13(b) of the CEA does not specifically list a corner as a particular form of price manipulation. However, Section 7(d) of the Act requires exchanges to prevent corners, Section 8a(9) allows the CFTC to intervene in order to prevent corners, and Section 7a(10) requires exchanges to establish delivery systems and delivery differentials in order to reduce the likelihood of a corner. Thus, it is apparent that the statute regards exercise of market power--a corner--as an important form of market manipulation. In fact, it is the only kind of manipulation that is listed by name. Moreover, the cases discussed in Section 5.4 all clearly state that a corner is a form of market manipulation.

[30] Philip McBride Johnson and Thomas Hazen, 3 Commodities Regulation 32-54 (1989).

[31] The model of Albert Kyle, A Theory of Futures Market Manipulation, in The Industrial Organization of Futures Markets (R. Anderson ed. 1984), assumes that a single trader knows the orders submitted by other traders and can choose a trading strategy that exploits this information and allows him to acquire market power without the knowledge of those trading with him.

[32] Easterbrook, supra note 21.

[33] Ronald Anderson, The Industrial Organization of Futures Markets: A Survey, in The Industrial Organization of Futures Markets 13-14 (R. Anderson ed. 1984).

CHAPTER 2
THE ECONOMICS OF MARKET POWER IN A FUTURES CONTRACT: THE DELIVERY "END GAME"

2.1. Introduction

Economists have long known that corners and squeezes result from the exercise of market power during the delivery period of a futures contract but have not rigorously detailed either the factors that make it possible for traders to exercise such power or the implications of this behavior. This chapter examines these issues in detail. It answers several crucial questions about manipulation. How does it work? What structural conditions facilitate it? What are the empirical implications of this conduct? Specifically, what are the effects of manipulation on prices, consumption, production, and storage? What are its welfare effects?

This analysis is the foundation for all the remaining material in this book. The effects of market power during the delivery period affect how rational traders behave prior to the delivery period. Even prior to the delivery period traders will condition the prices at which they are willing to buy and sell on the information available to them concerning the probability that a manipulation will occur in the future and the effect of a manipulation on prices. As a result, the mere prospect for manipulation affects futures prices prior to the delivery period. In order to understand this linkage it is necessary to understand how manipulation affects prices in the delivery period. Moreover, the economic incentive to engage in manipulation depends on the profitability of this activity. An analysis of the likelihood of manipulation therefore requires a firm understanding of the factors that determine this profitability. The present chapter examines these issues in detail; Chapter 3 builds on these results to determine how the prospect of manipulation and the profitability thereof affect prices and trader behavior prior to the delivery period.

Furthermore, an analysis of the optimal deterrence of manipulation requires a firm grasp of its empirical and welfare effects. The optimal deterrence mechanism depends in large part on the ability of adjudicators to detect whether a manipulation has occurred; *ceteris paribus,* deterrence through harm-based sanctions is more desirable, the easier it is to detect market-power manipulation. Detection is possible to the extent that manipulation has unique effects on prices and quantities. The present chapter examines the observable effects of market power on these variables in detail. These empirical implications provide the basis for the critique contained in Chapter 5 of decisions in United States manipulation cases brought under the Commodity Exchange Act. The welfare effects analyzed here and in the subsequent chapter are also important in an analysis of deterrence because a primary purpose of any law (including commodity law) is to improve economic efficiency. Therefore, the benefits of deterrence depend crucially on the extent to which market-power manipulation impairs efficiency. The analysis of this chapter demonstrates in detail what these effects are.

The analysis proceeds by deriving several models of the delivery end game. The first set of models focus on the role of economic frictions in facilitating manipulation. Section 2.2 provides a very simple reduced form model of market-power manipulation. This model shows that an increasing marginal cost of delivery is a necessary (but not sufficient) condition for a profitable market-power manipulation to occur. Sections 2.3 and 2.4 derive structural models of long market-power manipulation which show how economic frictions–such as transportation and storage costs–can cause an increasing marginal cost of delivery. These sections also examine the effects of a long market-power manipulation on prices and quantities. The models in Section 2.3 assume that all traders but one are atomistic during the delivery period. That is, these models are essentially monopoly models. Section 2.4 expands the analysis by allowing several large long traders. That is, this section contains an oligopoly model of market manipulation.

Subsequent sections extend the analysis beyond the canonical case of the frictional long manipulation of a commodity settled by delivery. Section 2.5 analyzes whether holders of large short positions can exercise market power during the delivery period. Section 2.6 examines the profitability of manipulation in the absence of economic frictions. This analysis shows that these alternative forms of manipulation are unlikely to be important because the conditions that make them profitable are unlikely to prevail in practice. Thus, the frictional long manipulation is theoretically the most worrisome form of market power in futures markets. This comports with historical experience.

2.2. The Basics of Long Manipulation

Long manipulation, that is, the manipulation of the futures price by an owner of a long futures position, results from the exercise of monopoly power. To see how such a long manipulation works, consider a market where one futures trader—"trader 1"—has amassed X long futures positions, while a continuum of traders has accumulated the remaining Y open long positions. The $X+Y$ open short positions are held by a continuum of traders.

At the expiration of a futures contract, the holder of a short position can either liquidate his position or deliver against it. The cost of making delivery therefore bounds the price that the short is willing to pay to liquidate. As a result, the demand curve for futures contracts at the expiration of a contract—the *liquidation demand curve*—depends on the cost of making delivery, which include the price and transactions costs the short must pay to acquire the commodity, transport it to the delivery point, and ensure that its quality meets contract specifications.

At contract expiration a long trader can close her position either by selling futures contracts or by accepting delivery. Thus, the supply curve of futures positions at the expiration of a contract, the *liquidation supply curve,* depends on the costs and benefits of taking delivery. The costs include the costs of transporting it from the delivery point to where it is consumed, stored, or processed, and the transactions costs of selling it if the long chooses to do so. The benefits equal the value of the commodity received.

If shorts act competitively at contract expiration the liquidation demand curve of bids will correspond to the mirror image of the marginal cost of delivery curve. That is, if the marginal cost of delivery rises as the number made increases, the price at which shorts are willing to liquidate will fall as the number of liquidations increases because liquidations vary inversely one for one with deliveries. Similarly, if longs behave competitively, the liquidation supply curve will equal the mirror image of the marginal benefit of taking delivery curve.

For simplicity, assume that trading for liquidation occurs in a call auction. When all traders act as perfect competitors, the expiration futures price equates the marginal cost of making delivery with the marginal benefit of taking delivery as illustrated in Figure 2.1. Here the equilibrium futures price equals F^*, L^* positions are liquidated, while $Q_D = X + Y - L^*$ deliveries occur. This result is efficient, as the marginal cost of delivery equals the marginal benefit of delivery. Deliveries occur because some shorts face costs of making delivery that are less than the benefits some longs receive from taking them.

Traders need not act competitively at expiration, however, and this can disrupt this efficient equilibrium. To see how, consider Figure 2.2. Here for simplicity it is assumed that the marginal benefit of taking delivery is constant. If other traders continue to act competitively, and trader 1 offers to liquidate his position only at a price $F_1 > F^*$, the supply curve of futures contracts perceived by the shorts is given by the hatched line, and the futures price will equal F_1: L_1 shorts will liquidate at that price, as the marginal cost of making delivery equals F_1 when $X + Y - L_1$ deliveries occur.

The foregoing implies that trader 1 faces a demand curve to liquidate his positions equal to the segment GH of the overall liquidation demand curve. Therefore, by liquidating *fewer* positions, trader 1 accepts *more* deliveries and increases the marginal cost of making further deliveries. This drives up the price that shorts are willing to pay to liquidate their remaining contracts in order to avoid making even costlier additional deliveries.

Figure 2.1

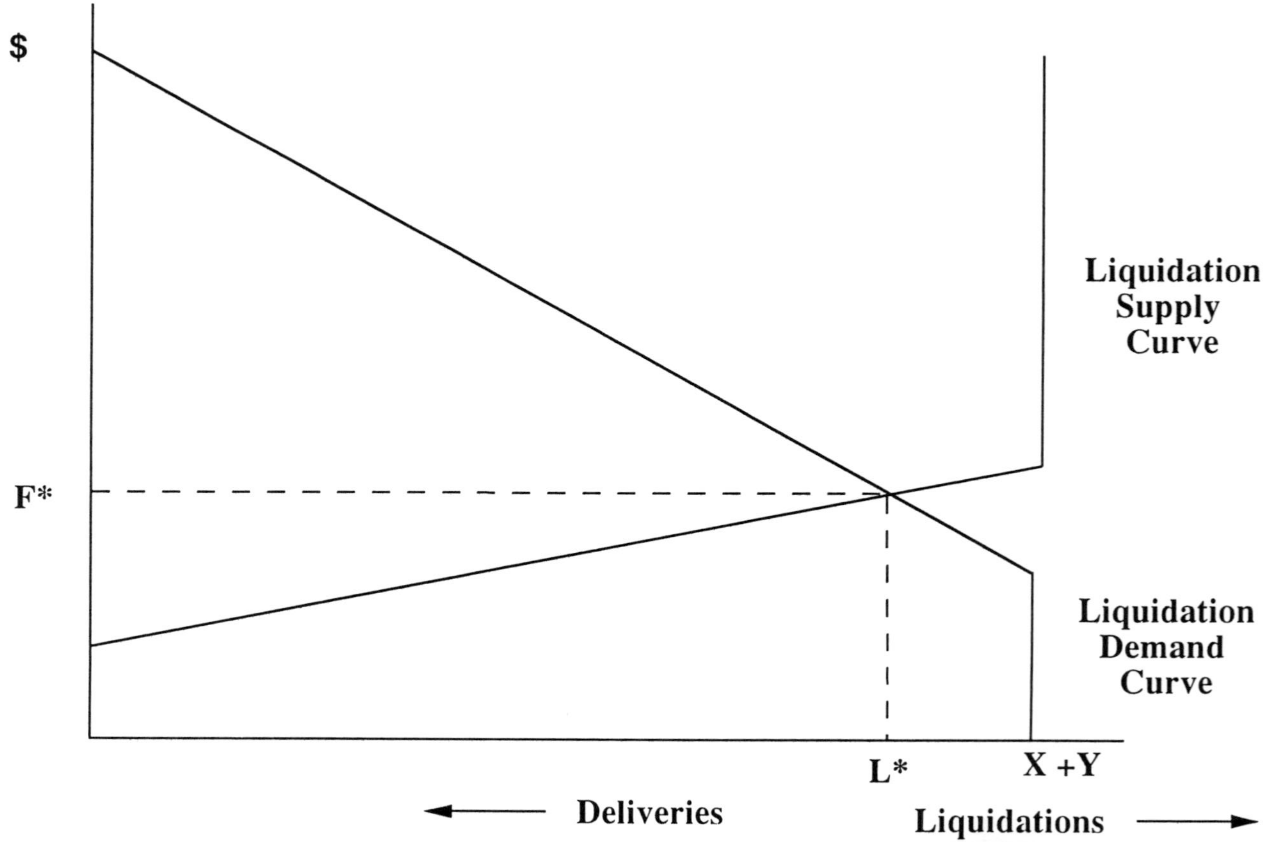
$
F*
Liquidation
Supply
Curve
Liquidation
Demand
Curve
L*
X +Y
Deliveries
Liquidations

Figure 2.2

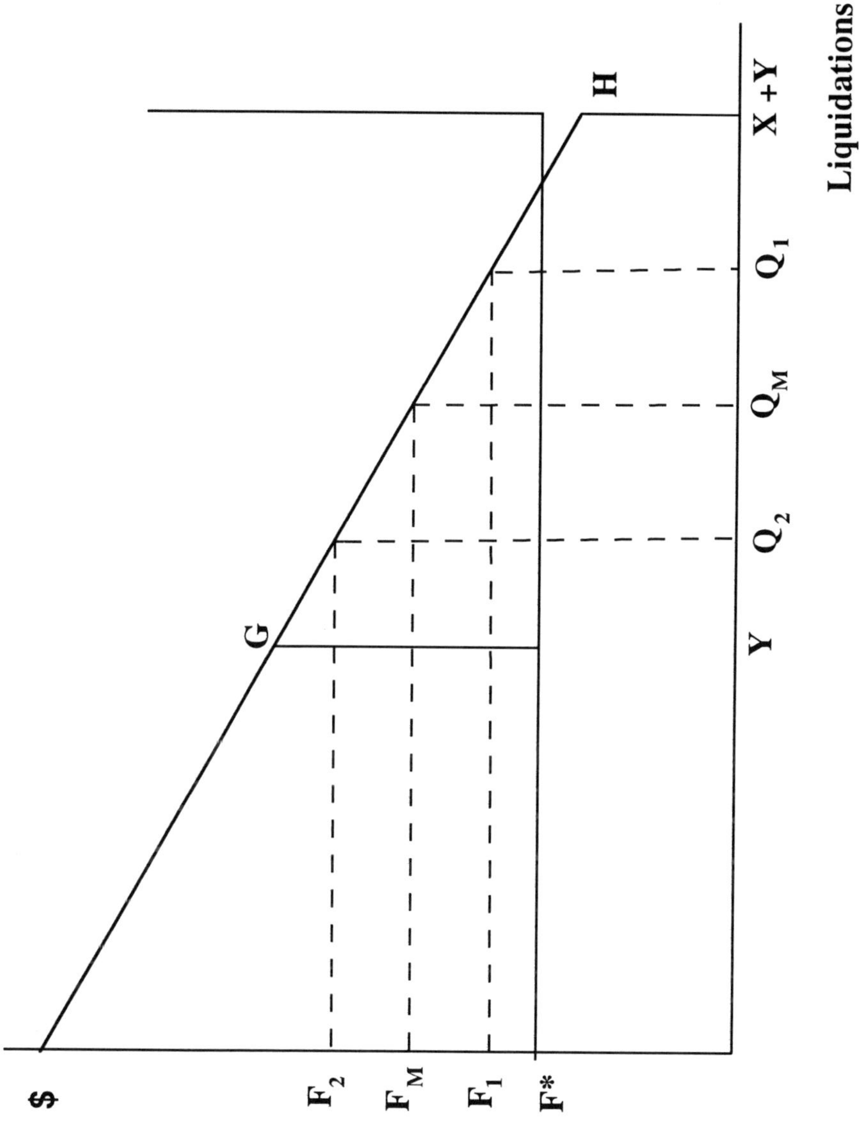

Since trader 1's liquidation demand curve slopes down, he can act as a monopolist toward the shorts standing on the opposite side of the futures contract at expiration. He maximizes his wealth by equating the marginal revenue from an additional liquidation to the marginal cost of a liquidation, which equals the marginal benefit of a delivery. In Figure 2.2, trader 1 liquidates $L_m - Y$ positions at a price of F_m and accepts delivery on $X - L_m + Y$ contracts.

The equilibrium futures price in this market exceeds the competitive futures price when trader 1 exploits his monopoly power. Moreover, too many deliveries occur as the monopolist restricts his "output" of liquidations. A welfare loss given by triangle LHM results. The area of this triangle equals the cumulative difference between the marginal cost and marginal benefit of delivery over the range of uneconomic deliveries.

It is obvious that just like any would-be monopolist, a trader with outstanding long futures positions must face a downward-sloping residual liquidation demand curve in order to increase the futures price. Since a downward-sloping liquidation demand curve results when the marginal cost of delivery is increasing, this raises the question: what determines the shape of the marginal cost of delivery function? The following sections examine the marginal cost of delivery function under various assumptions concerning transportation and transactions costs in spot and futures markets.

2.3. Frictional Long Manipulations

2.3.1. Introduction

What factors contribute to an upward-sloping-marginal cost of delivery and therefore make long manipulation possible? The model in Section 2.3.2 demonstrates that transportation costs facilitate long manipulation. Their effect is subtle. They make manipulation more likely not simply because shorts incur the direct costs of shipping supplies to the delivery market. Transport costs also serve to isolate markets and therefore make it inefficient to return all additional deliveries to their points of origin. As a result, by demanding excessive deliveries a long induces distortions in the spatial and temporal distribution of consumption, transportation, and storage. Shorts must pay current owners of the commodity increasingly higher prices in order to compensate current owners of the commodity for the surplus foregone as a result of these distortions. This causes the marginal cost of delivery to increase with the number of deliveries.

Although the formal analysis examines transportation costs as the source of friction, the consumption distortion results suggest that any friction that makes it costly to return the commodity to its original owners (such as, storage costs or search costs) may facilitate manipulation. When such frictions exist, shorts must bid up the price in order to increase the number of deliveries as the current owners of the commodity anticipate that they will incur search costs themselves or forgo some consumption. This bidding up of the price leads to an increasing marginal cost of delivery, which may make manipulation profitable.

2.3.2. A Spatial Model of Long Manipulation

Consider a spatial market where transportation is costly. The model is intended to represent the market for a physical commodity such as soybeans, oil, or copper where production and consumption of the deliverable commodity take place at several spatially separate locations and where the cost of transport is large relative to value. (Where transport costs are unimportant as in currencies, securities, or precious metals, the analysis of Section 2.5 is relevant). The source of friction in this model is the cost of transportation.

All consumers and producers of the product against which a futures contract is traded are located along a line segment illustrated in Figure 2.3. The delivery point for the futures contract is point $D = 0$, the left endpoint of the segment. Production of the commodity takes place along the open interval $(0, C_1)$. Production is seasonal: it takes place in odd-numbered periods of time. During these odd-numbered periods, production at each point x along the interval equals ρdx, so total production equals ρC_1. Output equals 0 during even-numbered periods. The commodity is transported to the consumption points immediately after the harvest. Output arrives at these sites in the subsequent even-numbered period. It costs t dollars to move one unit of the commodity one unit of distance.

The commodity is consumed at n distinct points located in the interval $[C_1, C_n]$, as well as at point D. The demand curve at a point C_i, $1 \leq i \leq n$ equals $P_i(q_i)$, where q_i is the quantity consumed at C_i, while P_i is the market price there. The demand curve at D is $P_D(q_D)$. The $P_i(q)$ and $P_D(q)$ are decreasing in q.[1]

Given t, the distances between consumption and production points, and the demand curves at each of the consumption sites, there is a point x^* such that all output produced in the interval $(0, x^*)$ is optimally shipped D while all output produced in $[x^*, C_1)$ is shipped to C_1 and beyond. This optimal distribution q_D^*, $\{q_i^*\}_{1 \leq i \leq n}$ implies the following price relations:

$$-tC_1 \leq P_1 - P_D = tC_1 - 2tx^* \leq tC_1 \tag{2.1}$$

$$P_i - P_1 = t(C_i - C_1) \qquad i = 2, 3, \ldots, n. \tag{2.2}$$

Thus, depending on whether demand is high or low at the delivery point relative to the other consumption points, the price there can be higher or lower than at point C_1.

These pricing and spatial distribution relations affect the incentive to manipulate the futures contract because they determine the marginal cost of delivering the commodity and the price the long receives on sale of the units delivered to him. Marginal cost equals the sum of the price a short pays when buying the commodity from the owner of the marginal unit thereof and the cost of transport of this unit to the delivery market.

First consider the economics of the manipulation of a contract expiring in an even-numbered period. Assume that the commodity stock is distributed optimally among the consumption points, and thus expressions (2.1) and (2.2) hold. Also, without loss of generality assume that $q_D^* > 0$ and $q_i^* > 0$ for all $i = 1, \ldots, n$.

Figure 2.3

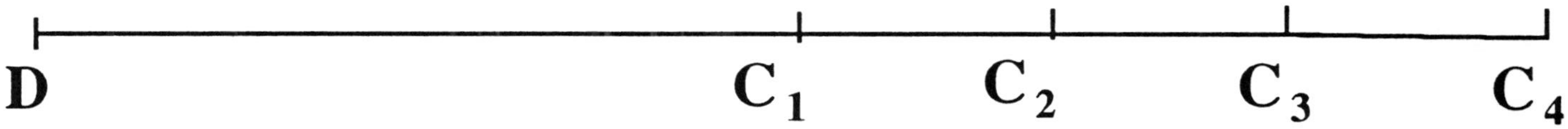

The price that shorts pay to acquire the commodity depends on what its current owners expect to happen after any sale. If sellers at location i sell y_i units to shorts for delivery and anticipate that they will not be able to repurchase any, they charge a price equal to $P_i(q_i^* - y_i)$. If the sellers anticipate, however, that s_i units will be returned to their market after delivery, they sell at a price of $P_i(q_i^* - y_i + s_i)$.

These considerations imply that in order to determine the price at which the current holders of the commodity are willing to sell to shorts to permit delivery, one must make assumptions about the price determination processes *after* as well as before the manipulation, and the valuation that the manipulator places on the commodity received via delivery. I assume that shorts buy the commodity at a perfectly competitive auction prior to delivery. The manipulator sells all that shorts deliver to him at the price that clears the delivery market; that is, he behaves competitively in the postdelivery spot market.[2] All other market participants have perfect foresight about the long's behavior and other relevant variables. In other words, in the delivery period shorts and the current owners of the commodity are aware that a manipulation is in progress.

Current owners of the commodity sell only if they are compensated for any loss of surplus they suffer. Competition between them at the predelivery auction to sell to shorts to permit the latter to make delivery minimizes the total cost of delivering Q units.

First consider the marginal cost of delivery when $Q < q_D^*$. In this case all deliveries are made from stocks on hand at D. Shorts need not pay for transport here, nor is consumption distorted. Current holders of the commodity therefore know that they can repurchase what they deliver at the postdelivery auction for the current market price of $P_D(q_D^*)$, so they are willing to sell to the shorts at that price. As a consequence the marginal cost of delivery equals $P_D(q_D^*)$ as long as $Q \leq q_D^*$. This implies the following:

Result 1. *To manipulate, a trader who cannot exert monopoly power in the spot market must be able to demand delivery of more* *supply than is available in the delivery market.*

The problem of determining the marginal cost of delivery, and the receipts from the sale of deliveries, is more complicated when the total number of deliveries exceeds stocks on hand in the delivery market. Now a transportation cost must be incurred in order to increase deliveries. Deliveries affect the spatial distribution of the commodity, moreover, and therefore prices in the various markets change. If during the postdelivery auction a unit delivered from market j is bought by a consumer located at D, prices rise and consumer surplus falls at j, while prices fall and consumer surplus rises at D. If instead a unit shipped from j is repurchased by a consumer there, another transport cost is incurred to "backhaul" the commodity, but prices in the two markets are unchanged.

Formally, if current owners at j, $j = 1, \ldots, n$ sell y_j units for delivery and repurchase s_j units after the delivery process ends then consumption at j falls from q_j^* to $q_j^* - y_j + s_j$. This reduces consumer welfare at location j by:

$$F_j - \int_{q_j^* - y_j + s_j}^{q_j^*} P_j(w)dw.$$

The total transport cost incurred by this movement of the commodity between D and j equals

$$T_j = tC_j(s_j + y_j).$$

If $q_D^* + \sum_{j=1}^n y_j \equiv Q$ and $\sum_{j=1}^n s_j \equiv V$ then the total increase consumption at D rises from q_D^* to $Q - V$, so consumer welfare at D rises by

$$B_D = \int_{q_D^*}^{Q-V} P_D(u)du.$$

The foregoing implies that total cost of delivering Q units equals:

$$C(Q) = \sum_{j=1}^{n} [T_j + F_j] - B_D. \tag{2.3}$$

Competitive interactions between shorts and the current owners in the predelivery auction minimize this cost subject to the following constraints:

$$q_j^* \geq y_j(Q) \quad \forall \quad j \tag{2.4}$$

$$\sum_{j=1}^{n} y_j(Q) + q_D^* \geq Q. \tag{2.5}$$

The first constraint states that the number of deliveries from a particular location cannot exceed the stocks on hand there, while the second ensures that the total quantity delivered equals at least the amount required. There is a Lagrangean multiplier μ_j associated with each of the n constraints of the form (2.4), and a multiplier λ associated with constraint (2.5).

Assume $y_j^*(Q)$, $s_j^*(Q)$, $\mu_j^*(Q)$ and $\lambda^*(Q)$ solve this program. Defining $P_j(Q) = P_j[q_j^* - y_j^*(Q) + s_j^*(Q)]$, and $P_D(Q) = P_D[Q - V(Q)]$ the functions satisfy the following first-order conditions:

$$P_j(Q) + tC_j \geq P_D(Q) + \lambda^*(Q) + \mu_j^*(Q) \quad \forall \quad j \tag{2.6}$$

$$P_D(Q) \geq P_j(Q) - tC_j \quad \forall \quad j \tag{2.7}$$

$$\mu_j^*(Q) \leq 0 \quad \forall \quad j \tag{2.8}$$

$$\lambda^*(Q) \geq 0 \tag{2.9}$$

Equation (2.6) holds as an equality if $y_j^*(Q) > 0$, and as a strict inequality otherwise. Equation (2.7) holds as an equality if $s_j^*(Q) > 0$ and as a strict inequality otherwise. The multiplier $\mu_j^*(Q) < 0$ if $y_j^*(Q) = q_j^*$ and equals 0 otherwise.

These first-order conditions imply the following propositions, which are proved in the appendix:

Proposition 1. *Assume the distribution of the commodity is initially optimal. Then there are n intervals $[D_i, U_i]$ in which the marginal cost of delivery is increasing in Q when $D_i \leq Q \leq U_i$.*

Proposition 2. *Assume $s_j^*(Q) > 0$ for $Q \geq Q'$, and $s_j^*(Q) = 0$ for $Q < Q'$. If $y_j^*(Q') < q_j^*$ (and thus $\mu_j^*(Q) = 0$), then there is an interval $[Q', Q' + q_j^* - y_j^*(Q')]$ such that the marginal cost of delivery is constant and equal to $P_j(Q') + tC_j$.*

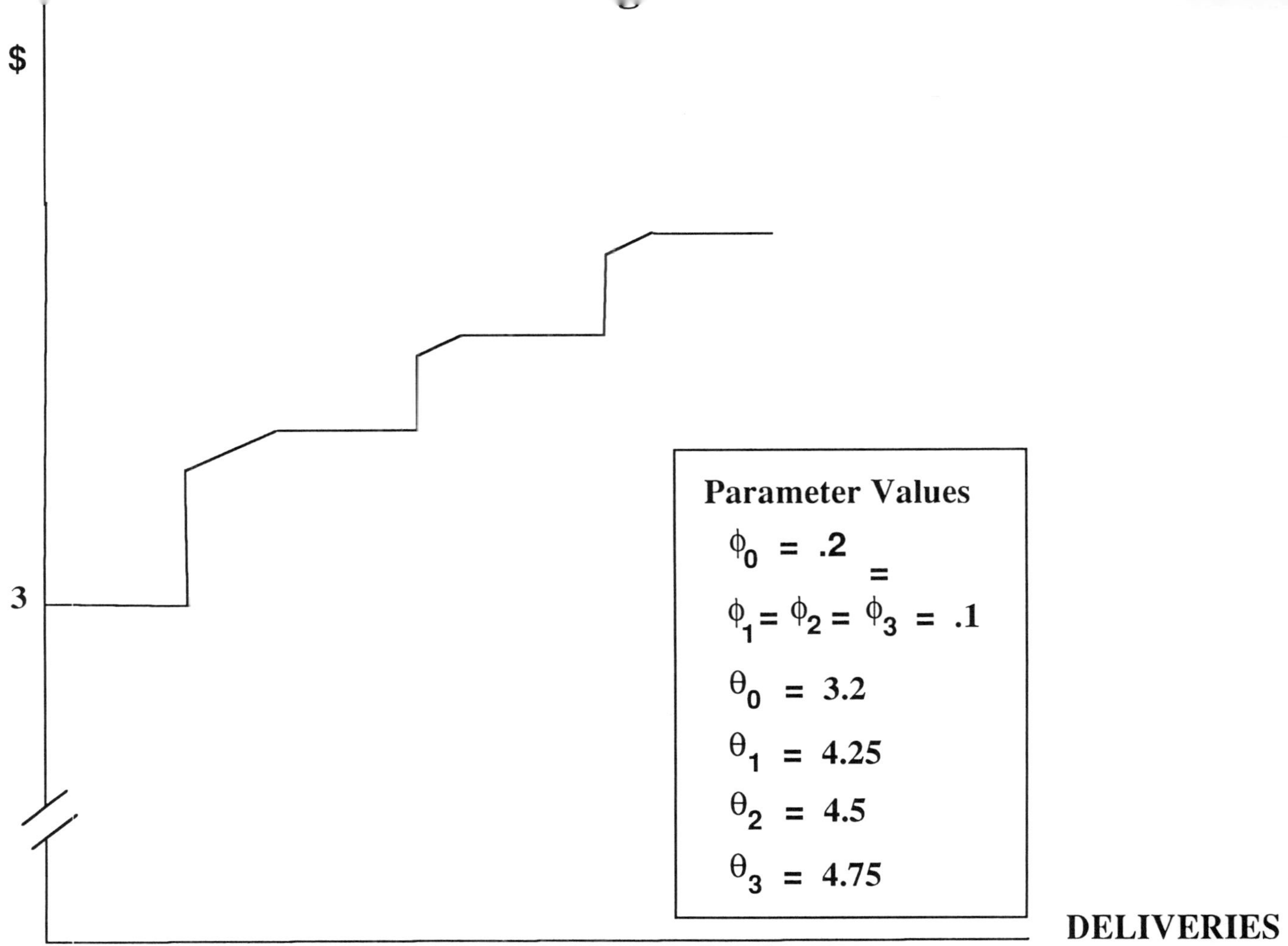
$
3
DELIVERIES
Parameter Values
ϕ_0 = .2
$\phi_1 = \phi_2 = \phi_3$ = .1
θ_0 = 3.2
θ_1 = 4.25
θ_2 = 4.5
θ_3 = 4.75

Figure 2.4 depicts the marginal cost of delivery function for the following simple example. Assume that there are four consumption locations, the delivery point and $C_1, \ldots, C_3$. Total production equals four units; that is, $\rho = 8$. Demand is linear at each location, with the values of the intercept parameters θ_i and slope parameters ϕ_i provided in the figure. Given these assumed values, under the optimal distribution one unit of the commodity is consumed at each location under the optimal distribution.

The propositions demonstrate, and Figure 2.4 illustrates, that the marginal cost of delivery curve consists of a combination of flat and upward-sloping segments. There are as many upward-sloping segments as there are consumption locations. These upward-sloping segments occur for those Q such that the units shipped from the marginal source of deliveries are purchased by consumers at D during the postdelivery auction. The flat segments occur for those Q where the marginal deliveries are repurchased by consumers at the marginal source of deliveries during that auction. The discontinuous jumps occur when shorts must go to a higher priced, more distant location to acquire the commodity.

Taken together, these propositions imply the following:

Result 2. *In the spatial market, the marginal cost of delivery is increasing if $X > q_D^*$. Thus, the holder of such a position satisfies a necessary condition for a successful manipulation even if he does not exert monopoly power in the postdelivery spot market.*

Increasing the number of deliveries also affects the postdelivery price at D, as the following proposition (proved in the appendix) demonstrates:

Proposition 3. *Given the assumptions of Propositions 1 and 2, the postdelivery price in the delivery market is decreasing in Q when $D_i \leq Q \leq U_i$ and is constant when the marginal cost of delivery is constant.*

The intuition behind Propositions 1 through 3 is as follows. Increasing the number of deliveries forces current owners of the commodity to reduce their consumption because transportation costs make it inefficient to return all they supply to them after delivery. As a result, they provide the commodity to the shorts only if compensated for their lost surplus. Since $P_i'(q) < 0$, the compensation required rises as more units are bid away. Moreover, shorts must pay a higher transport charge when they go to more distant markets to obtain the commodity. Finally, due to transport costs, prices are higher in some markets, and shorts must purchase in these more expensive locations when supplies in cheaper markets are exhausted. Each of these factors causes the marginal cost of delivery to rise with Q.

The price declines at D in the postdelivery auction as Q increases for similar reasons. Transport costs make it optimal to retain some of the additional units delivered at D rather than return them to the market of origin. These additional supplies depress price. Market slang refers to this as the problem of *burying the body* or *disposing of the corpse.*

Finally, if the price increase at a source of deliveries j and the price decrease at D are so large that the price difference equals the cost of transport between these points, it is efficient to return the commodity to j. As long as supplies of the commodity at j are not exhausted, therefore, the marginal cost of delivery is constant, as prices at j and D cannot differ by more than the cost of transport.

Given the just-derived relations between the number of deliveries, the prices at which shorts are willing to liquidate, the prices at which a long will be able to sell the stocks tendered to him, and the number of contracts he owns, the large long chooses the number of deliveries (or equivalently the number of liquidations) in order to maximize his delivery-period revenues.[3] If, given Q, location j is the source of the marginal delivery, these revenues equal

$$R(Q) = (X - Q)[P_j(Q) + tC_j] + QP_D(Q). \tag{2.10}$$

The first term of this expression is the total revenue earned from the sale of futures positions, while the second term is the revenue from sale of units delivered to the long. Note that it may be optimal for the long to choose $Q = 0$, in which case $R(Q) = XP_D(0)$.

Maximizing (2.10) with respect to Q yields

$$P_j(Q) + tC_j - (X - Q)\frac{dP_j}{dQ} = P_D(Q) + Q\frac{dP_D}{dQ}. \qquad (2.11)$$

That is, at a maximum the marginal revenue from a delivery (given by the r.h.s. of (2.11)) is equal to the marginal cost of a delivery (given by the l.h.s. of (2.11)). Since the number of liquidations, L, equals $X - Q$, $dP_j/dL = -dP_j/dQ$, and (2.11) can be rewritten to imply that the profit-maximizing choice of Q (and hence L) equates the marginal revenue from a liquidation to the marginal cost thereof. It is straightforward to show that such a maximum occurs in one of upward-sloping portions of the marginal cost of delivery curve and therefore in one of the downward-sloping portions of the liquidation demand curve.

There are many important implications of this analysis, including:

Result 3. *Too many deliveries occur during a long manipulation in the spatial market, but the large long accepts delivery on only a fraction of his position, that is,* $q_D^* < Q < X$ *and* $0 < L < X$.

Note that if $X = Q$, since $dP_D/dQ < 0$, (3.6) implies that the l.h.s. of (3.11) exceeds the r.h.s., therefore violating the first-order condition for a maximum. Intuitively, the manipulator exploits his market power by restricting the number of liquidations in order to elevate the liquidation price. Nonetheless, in order to profit he must liquidate some contracts. If he were to take delivery on his entire position, he would suffer a loss due to the burying-the-body effect. As a result, he takes delivery on only a part of it.

Result 4. *Long manipulation in the spatial market imposes a welfare loss because it distorts the spatial pattern of consumption and induces excessive transportation.*

It is evident that there is excessive transportation of the commodity during a manipulation. Moreover, Propositions 1 through 3 imply that a manipulation distorts the distribution of the commodity. This causes a deadweight loss: there is too much consumption in the delivery market and too little at the nondelivery points.

This distortion of consumption is important. The result implies that transportation costs facilitate manipulation in several ways. The direct effect of transport costs on the costs of delivery is readily understood. These costs also serve to isolate the various consumption points. As a result, it is inefficient to return all units delivered to their original owners, so shorts must pay supercompetitive and rising prices to acquire the commodity. Moreover, even under the efficient distribution of the commodity transport costs ensure that prices differ across markets. When shorts exhaust supplies at low-price locations they must travel to higher-priced locations to obtain the commodity. Thus, transport costs contribute to an increasing marginal cost of delivery in three ways in this model.

Result 5. *Long manipulation distorts spatial price relationships and depresses the deferred futures price absolutely and relative to the price of the expiring contract.*

Post-manipulation prices rise above the competitive level at source of the marginal delivery due to the decline in consumption there. Prices at inframarginal sources of deliveries may either rise or fall due to manipulation. Price after delivery falls at the delivery point due to the burying-the-body effect.

Figure 2.5 illustrates these various results assuming that $X = 2.4$ given the parameters assumed in Figure 2.4. (The kinks in the liquidation demand curve and delivery market price functions, which occur when the marginal source of delivery changes and when backhauls commence, induce the discontinuities seen in the marginal revenue and marginal cost curves.) Note that the no-manipulation equilibrium price equals 3, but when the manipulator equates the marginal benefit (cost) of a liquidation (delivery) to the marginal cost (benefit) of a liquidation (delivery), the futures price equals 3.9375 and the postdelivery price at D equals 2.9625. Moreover, the long accepts deliveries in excess of the original stocks at D but takes fewer than X deliveries. Finally, it is possible to show that the long's actions create a deadweight loss of .1833 due to the resulting distortion in consumption (consumption rises at D and falls at C_1 and C_2) and the excessive transportation.

Figure 2.5

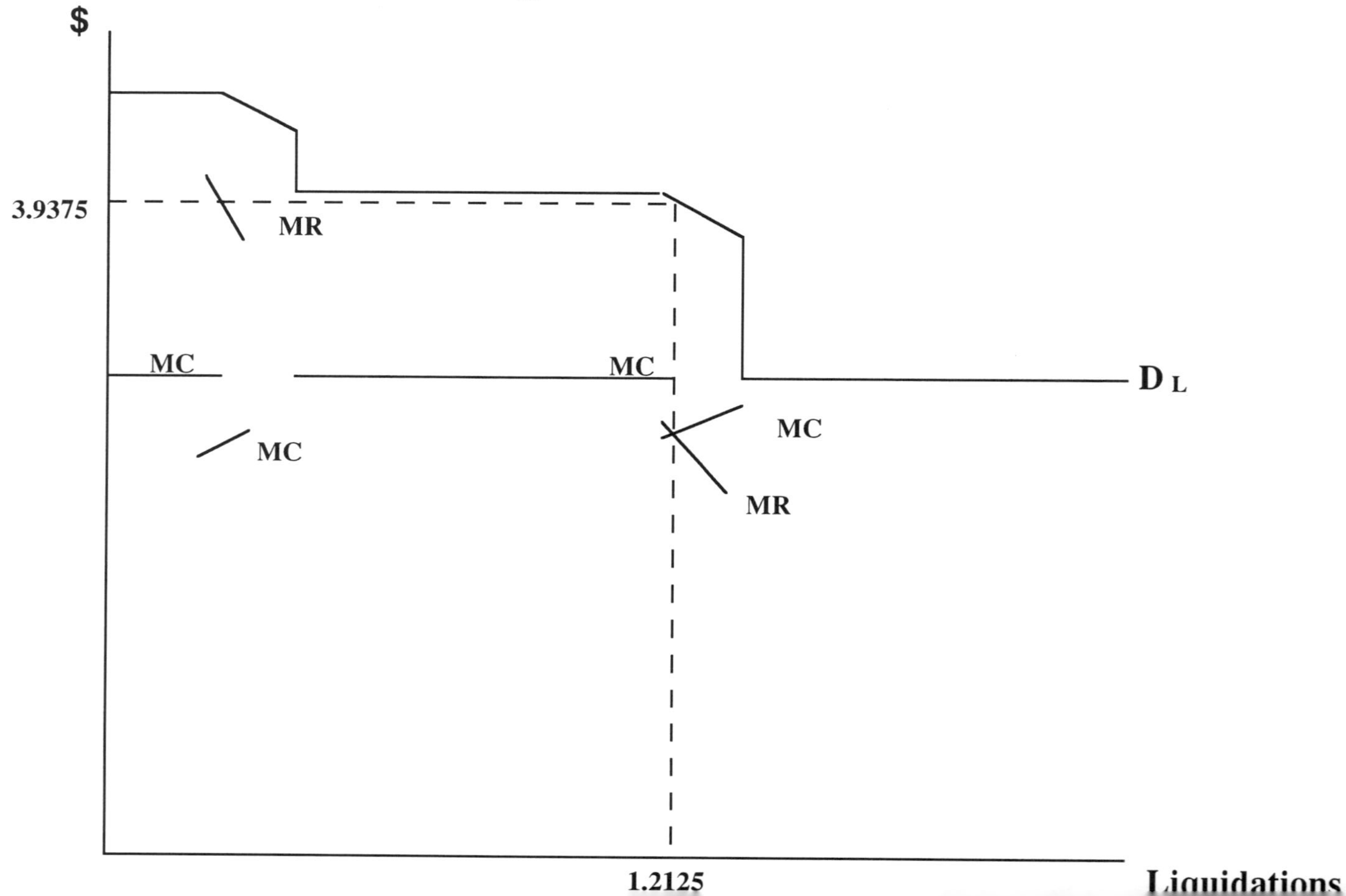

The burying-the-body effect also produces distortions in intertemporal price relationships. Prior to contract expiration the price of the commodity in the delivery market rises to equal the marginal cost of a delivery, as this is what shorts are willing to pay for a unit located there. The price then falls at D after the delivery process ends. Since this decline in P_D is an anticipated consequence of manipulation, the deferred month futures price is depressed relative to the artificially inflated expiring month futures price. Indeed, manipulation may result in a backwardation in which the expiring contract's price exceeds the price for deferred delivery.

Together, Results 3, 4 and 5 describe how a manipulation distorts price and quantity relations. Market-power manipulation causes excessive flows of the commodity *to* the delivery market before the completion of a corner, excessive flows *from* the delivery market after it is over (due to the backhauls), a *temporary* increase in the price in the delivery market relative to the prices in other markets, and a *temporary* increase in the spot price of the commodity relative to the deferred futures price. All of these symptoms distinguish price and quantity patterns during a manipulation from competitive price and quantity patterns. The burying-the-body effect is particularly distinctive; absent the release of any new fundamental information, a large price decline immediately following the liquidation of a futures contract is extremely difficult to reconcile with a competitive model of the futures market.

Furthermore, it is very improbable that these effects would occur simultaneously in a competitive market. Specifically, the theory of storage implies that in a competitive market, increases in deliverable supply are typically associated with a *decline* in the spot price relative to the deferred futures price. In a manipulation, the exact opposite is true. In sum, the behavior of prices and quantities during a corner differs starkly from their behavior under competitive conditions.

Chapter 5 demonstrates how the distinctive price and quantity patterns that prevail during a squeeze make it possible to detect a corner with high probability. Specifically, empirical documentation of these patterns allows a fact-finder to reject with high confidence the null hypothesis that the futures market was competitive at the expiration of a futures contract. Decisive rejection of the competitive null in favor of the manipulative alternative makes it possible to punish manipulators while largely avoiding mistaken convictions. Chapter 6 shows that this makes harm-based *ex post* sanctions an efficient way to deter manipulation.

In conjunction with Results 3 and 5, Result 4 assists in the identification of a manipulator. A manipulator liquidates many futures contracts at the same time that he accepts a large number of deliveries. Moreover, if a fact-finder documents a burying-the-body effect, it is highly unlikely that any trader who acts in this fashion could have competitive motivations. The simultaneous purchase and sale of a commodity by a competitive trader implies that the marginal value of the units purchased equal the marginal value of the units sold. If anticipated, a sudden collapse in the spot price of a commodity at the end of the delivery period implies that the value of the last futures contract sold is substantially higher than the value of the last deliveries taken. As a result, unless there is convincing evidence that the decline in the spot price is a surprise, the combination of simultaneous purchase and sales of a commodity and the burying-the-body effect is consistent with the exercise of market power and clearly inconsistent with competitive behavior. If the deferred futures price is very low relative to the preexpiration spot price, moreover, it is unlikely that a price collapse at contract expiration is a surprise. Thus, an examination of a suspected manipulator's behavior during the delivery period makes it possible to determine whether he exercised market power. Another form of trading activity also sheds light on the motivations of a trader suspected of manipulation. Specifically, we have the following:

Result 6. *A large time spreading manipulator who is long the expiring future and short the deferred contract is an especially dangerous manipulator.*

This is also a consequence of the burying-the-body effect, which increases the value of the deferred-month short futures positions. The manipulator can therefore hedge himself against the costs of burying the body by shorting contracts. Indeed, a spreader takes more deliveries as the increased profit on the deferred-month short futures positions resulting from higher stocks in the delivery market increases the marginal benefit of delivery. Thus, a time spreader has a stronger motive to take excessive deliveries and exercise market power. This is information that can be used to evaluate a suspected trader's motivation and behavior.

Result 7. *$X > q_D^*$ is not a sufficient condition for profitable manipulation.*

This is yet another manifestation of the burying-the-body effect. If the manipulator's position is only slightly larger than q_D^*, for instance, he can liquidate only a small number of contracts at a supercompetitive price, but he must sell more than q_D^* units on the delivery market at an artificially depressed price. The losses on spot market sales may exceed the gains from the liquidations at the artificially inflated price. In this case the long chooses $Q \leq q_D^*$.

The comparative statics of the model are also important because they demonstrate the factors that make manipulation more profitable and therefore more likely. Such information is necessary to determine the how efforts to prevent or deter manipulation should vary with changes in market conditions.

In particular, it is of interest to determine how changes in various parameters affect the gains from long manipulation, where gains are defined as

$$G_L \equiv R(Q) - XP_D(0). \tag{2.12}$$

The last term in this expression equals the revenues the long would earn if he were to act competitively at contract expiration. Examining manipulative revenues relative to competitive revenues allows the separation of the effects of structural changes on the value of market power per se from their effects on the value of long positions in general.

Result 8. *The gains from manipulation are increasing in t.*

By the envelope theorem and (2.10), if j is the source of the marginal delivery, then

$$\frac{dG_L}{dt} = (X - Q)C_j = LC_j > 0.$$

The gains from manipulation also depend on the nature of demand. This is most easily seen when demand functions are linear, that is, $P_D(q) = \theta_D - \phi_D q$ and $P_i(q) = \theta_i - \phi_i q$, with $\theta_D > 0$, $\theta_i > 0$, $\phi_D > 0$ and $\phi_i > 0$, for all i. Then,

Result 9. *Holding the unmanipulated prices in each market constant, if the manipulator is not short the deferred month contract, then his gains vary inversely with ϕ_D and directly with ϕ_i, where i is the source of the marginal delivery.*

This result pertains to the effect of changes in the slope of demand curves alone, holding prices given q_D^* and q_i^* constant for all i. That is, it examines the effect of rotating demand curves around the original price-quantity point. If the demand curve is rotated around its intercept instead, the *unmanipulated* price at D—P_D^*—varies inversely with ϕ_D. This confounds the effect of changing demand parameters on the profitability of manipulation per se with its effect on the value of long positions in competitive conditions.

In order to hold nonmanipulated prices constant as the slopes of the demand curves change, it is necessary to vary the θ's along with the ϕ's. In particular, if

$$\theta_D \equiv P_D^* + \phi_D q_D^*$$

and

$$\theta_i \equiv P_i^* + \phi_i q_i^*,$$

where P_i^* is the unmanipulated price prior to the change in the slope parameter at i, then any variation in the ϕ's will leave the unmanipulated prices unchanged. Here the θ's rise in order to offset the price depressing effects of increases in the ϕ's. This can be called a *compensated* change in the slope parameters.

Consider the effect of a compensated change in ϕ_D on G_L. The envelope theorem implies

$$\frac{dG_L}{d\phi_D} = Q\{q_d^* - [Q - \sum_{j=1}^{n} s_j^*(Q)]\} < 0.$$

The inequality holds because manipulation increases the stock of the commodity in the delivery market. This result obtains because the steeper the demand curve in the delivery market, the more acute the burying-the-body effect. Indeed, the larger decline in the price at D resulting from the steeper demand curve at D implies that (1) backhauls to any location j commence at a smaller Q, and (2) a buyer at j pays a lower price to reacquire the commodity in the postdelivery auction for those Q where backhauls are efficient. The fall in elasticity therefore causes a downward shift in the marginal cost of delivery curve. The combination of a greater cost of burying the body and a lower liquidation demand curve makes manipulation less profitable.

Next consider the effect of a compensated change in ϕ_i, where i is the source of the marginal delivery. Here,

$$\frac{dG_L}{d\phi_i} = (X - Q)\{q_i^* - [q_i^* - y_i^*(Q) + s_i^*(Q)]\} > 0.$$

The inequality holds because consumption falls at the source of the marginal delivery. Manipulation is more profitable with a steeper the demand curve at nondelivery points because shorts must bid up the price more in order to induce owners at these points to sell a given quantity of the commodity.

The size of the manipulator's futures position, and the size and spatial distribution of his ownership of the physical commodity also affect the profitability of manipulation. In particular,

Result 10. *The gains from manipulation increase with the size of the futures position, and the ownership of a unit of the commodity at D increases the manipulator's gains by exactly the same amount as the ownership of an additional futures contract.*

Applying the envelope theorem to (12):

$$\frac{dG_L}{dX} = (X - Q)\frac{dP_j}{dQ} + P_D(Q) + Q\frac{dP_D}{dQ} - P_D(0),$$

which by (2.11) equals $P_j(Q) + tC_j - P_D(q^*_{D}) > 0$. That is, the manipulator can liquidate the additional contract and receive the marginal cost of delivering the commodity, which exceeds the unmanipulated futures price; a larger position thus enhances his market power.

If a manipulator purchases ϵ units of the deliverable commodity, retains it until after the manipulation is complete, and takes delivery on Q of his X positions, his gains equal

$$G_L = (X - Q)[P_j(Q + \epsilon) + tC_j] + (Q + \epsilon)P_D(Q + \epsilon) - (X + \epsilon)P_D(0). \qquad (2.13)$$

Applying the envelope theorem to (2.12) and using (2.11) implies that when $\epsilon = 0$,

$$\frac{dG_L}{d\epsilon} = (X - Q)\frac{dP_j}{dQ} + P_D(Q) + Q\frac{dP_D}{dQ} - P_D(0) = P_j(Q) + tC_j - P_D(0).$$

This is the same as the marginal gain from an additional futures contract, which is unsurprising inasmuch as they are perfectly substitutable claims on the commodity in the delivery market.

Result 10 shows that ownership of the deliverable stock is neither necessary nor sufficient to consummate a manipulation. This contradicts some assertions in the academic literature and much of existing legal doctrine on manipulation. That doctrine requires a finding of an intent to manipulate at the time a trader *initiates* a position, and uses ownership of the deliverable as an indicator of intent. (Chapter 5 discusses this issue in detail.) Besides the fact that a trader's intent at contract initiation has no bearing on whether he exerts market power at contract expiration, Result 10 implies that assuming the costs of obtaining a unit of the deliverable stock and a futures contract are equal, a trader with intent to manipulate may do so without purchasing the deliverable stock.

Since accused manipulators may own considerable amounts of the deliverable, this finding suggests that there is some other reason for purchasing deliverables. One possible explanation is that a trader may be able accumulate cash stocks without attracting attention, whereas very large futures trades are quickly noticed in the pit. If a trader is observed attempting to acquire a large long position, shorts may infer that a manipulation may occur and raise their prices as a result. Chapter 3 shows that secrecy facilitates manipulation by reducing the costs a trader must incur to acquire a position large enough to squeeze the market. If spot purchases indeed facilitate secrecy, they would allow a would-be manipulator to acquire his positions at a lower cost.

Result 11. *Under certain circumstances a manipulator may prefer to purchase a unit of the commodity in a non-deliverable location that is the source of deliveries during a manipulation to the purchase of a unit of the deliverable stock.*

Consider a trader long X futures contracts who purchases ϵ units of the commodity at location C_i where $y_i^*[Q(X)] > 0$. If the long holds onto the good until after the delivery process ends and then sells it, his delivery period revenue equals:

$$R(Q) = (X - Q)[P_j(Q + \epsilon) + tC_j] + QP_D(Q) + \epsilon P_i(Q).$$

Substituting from (2.11), and evaluating at $\epsilon = 0$,

$$\frac{dR(Q)}{d\epsilon} = P_j(Q) + tC_j - P_D(Q) - Q\frac{dP_D}{dQ} + P_i(Q).$$

Assume that prior to the revelation of an impending corner or squeeze a large trader can purchase a unit of the physical commodity at the competitive price.[4] In order for the incremental profit from this strategy to exceed the profit earned from purchasing a unit of the deliverable stock or an additional futures contract at the competitive price $P_D(0)$, the following expression must hold:

$$P_j(Q) + tC_j - P_D(Q) - Q\frac{dP_D}{dQ} + P_i(Q) - P_i(0) \geq$$
$$P_j(Q) + tC_j - P_D(0).$$

Thus, it is more beneficial to own the unit at C_i than an additional futures contract or a unit of the deliverable if:

$$[P_i(Q) - P_i(0)] - [P_D(Q) - P_D(0)] - Q\frac{dP_D}{dQ} \geq 0.$$

Note that $[P_i(Q) - P_i(0)] - [P_D(Q) - P_D(0)] > 0$ because manipulation raises the postdelivery price at C_i relative to that prevailing at D. Moreover, $dP_D(Q)/dQ < 0$ due to the burying-the-body effect. Therefore, the long may favor spot purchases outside the delivery market to purchases in it because the price at the former point rises relative to the price at the latter, and purchases in outside the delivery market do not exacerbate the burying-the-body effect.

By buying stocks outside the delivery market, a manipulator increases the marginal cost of delivery. This increases his profit. This result is quite general. Other actions that increase the marginal cost of delivery also enhance manipulative profit. For example, a long who increases transport costs by interfering with the transportation facilities will, by Result 8, make manipulation more profitable. As an example of this, consider the events on the New York Mercantile Exchange's potato futures contract in 1976. One trader accumulated as many railcars as possible on the only rail line where shorts could deliver. As a result, shorts could not enhance deliverable supplies and were forced to default on their contractual obligations. Although such activities can make manipulation more profitable, such actions alone are not sufficient to manipulate the market. In addition, the large long must restrict the number of contracts he liquidates in order to squeeze the market. Thus, raising delivery costs is a special case of the market-power manipulation analysis of this chapter.

The profitability of manipulation also depends on seasonal factors. Specifically,

Result 12. *Even-period manipulations are more profitable than odd-period manipulations, and Results 1 through 10 derived for even-period manipulations hold for odd-period ones.*

The appendix contains the proofs for an odd-period (that is, immediately following the harvest) manipulation corresponding to those for Propositions 1 through 3 and Results 1 through 10. The comparison of even- and odd-period manipulations is of interest because it forcefully demonstrates the importance of consumption distortions in facilitating manipulation in a spatial market.

Recall that in even-periods shorts purchase stocks to deliver from C_1, C_2, and so on *in turn* so the entire consumption response falls on each market separately. In the odd-period, in contrast, shorts bid away the commodity from all markets *simultaneously.* As a result, there is a more equal sharing of consumption losses in the odd-period, so a smaller increase in price is required at that time to increase deliveries by a given amount. Put another way, before the commodity has flowed to the final consumption points agents can respond more flexibly to an increase in the number of deliveries and this reduces the cost of satisfying this demand. The appendix also proves that the burying-the-body effect is more acute in the odd period, which is also due to the smaller consumption distortion in markets $C_1, \ldots, C_n$.[5]

The spatial model also contains insights concerning how the design of a futures contract can influence the profitability of a manipulation. In particular, it demonstrates that locating delivery points at low-price locations and allowing delivery at several locations can make manipulation less profitable and thus less likely, *ceteris paribus.*

Consider first the effect of the choice of a delivery point. Delivery points located in high-price markets that are along the same transport routes as low-price markets (i.e. markets at the terminus of significant flows of the commodity) are less susceptible to long manipulation even if both are equidistant from stocks of the commodity. The intuition behind this result is straightforward. Compare two markets distance d apart along a particular line segment, such that the prices in the markets differ by td, that one market is the highest price market along the segment, and that the other is the lowest price market on that segment. Here the commodity flows toward the high-price market and away from the low-price one. Thus delivery to the low-price market must come from higher price markets, while delivery to the low-price market comes from lower price ones.

The marginal cost of delivering a unit of the commodity to the low-price market from distance l away exceeds the no manipulation price in that market by $2tl$ because the price at the source of the delivery exceeds the price at the delivery point by tl, and the cost of transport equals tl.

The marginal cost of delivering a unit of the commodity to the low-price market from a point i distance l away, on the other hand, exceeds the no manipulation price in the low-price market by *at most* $2tl$. Increasing deliveries to the low-price market must depress the price there after deliveries are complete for some $Q > 0$ as backhaul cannot be efficient for all units delivered. Thus if the postdelivery price in the low-price market as a function of Q equals $P_H(Q)$, $P_H(0) > P_H(Q)$ for all $Q > 0$. Moreover, $P_H(Q) + tl \geq P_i(Q)$, where $P_i(Q)$ is the price at i, as otherwise it would be efficient to backhaul the commodity after the end of the delivery process. Since the marginal cost of delivering the commodity from i equals $MC_i = P_i(Q) + tl$, together these results imply $MC_i < P_H(0) + 2tl$ as asserted.

This analysis implies that the difference between the marginal cost of delivery and the no-manipulation spot price is always lower in the high-price market for given Q. Since it is costly to bury the body in the high-price market but costless to do so in the low-price one (as it is always efficient to return deliveries to their origin from the low-price market after a manipulation while some units remain in the low-price market afterward), the high-price market is unambiguously less vulnerable to manipulation than the low-price one.

This reasoning also implies that it is desirable to locate delivery points at the terminus of considerable commodity flows, rather than at markets near the origin of said flows. Prices in markets at the terminus exceed prices in markets at the origin by the cost of transport in order to attract these commodity flows. Since a manipulator exploits the cost of distorting natural commodity flows, and the degree of distortion—and hence the cost—is greater when these flows are reversed, manipulation is more profitable when deliveries must occur in the low-price market.

Recent developments in the grain market illustrate the importance of this factor. During its heyday as a grain market, Chicago was a low-price location on the major United States grain transport route, and attracted grain from a large tributary area. A variety of factors have dramatically altered the position of Chicago as a grain market over the past decades, however. Most important, changes in grain ocean shipping technology and grain shipping patterns have made it efficient to export grain via the Gulf of Mexico rather than via the Great Lakes or the East Coast. Panamax-size ships and very large bulk carriers economize on ocean transport costs, but these ships cannot navigate the Great Lakes. In addition, the relative decline of Europe as a grain importer, and the concomitant rise of Asia as a purchaser of United States grain have undercut the position of Great Lake and Northeast American. ports. It is cheaper to use Gulf ports rather than Great Lake or Eastern ports to ship grain to the new importing regions. Chicago is on the natural route to ship grain from the producing regions in the Midwest through the Great Lakes or the Northeastern ports. In contrast, it is peripheral to the transport route to the Gulf. Thus, Chicago has become a relatively low-price point near the origin of grain flows rather than a high-price point near the destination of these flows. *Ceteris paribus,* this made the Chicago Board of Trade contract, which employed Chicago as its primary delivery point, more manipulable.

Deregulation also contributed to this effect. The proportional rate system in effect prior to the deregulation of the railroads provided an artificial incentive to attract grain to Chicago. Under proportional rates, it was possible to ship grain from some location I to Chicago, store it, then ship it later to location J and pay the I to J through-shipment rail rate rather than the sum of the I–Chicago and Chicago-J rates. The through rate was lower than the sum of the rates on the individual legs. This is not possible under deregulated rates. The proportional rate therefore reduced the opportunity cost of storing grain in Chicago. This attracted grain shipments to Chicago and thereby reduced the vulnerability of the market to manipulation.

It should be noted that other changes in transport have had countervailing effects. Deregulation, for example, has reduced transport costs. According to Result 8, this would tend to reduce the susceptibility of Chicago Board of Trade grain contracts to corners. The important point to note in this regard, however, is that the decline in transport costs benefits all potential delivery points, whereas the effects examined in the two previous paragraphs has had an adverse effect on Chicago alone. Thus, the changes in the United States grain market suggest that a change in delivery points would reduce the susceptibility of grain futures contracts to manipulation.

It is also possible to show that the designation of several locations as eligible for delivery can reduce a contract's vulnerability to market-power manipulation. In the foregoing example of an odd-period manipulation, for instance, the addition of C_o as a delivery point dramatically alters the shape of the marginal cost of delivery curve.

In this case, for $1 \leq Q \leq 2$ the marginal cost of delivery equals the price at C_o, 3.25, as the commodity could be purchased there for that price. Since under the assumption that the distribution of the commodity is optimal prior to the attempted manipulation, prices at C_1 and C_2 exceed the price at C_o by the cost of transportation. Thus any units delivered from these points will be immediately shipped back to the point of origin. Thus for $Q \in (2, 3]$ the marginal cost of delivery equals the price at C_1, 3.5 plus the cost of transport between C_o and C_1 of .25 for a total of 3.75. Similarly, for $Q \in (3, 4]$ the marginal cost of delivery equals 4.25.

Although the marginal cost of delivery curve is increasing in this case, a comparison of this curve with that relevant in the case where delivery is allowed only at D demonstrates that the marginal cost of delivery is appreciably less when delivery can occur at either D or C_o. This is because this delivery specification reduces both transport costs and consumption distortions.

Making C_o, C_1, and C_2 delivery points and giving those making deliveries at C_i a premium equal to the cost of transport between C_i and D reduces the profitability of manipulation even further. Thus a short making delivery at C_1, for example, receives .75 more per unit delivered than a short making delivery at D. In the context of the previous example, such a set of premia makes the marginal cost of delivery curve perfectly elastic for all $Q \leq 4$. Manipulation is consequently unprofitable unless a long can amass a position larger than the stocks held at all four points.

This analysis implies that the use of multiple-delivery-point contracts is another way to reduce the vulnerability of futures markets to manipulation. Historically, exchanges have employed this measure, although they have sometimes done so only under pressure from the government. In 1992, the Chicago Board of Trade responded to the changes in the grain market discussed earlier by adding St. Louis as a delivery point. This city is on the primary United States grain transport route. The attempt by Ferruzzi S.A. to squeeze the CBT's soybean futures contract provided the impetus for this change. Similarly, under the Cotton Futures Act of 1916, the government required the New York Cotton Exchange to allow deliveries of cotton at several Southern ports, rather than at New York alone. This change was also motivated by several manipulations.

In summary, this section has shown that in spatial markets increasing the number of deliveries can induce distortions in consumption and transport. A large long trader can exploit this fact by standing for an excessive number of deliveries and force shorts to pay a premium to attract the commodity from its high-valued uses in order to obtain additional deliverable supplies. Shorts are willing to pay a premium to liquidate their futures positions in order to avoid paying this cost. This allows the large long to liquidate some of his contracts at a favorable price.

The model of this section demonstrates that manipulation can occur if increasing deliveries requires a distortion in the spatial pattern of consumption. Other factors may also facilitate manipulation. The following sections discuss briefly some of these factors.

2.3.3. An Intertemporal-Spatial Model of Manipulation

The previous section shows that the marginal cost of delivery is increasing if it is necessary to distort the *direction* of commodity flows in order to increase deliverable supplies. This section demonstrates that directional distortion is not a necessary condition for a successful manipulation in a spatial market. Temporal distortions may also facilitate manipulation.

Consider the following representation of a different one dimensional spatial market. Consumers are located at the right endpoint (location R) of a line segment. A commodity is produced at the left endpoint (location L) of the segment. The commodity is produced in odd-numbered periods only and is consumed in both odd and even-numbered periods (this contrasts with the model of the previous section). Production is nonstochastic, and equals H in each odd-numbered period. Demand is also nonstochastic, and the demand curve is given by $P_1 = \theta_1 - \phi q_1$ in the odd-numbered periods (where q_1 is odd-period consumption) and $P_2 = \theta_2 - \phi_2 q_2$ in even-numbered periods. The discount rate equals r.

The commodity must be stored between the odd and the even-periods in order to allow consumption in the even-periods. The commodity may be stored at location L and at the midpoint of the segment (location C). The latter location is the delivery point for a futures contract.

In contrast to the model of the previous section, commodity flows in this market are one-directional, that is, the commodity moves from the left endpoint to the right endpoint. As a result, manipulation in this market cannot result from distortions in the location of consumption, but only its timing.

The commodity is costly to transport and store. Total costs of transportation and storage are quadratic: the cost of storage at L equals $s_L q_L^2$, the cost of storage at C equals $s_C q_C^2$, the cost of transport between L and C equals $t_{LC} q_{LC}^2$, and the cost of transport between C and R equals $t_{CR} q_{CR}^2$ where s_L, s_C, t_{LC}, and t_{CR} are parameters; q_L and q_C are the amount stored at L and C respectively; and q_{LC} and q_{CR} are the quantity transported between the L and C, and C and R, respectively.

The commodity is costly to handle in the delivery market. The costs of in-bound and out-bound elevation in grain markets are examples of handling costs. These costs are also assumed quadratic. In particular, the cost of unloading q units of the commodity into the delivery facilities equals $e_I q^2$, while the cost of loading q units of the commodity from the delivery storage facilities for transport from C to R equals $e_o q^2$.

Perfect competition among buyers and sellers of the commodity, storage services, and transportation ensures that the equilibrium spatial and temporal distribution of consumption, storage, and transportation will maximize the net social surplus. To determine the optimal surplus, note that odd-period consumption equals $H - q_C - q_L$, and even-period consumption equals $q_C + q_L$. Moreover, $q_{LC} = H - q_C - q_L$ in the odd-period and $q_{LC} = q_L$ in the even-period. Finally, $q_{CR} = H - q_C - q_L$ in the odd-period and $q_{CR} = q_L + q_C$ in the even-period.

Social surplus equals the difference between the surplus enjoyed by consumers and the costs of handling, storage and transportation. Since all conditions repeat every two periods, it is only necessary to examine a single odd (first) period and the subsequent even (second) period. Formally, total surplus equals

$$
\begin{aligned}
W \equiv \int_0^{H-q_L-q_C} [\theta_1 - \phi q]dq + f \int_0^{q_L+q_C} [\theta_2 - \phi q]dq - s_L q_L^2 \\
s_C q_C^2 - t_{LC}(H - q_L - q_C)^2 - t_{CR}(H - q_C - q_L) - f t_{LC} q_L^2 - \\
f t_{CR}(q_L + q_C)^2 - e_I q_C^2 - f e_o q_C^2,
\end{aligned}
$$

where $f = 1/(1 + r)$.

Assume that q_C^* and q_L^* maximize this expression. It is possible to show that given these quantities prices reflect full carrying charges. That is, competitive prices at R in the even-period exceed prices there in the odd-period by the cost of money, the cost of storage, and the difference in marginal transport costs between even and odd-periods.

Now consider the maximum market surplus when shorts must

deliver $Q > q_C^*$ in the odd (first) period:

$$W_{eQ} \equiv \int_0^{H-q_L-q_C} [\theta_1 - \phi q]dq + f \int_0^{q_L+q_C} [\theta_2 - \phi q]dq +$$
$$s_C q_C^2 - t_{CR}(H - q_C - q_L) - f t_{LC} q_L^2 - f t_{CR}(q_L + q_C)^2 -$$
$$e_I Q^2 - e_o(Q - q_C)^2 - f e_o q_C^2. \tag{2.14}$$

Maximization of (2.14) subject to the constraint $Q \leq H - q_L$ implies the following first-order conditions:

$$\begin{pmatrix} a_{11} & a_{12} & 1 \\ a_{21} & a_{22} & 0 \\ 1 & 1 & 0 \end{pmatrix} \begin{pmatrix} q_L(Q) \\ q_C(Q) \\ \lambda(Q) \end{pmatrix} \leq \begin{pmatrix} c_1 \\ c_2 \\ -Q \end{pmatrix},$$

where $\lambda(Q)$ is the lagrangean multiplier on the constraint, and

$$\begin{aligned} a_{11} &= -(1+f)(\phi + 2t_{LC} + 2t_{CR}) - 2s_L \\ a_{12} = a_{21} &= -(1+f)(\phi + 2t_{CR}) \\ a_{22} &= -(1+f)(\phi + 2t_{CR} + 2e_o) - 2s_C \\ c_1 &= \theta_1 - f\theta_2 - H(\phi + 2t_{LC} + 2t_{CR}) \\ c_2 &= \theta_1 - f\theta_2 - H(\phi + 2t_{CR}) - 2e_o Q. \end{aligned}$$

Consider the case where $\lambda(Q) = 0$. (The analysis is very similar when $\lambda > 0$, so for brevity I restrict my attention to this case). Here

$$q_L(Q) = \frac{c_1 a_{22} - c_2 a_{12}}{a_{11} a_{22} - a_{12}^2} > 0$$

$$q_C(Q) = \frac{c_2 a_{11} - c_1 a_{12}}{a_{11} a_{22} - a_{12}^2} > 0.$$

Recall that the marginal cost of delivery equals the sum of the price of the commodity at L plus the cost of moving the commodity to the delivery point. This latter cost equals the sum of the cost of transport from L to R and the cost of inbound handling at C. Formally, if $P_{i,j}(Q)$ is the price at location i in period j given Q deliveries:

$$MC(Q) = P_{L,1}(Q) + 2t_{LC}(H - q_L) + 2e_I Q. \tag{2.15}$$

Consequently

$$\frac{dMC(Q)}{dQ} = \frac{dP_{L,1}(Q)}{dQ} - 2t_{LC}\frac{dq_L(Q)}{dQ} + 2e_I.$$

Note that

$$P_{L,1}(Q) = fP_{R,2}(Q) - 2s_L q_L(Q) - 2ft_{LC}q_L(Q) - 2f_{CR}[q_L(Q) + q_C(Q)]$$

$$P_{R,2}(Q) = \theta_2 - \phi[q_L(Q) + q_C(Q)].$$

Thus

$$\frac{dP_{L,1}(Q)}{dQ} = f\frac{dP_{R,2}(Q)}{dQ} - \frac{dq_L(Q)}{dQ}[2s_L + 2t_{LC}(1+f) + 2ft_{CR}] - \frac{dq_C(Q)}{dQ}2ft_{CR} + 2e_I$$

$$\frac{dP_{R,2}(Q)}{dQ} = -\phi[\frac{dq_L(Q)}{dQ} + \frac{dq_C(Q)}{dQ}].$$

These imply

$$\frac{dMC(Q)}{dQ} = -[\frac{dq_L(Q)}{dQ} + \frac{dq_C(Q)}{dQ}]f[\phi + 2t_{CR}] - \frac{dq_L(Q)}{dQ}[2s_L + 2(1+f)t_{LC}] + 2e_I.$$

Since

$$\frac{dq_L(Q)}{dQ} = -\frac{2e_o(1+f)(\phi + 2t_{CR})}{a_{11}a_{22} - a_{12}^2} < 0$$

$$\frac{dq_C(Q)}{dQ} = \frac{2e_o[(1+f)(\phi + 2t_{LC} + 2t_{CR}) + 2s_L]}{a_{11}a_{22} - a_{12}^2} > 0,$$

the following is true:

$$\frac{dMC(Q)}{dQ} = \frac{2e_o(\phi + 2t_{CR})[2t_{LC}(1+f) + 2s_L]}{a_{11}a_{22} - a_{12}^2} + 2e_I > 0. \quad (2.16)$$

The intuition behind this increasing marginal cost of delivery is as follows. Increasing the number of deliveries beyond q_C^* forces distortions in the spatial pattern of storage, the temporal pattern of transportation and of consumption at R, and the amount of handling at C. These changes raise both the price shorts must pay to acquire the commodity ($P_{L,1}$) and the marginal costs of moving the commodity into deliverable position.

In particular, $q_C > q_C^*$ and $q_L < q_L^*$ when $Q > q_C^*$. This increases the marginal cost of storage at the former point and lowers it at the latter, increases the first period marginal cost of transport between L and C, lowers the second period marginal cost of transport between L and R, and increases the marginal cost of handling. Finally, $q_C + q_L$ is increasing in Q. Thus consumption at R rises in the second period and falls in the first period when Q increases, so $P_{R,1}$ rises and $P_{R,2}$ falls. Together the decline in the marginal cost of storage at L and the decline in the second period marginal cost of transport between L and R are larger than the decline of the $P_{R,2}$. Therefore $P_{L,1}$ rises. Finally, the change in the pattern of shipments alters the marginal transport costs in each segment and each period.

Together these changes create the necessary conditions for manipulation. The increase in the first period price at L, the increase in the first period marginal cost of transport between L and C, and the higher marginal cost of handling, lead to a rising marginal cost of delivery.

There is also burying-the-body effect in this model. To see this, note that

$$P_{C,1}(Q) = fP_{R,2}(Q) - 2s_C q_C(Q) - 2ft_{CR}(q_L + q_C) - 2fe_o q_C(Q). \quad (2.17)$$

Consequently,

$$\frac{dP_{C,1}(Q)}{dQ} = -f(\phi + 2t_{CR})[\frac{dq_C(Q)}{dQ} + \frac{dq_L(Q)}{dQ}] - 2(s_C + 2fe_o)\frac{dq_C(Q)}{dQ} < 0.$$

There are clear similarities between the implications of this model and the one previous despite the significant structural differences between them. Again, when a large long trader demands deliveries in excess of the stocks optimally held in the delivery market, shorts must disrupt efficient patterns of consumption, transport, and storage. They must pay increasing prices to bid resources from their highest-value uses. This causes the marginal cost of delivery to increase with the number made. Moreover, the excessive quantity stored in the delivery market depresses the price there after the corner is over.

It is straightforward to demonstrate that Results 1 through 12 are true for this model as well; for brevity the relevant derivations are omitted. Most important, the implications concerning the behavior of prices and quantities during a manipulation discussed earlier obtain. Specifically, a market-power manipulation in this model causes a temporary rise in the delivery market spot price relative to prices in other markets and prices for deferred delivery, followed by a drop in the relative price at the delivery market when the contract is liquidated. Moreover, manipulation artificially stimulates shipments to the delivery market prior to contract expiration and stimulates shipments from the delivery market after expiration as the commodity is shipped to higher-value locations. Finally, a corner increases the amount stored in the delivery market. This inflation in stocks is especially acute when one takes into account the distortion of intertemporal price relations that result from the exercise of market power. That is, in competitive markets the spot price is highest relative to the futures price when deliverable stocks are very small; therefore, a combination of a high spot price relative to deferred futures prices and large deliverable stocks is inconsistent with competitive behavior and indicative of a market-power manipulation.

The main distinctions between this model and the one previous are the intertemporal nature of the former and the differences in the structural parameters. Results pertaining specifically to this model include the following,

Result 13. *Due to manipulation* $P_{R,1}$ *rises and* $P_{R,2}$ *falls.*

This is due to the fact that consumption rises in the even-period, while consumption falls in the odd-period, due to the manipulator's actions.

Result 14. *Manipulation increases both* $P_{L,1}$ *and* $P_{L,2}$, *and reduces* $P_{L,2}/P_{L,1}$.

Prices rise at L because manipulation decreases stocks there. Since a positive quantity is stored there, even and odd-period prices can differ only by the cost of carry, which consists of a time value of money component and a storage cost component. Therefore

$$\frac{P_{L,2}}{P_{L,1}} = 1 + r + \frac{2s_L q_L}{P_{L,1}}.$$

Since manipulation reduces q_L and increases $P_{L,1}$ this expression implies that manipulation reduces the even-period price relative to the odd-period price.

Result 15. *The structural parameters in the model affect the marginal cost of delivery and thus the profitability of manipulation.*

An examination of (2.16) reveals that the marginal cost of delivery rises more rapidly: the higher the discount factor (that is, the lower the interest rate), the larger is ϕ (that is, the steeper the demand curve), the larger the transport cost parameters, and the larger the storage cost parameter. All of these results are quite intuitive. The lower the interest rate, the higher the present value of receipts from sales in the even-period. The larger ϕ, the greater the price response at R in the even-period to a fall in consumption, and hence the greater the odd-period price response at L. The larger the transport cost parameters, the larger the fall in marginal transport costs when shipments between L and R decline in the even-period. Similarly, the larger the storage cost parameter, the greater the fall in marginal storage costs at L as the quantity stored there declines.

In sum, this intertemporal-spatial model again highlights the central role of consumption distortions in facilitating manipulation. A large long trader who demands deliveries in excess of the stocks optimally held in the delivery market forces inefficient flows of the commodity to that place. This alters the temporal pattern of consumption and transport and the spatial distribution of storage and induces excessive handling of the commodity. A distortion on each of these margins is costly, and shorts are willing to liquidate their futures positions at high prices in order to avoid bearing these costs.

Some historical examples of this sort of phenomenon exist. Specifically, manipulators on the Chicago Board of Trade sometimes exploited storage space shortages and transportation difficulties in order to squeeze the Board's grain markets. Note that capacity constraints in both storage and transportation cause the marginal costs of storage and transportation to increase. The model of this section implies that such increasing marginal costs can make manipulation possible. Thus, this model shows how a manipulation could succeed on the Chicago Board of Trade even during an era when Chicago was a high-priced market with a large tributary region that lay along the primary grain transportation route.

The addition of nonlinear transport and storage costs therefore implies that although locating the delivery point in a low-price location along a transportation route can reduce the profitability of manipulation (as was demonstrated in the previous section), this does not immunize a contract from manipulation if there are rigidities in storage or transportation. Moreover, the model demonstrates that the efficiency and capacity of transportation and storage are important determinants of the profitability of manipulation. Specifically, the more elastic the marginal costs of transport and storage, the more elastic the marginal cost of delivery. This increased elasticity, in turn, makes manipulation less profitable. Thus, the nature of transportation and storage technologies is an important determinant of the frequency and severity of corners.

This last finding strongly suggests that important changes that have occurred in the American commodity markets over the last three decades have, *ceteris paribus*, reduced the vulnerability of grain, oilseed, and cotton futures markets to corners and squeezes. Specifically, the efficiency of rail transport has improved dramatically. This is primarily due to the deregulation of rail transport under the Staggers Act of 1981. Deregulation has increased the flexibility of rail transport. In the regulated era, rail-car shortages were not uncommon. Moreover, the inflexibility of rail rates diminished the incentives of railroads to make additional capacity available to shippers in the event of an increase in the demand for rail transport; a market-power manipulation causes just such an increase in demand. In contrast, in the deregulated rail market, transport resources flow to their highest-value uses. Moreover, it is now possible and profitable for railroads to operate so-called unit trains consisting of approximately 100 rail cars in order to haul large quantities of cargo for a single shipper. This form of transport is extremely efficient and therefore tends to reduce the marginal cost of delivery. This, in turn, makes manipulation less profitable.

Although the improved efficiency of transport attributable to deregulation would tend to reduce the vulnerability of spatial markets to manipulation, one cannot make inferences concerning the likelihood of manipulation in contemporary American futures markets on the basis of this fact alone. Indeed, Section 2.3.2 showed that secular changes in shipping patterns have had offsetting effects on the manipulability of Chicago Board of Trade grain futures contracts. Moreover, Chapter 3 demonstrates that other factors such as the volume of futures trading and the volatility of the order flow affect a contract's vulnerability to corners. Changes in these variables may have offset the effect of reduced transport costs in whole or in part.

As noted earlier, moreover, these results imply a trader who can raise transport or storage costs (by withholding transport or storage capacity, for instance) is a very dangerous manipulator. Thus, if transportation markets or storage markets are very concentrated, manipulation is more likely. If these markets are concentrated, the party who controls a substantial portion of transport or storage capacity can withhold this capacity from the market, raise the marginal costs of transport or storage, and therefore increase the profitability of manipulation. This party can exploit this advantage by acquiring a large long futures position.

2.3.4. Other Sources of Frictional Manipulation

The preceding model demonstrates that transportation costs create the potential for profitable manipulation if a futures trader can amass a position sufficiently larger than the supply available at the delivery point. The extent of his market power depends on supply and demand conditions, seasonal factors, and transport costs. These transport cost related frictions are likely to be important in many markets, including grains, non-precious metals, and petroleum products.

Transportation costs are an example of an economic friction that isolates geographically dispersed consumers. The results therefore suggest that any form of transactions cost that impedes the transfer of a commodity among consumers can make manipulation possible. Given such costs, an increase in the number of deliveries forces a reallocation of the commodity from those who value it highly to those who do not. As a result, to obtain the good for delivery shorts must bid it away from high-value owners at increasing prices. This causes the marginal cost of delivery to increase and facilitates manipulation. Any friction that makes it inefficient to return to the *status quo ante* may therefore favor manipulation.

As one example of a friction that can facilitate manipulation, shorts may have to incur search and negotiation costs to obtain the commodity. Moreover, the existence of search costs may make it inefficient to return the commodity to the original owners, which implies that excessive deliveries may induce a consumption distortion similar to that found in the spatial market.

Institutional factors may also create frictions. As one example, certain participants in the Treasury securities market cannot lend these securities through the repurchase market. Specifically, some pension and mutual funds cannot lend securities. Security loans through the repurchase market are frequently the low-cost way to supply T-bonds and T-notes for delivery against derivative contracts such as when-issued agreements. Thus, the funds so restricted must sell securities in order to make them available for delivery. They incur transactions costs to do so. Moreover, the funds tend to follow *buy and hold* strategies for Treasuries in order to meet cash flow management objectives. This suggests that they incur high explicit or implicit costs to trade their portfolio. Also, tax considerations make it uneconomical for some investors to sell Treasuries unless they receive a large price premium; sale may require them to extinguish a tax-timing option, which is particularly valuable (that is, *in-the-money*) when the security is selling at a substantial premium over the acquisition price. As a result, the institutional restriction on security lending and tax-induced frictions make it costly to acquire Treasuries for delivery against Treasury derivative positions. This inflates the marginal cost of delivery. To take another example from the Treasury market, some T-notes and T-bonds are stripped. That is, the interest and principal on these securities are split and traded separately. It is costly to re-assemble a stripped security. Moreover, the strips market is less liquid than the market for whole securities. Therefore, transactions costs in strips are higher than for whole securities. It is thus costlier to use stripped securities to make deliveries against derivative contracts than it is to use whole securities. This in turn contributes to an increasing marginal cost of delivery.

2.4. Manipulation With Several Large Traders

Section 2.3 assumes that all traders but the large long are atomistic. In real-world markets, however, there may be several large traders. This section examines the economics of market power in a derivatives market when there are several large long traders. I continue to assume that shorts are atomistic.

Consider the following model of the market during the delivery period. Traders have already initiated a total of X positions in the futures market; that is, shorts have undertaken obligations to deliver X units of the security, and longs have assumed obligations to purchase X units of the security. There are $N \geq 1$ long traders and a continuum of short traders. Shorts are therefore atomistic, whereas the longs may be either large and concentrated or small and diffuse. The concentration on the long side of the market varies inversely with N.

During the delivery period longs and shorts can settle their outstanding positions either making a reversing transaction or making or taking delivery. By assumption, the marginal cost of delivery is given by the function $MC(Q)$, where Q is the total amount of deliveries demanded by the N longs. For $Q > q_D^*$, $MC'(Q) > 0$, where as before q_D^* is the deliverable stock under perfect competition; otherwise, $MC'(Q) = 0$.

For simplicity, I assume trading for liquidation in the futures market takes place in the following way. Longs submit market orders to sell their outstanding positions. Since there are N identical longs, any long i may submit a market order to sell $Z_i \leq X/N$ units of the derivative. Put another way, they stand for $\Delta_i = X/N - Z_i$ deliveries. The identical, atomistic shorts submit bids to buy the $X - \sum_{i=1}^{N} \Delta_i = \sum_{i=1}^{N} Z_i$ units offered by the longs. The price shorts are willing to pay depends on the costs of making delivery or defaulting. No short is willing to pay a price to purchase a unit of the derivative that exceeds the marginal cost of delivery or default. Competition between shorts thus implies that the equilibrium price in the derivative market equals the marginal cost of delivering or defaulting on a total of $\sum_{i=1}^{n} \Delta_i$ contracts.

An individual long i chooses Δ_i in order to maximize his total revenues. These revenues consist of two components: (1) his receipts on sale of the derivative security positions liquidated, and (2) the price he receives on resale of the underlying securities delivered to him. The resale price function equals $P(\sum_{i=1}^{n} \Delta_i)$. Due to the burying the corpse effect, if

$$\sum_{i=1}^{n} \Delta_i > q_D^*,$$

then

$$P(\sum_{i=1}^{n} \Delta_i) < MC(\sum_{i=1}^{n} \Delta_i)$$

and

$$P'(\sum_{i=1}^{n} \Delta_i) < 0 < MC'(\sum_{i=1}^{n} \Delta_i).$$

These assumptions allow the determination of the equilibrium liquidation price in the futures market at contract expiration. If longs choose their Δ's independently, given the choices of the other traders, long i chooses Δ_i to maximize:

$$\Pi_i = (\frac{X}{N} - \Delta_i) MC(\sum_{j=1}^{n} \Delta_j) + \Delta_i P(\sum_{j=1}^{n} \Delta_j).$$

The first term equals the long's revenues from the sale of positions in the derivative market. He sells $X/N - \Delta_i$ units of the derivative at a price equal to the marginal cost of delivery. The second term equals the long's receipts from reselling the securities delivered to him and from the damages shorts owe him on default.

The first-order condition for the maximization of Π_i is

$$\frac{d\Pi_i}{d\Delta_i} = 0 = -\ MC(\sum_{j=1}^{n} \Delta_j) + (\frac{X}{N} - \Delta_i) MC'(\sum_{j=1}^{n} \Delta_j) + P(\sum_{j=1}^{n} \Delta_j) + \Delta_i P'(\sum_{j=1}^{n} \Delta_j). \quad (2.18)$$

There are N expressions equivalent to (2.18), one for each of the N long traders. A Nash equilibrium set of $\{\Delta_i^*\}$ satisfies all N first-order conditions simultaneously. Since all long traders are identical, a symmetric Nash equilibrium specifies a $\Delta(N) = \Delta_j^*$ for all j such that

$$0 = -MC[N\Delta(N)] + [\frac{X}{N} - \Delta(N)] MC'[N\Delta(N)] + P[N\Delta(N)] + \Delta_i P'[N\Delta(N)]. \quad (2.19)$$

It is possible to show that in a symmetric Nash equilibrium the price of the future at contract expiration equals

$$MC[N\Delta(N)] \geq P(0) = P_c,$$

where P_c is the perfectly competitive price in the futures market. If X is sufficiently larger than q_D^*, then $N\Delta(N) > q_D^*$ and the inequality is strict. That is, there is an interior solution. The proof is omitted for the sake of brevity. The intuition behind the result is well known. This is essentially a Cournot model of competition. If the market liquidation demand curve is downward-sloping (as will be the case if the total number of deliveries taken exceeds q_D^*), given the amount of deliveries demanded by all other traders, an individual long may face a downward-sloping demand curve for liquidating his contracts. Given such a demand curve, he charges a supercompetitive price for his contracts. In equilibrium, all longs will behave in this manner, and therefore the equilibrium price will exceed the competitive price. The Cournot behavior of those long the derivative can therefore cause a supercompetitive price in the futures market.

It must also be emphasized that price distortions do not always occur even if the market is very concentrated. Recall from Result 7 above that even a monopolist cannot profitably exercise market power if his position is only slightly larger than q_D^*. Since competition is more acute when $N > 1$ than in the monopoly case, manipulation may not occur in the former case even when $X > q_D^*$. Indeed, the greater intensity of competition implies that for some values of open interest, manipulation will be unprofitable when $N > 1$ even though manipulation is profitable for a monopolist long. Therefore, for a given open interest, the less concentrated the market, the less likely is a market-power manipulation.

It is possible to derive the effects of changing the number of longs and the open interest on the equilibrium. If $N\Delta(N) > q_D^*$, (2) implies that

$$\frac{dN\Delta}{dN} = \frac{-MC[N\Delta(N)] + P[N\Delta(N)]}{-\frac{d^2\Pi_i}{d\Delta_i^2}} < 0.$$

The numerator of this expression is negative because the manipulated futures price exceeds the postdelivery cash price. The denominator of this expression is positive because $d^2\Pi_i/d\Delta_i^2$ is negative at a maximum.

In words, the total number of deliveries demanded by the N longs falls as the number of longs increases. This implies $dMC(.)/dN < 0$, that is, the derivative price varies inversely with the number of long derivative traders. This result is quite intuitive. Given X, the smaller the number of long traders in the futures market, the more market power these longs possess; that is, there is less competition in the futures market. As a result of this less intense competition among longs, they reduce their output of liquidations (that is, they demand more deliveries), and the futures price is higher. Indeed, it is possible to show that there exists a finite N such that $MC[N\Delta(N)] = P_c$. Therefore, as the number of longs increases and the concentration of long futures positions declines, eventually the competitive price obtains.

Next consider the relation between $MC(.)$ and X. Here

$$\frac{dN\Delta}{dX} = \frac{MC'[N\Delta(N)]}{-\frac{d^2\Pi_i}{d\Delta_i^2}} > 0.$$

This result is also very intuitive. The larger X, that is, the larger the open interest in the futures market, the greater the market power the longs can exercise.

This model implies that monopoly is not a necessary condition for a market-power manipulation to occur in a futures market (or more generally, a derivative securities market). Manipulation can occur if the long side of the futures market is sufficiently concentrated but not monopolistic. It is important to note, however, that competition among longs does reduce the severity of monopolistic distortions. Thus, price distortions may not exist if there is even a modest amount of competition among longs.

For simplicity, this model has assumed that all longs are identical. It is a simple matter to allow longs of different sizes. The standard Cournot analysis of heterogeneous firms applies in this case. Here the Herfindahl index of futures positions, rather than N, is the appropriate measure of competitiveness. The smaller the value of this index, the more competitive the market, and thus the lower the probability that a manipulation will occur, and the smaller the price distortion that obtains if traders do exercise market power.

2.5. Frictional Short Manipulations

Long manipulations receive considerably more attention, but manipulations by large short traders are sometimes alleged. Examples of alleged short manipulations include the Hohenberg cotton case of 1971, the 1976 Maine potato futures episode, and the infamous onion incident of 1956. In late 1991 a large grain processor alleged that regular warehousemen in Chicago were short manipulating Chicago Board of Trade grain futures contracts.

A short manipulator makes too many deliveries or inefficiently increases the stock of the commodity in the delivery market in order to decrease price there. This allows him to liquidate some of his futures positions at an artificially low price, since competitive longs are willing to sell their positions at a price equal to this depressed value.

Some of the same frictions that make a long manipulation profitable may contribute to short manipulation as well. It may occur, for example, in the spatial economy examined in Section 2.3.2.[6] A variant of the model examined there illustrates how short manipulation works in this case. To simplify the exposition, assume that there are only two consumption locations, D (the delivery point) and C_1, and that the stock in the former market equals q_D^* and that in the latter market equals q_1^*. The demand curves are $P_D(q_D)$ and $P_1(q_1)$, respectively. Assume that given q_D^* and q_1^* it is not profitable to ship the commodity from one market to the other. Therefore, $P_1(q_1^*) + t > P_D(q_D^*)$ and $P_D(q_D^*) + t > P_1(q_1^*)$, where t is the per unit cost of transport between the markets.

The short desires to minimize the cost of repurchasing his outstanding contracts. Recall that increasing supply in the delivery market forces down the spot price there due to the burying-the-body effect. A large short can exploit this effect by bringing more of the commodity into the delivery market. Price taking longs then submit bids to liquidate equal to this lower price. This favors the short trader by reducing the cost he incurs to close his outstanding contracts.

To increase the supply at D by Z units (and drive the price there to $P_D(q_D^* + Z)$) the short buys the commodity at C_1, which raises the price there to $P_1(q_1^* - Z)$. The total cost of purchasing the Z units and shipping them to D equals $Z[P_1(q_1^* - Z) + t]$.

If all traders are aware of the short trader's actions, the price at C_1 rises until the short ships Z' units between the two markets, where $P_D(q_D^* + Z') + t = P_1(q_1^* - Z')$. At this point traders recognize that any further units shipped to D will be returned to C_1, and therefore further shipments to D have no impact on prices. It is straightforward to demonstrate that

$$\frac{dZ'}{dt} = \frac{-1}{P_D'(q_D^* + Z') + P_1'(q_1^* - Z')} > 0.$$

Note that the short need not deliver these units to drive down the price at D. Simply selling them on the spot market there has the same effect. In fact, it is possible to show that the short's cost of closing his position is the same regardless of whether he disposes of the units he brings to D by sale or delivery. The expense the short bears when he closes his futures position while purchasing Z units at C_1 and disposing of them at D therefore equals

$$E_S(Z) = P_D(q_D^* + Z)S + [P_1(q_1^* - Z) + t - P_D(q_D^* + Z)]Z. \quad (2.20)$$

The first term equals the cost of repurchasing S contracts at the manipulated price, while the second term equals the cost of purchasing Z units at C_1 and reselling them at D. The short chooses Z to minimize $E_S(Z)$ subject to the constraint that $Z \leq Z'$. If an interior minimum exists, then there is a $Z^* \in (0, Z')$ that satisfies the following first-order condition:

$$\begin{aligned} SP_D'(q_D^* + Z^*) - P_D(q_D^* + Z^*) - P_D'(q_D^* + Z^*)Z^* = \\ P_1'(q_1^* - Z^*)Z^* - t - P_1(q_1^* - Z^*). \quad (2.21) \end{aligned}$$

Otherwise the short chooses either $Z^* = Z'$ or $Z^* = 0$. The first term on the l.h.s. equals the marginal decline in the cost of repurchasing the S short positions due to the depression in the price in the delivery market. The sum of the second and third terms is the marginal reduction in the short's expense due to the sale at D of a unit of the commodity purchased at C_1. The r.h.s. equals the cost of incrementally increasing the supply at D.

In order for the short to choose $Z^* > 0$, the following must be true:

$$E_S(Z^*) \leq SP_D(q_D^*).$$

The l.h.s. of this cost the short incurs when choosing a $Z^* > 0$ to satisfy (2.21). The r.h.s. side equals the cost short would pay when choosing $Z^* = 0$ and simply buying back his entire position at the competitive price $P_D(q_D^*)$. This implies that the following is a necessary condition for a short manipulation to occur:

$$Z^*[P_1(q_1^* - Z^*)+t - P_D(q_D^* + Z^*)] \leq S[P_D(q_D^*) - P_D(q_D^* + Z^*)]. \qquad (2.22)$$

It is possible to show that for a large enough S, there exists a $Z^* > 0$ that satisfies (2.21) and (2.22).

An analysis of the model yields several important results. It is again useful to examine the gains from short manipulation, defined as the difference between the short's offset expenses when he acts competitively and when he exerts market power:

$$G_S = SP_D(q_D^*) - E_S(Z^*).$$

The relevant results include the following:

Result 16. *If (given S) there exists a $Z^* \in (0, Z')$ that minimizes (2.20) and satisfies (2.22) then the gains from short manipulation vary inversely with t.*

This follows from an application of the envelope theorem to (2.20). Note that

$$\frac{dG_S}{dt} = -\frac{dE_S}{dt} = -\frac{\partial E_S}{\partial Z}\frac{dZ}{dt} - \frac{\partial E_S}{\partial t}. \qquad (2.23)$$

If an interior minimum exists $\partial E_S/\partial Z = 0$, and $\partial E_S/\partial t = Z > 0$; the short's offset expenses rise, and the gains to manipulation therefore fall.

Result 17. *If (given S) $Z^* = Z'$ (that is, the optimum is a corner solution), the gains from short manipulation may either increase or decrease with t. Moreover, given S, G_S is increasing in t for some t.*

If $Z^* = Z'$ then $dG_S/dZ = -dE_S/dZ > 0$. Since $dZ'/dt > 0$, (2.23) may be positive, negative, or zero. Using (2.20) and substituting extensively,

$$\frac{dG_S}{dt} = - P_D'(q_D^* + Z')S\frac{dZ'}{dt} + \\ [P_D(q_D^* + Z') - P_1(q_1^* - Z') - t]\frac{dZ'}{dt} - 2Z'.$$

The definition of Z' implies that the bracketed term equals 0. When $t = 0$ it is evident that $Z' = 0$, so for such a t

$$\frac{dG_S}{dt} = -P_D'(q_D^* + Z')S\frac{dZ'}{dt} > 0.$$

Together Results 16 and 17 imply that the profitability of short manipulation varies nonmonotonically with t; starting from small values of t the gains from short manipulation first increase with transport costs but eventually decline as these costs rise beyond a certain level. The intuition behind this is as follows. For very small t, the manipulator's ability to depress price at D is limited because he cannot distort consumption (and therefore prices) dramatically, as the level of t imposes a limit on the price difference between the two markets. Increases in t therefore allow him to dump larger quantities at D before backhauls commence, depressing the price at that point further. Over some range of t the advantages of doing so more than offset the effect of the higher costs of transporting the good to D the higher t implies. As t continues to grow, however, eventually a point is reached where the manipulator chooses a Z^* that is smaller than the quantity at which backhauls commence, that is, he chooses a $Z^* > Z'$. When this is true, the manipulator no longer imposes the largest possible price distortion. At this point, further increases in t only serve to increase the costs that the short must incur to transport the commodity to D without increasing his ability to depress prices.

These higher costs increase the expense the short bears to employ a manipulative strategy.

This result strikingly demonstrates the importance of consumption distortions in facilitating manipulation. A positive t is necessary for short manipulation to occur even though the short trader bears the direct cost of transporting the commodity to the delivery market because then it is inefficient to return it to the point of origin. As a result, these shipments depress price at D; if $t = 0$ all units would be returned to C_1 and the manipulator's actions would have no effect on price. Thus, it is the *indirect* effect of transportation costs—their effect on the spatial distribution of consumption—that facilitates short manipulation. This reinforces the conclusion derived in Section 3 that the costs of consumption distortions that arise in spatial markets are the fundamental source of manipulative profit.

Result 18. *If the trader chooses $Z^* > 0$, the gains from short manipulation are increasing in S.*

Note that

$$\frac{dG_S}{dS} = P_D(q_D^*) - P_D(q_D^* + Z^*) > 0$$

Result 19. *Short manipulation in the spatial markets distorts consumption and spatial price relationships, but does not cause a backwardation.*

The effect of short manipulation on these quantities is evident from the foregoing. There is too much consumption in the delivery market, and too little at points where the short acquires the commodity. This depresses price at the former point and increases it at the latter. Short manipulation in the spatial market does not induce a backwardation because the short dumps the commodity on the delivery market *prior to or contemporaneous with* delivery. This movement of excessive stocks to D therefore depresses both the expiring and deferred futures prices.

Result 20. *Holding the unmanipulated prices in each market constant, the short manipulator's gains vary directly with the slope of* *the demand curve at D and inversely with the slope of the demand curve at C_1.*

As in Section 2.3.2, for simplicity assume $P_D(q) = \theta_D - \phi_D q$ and $P_1(q) = \theta_1 - \phi_1 q$, and consider the effects of compensated changes in ϕ_D and ϕ_1. In this case,

$$\frac{dP_D(q_D^* + Z^*)}{d\phi_D} = -\frac{dP_1(q_1^* - Z^*)}{d\phi_1} = -Z^*.$$

It is possible to show that at an interior minimum $S > Z^*$. The envelope theorem then implies

$$\frac{dG_S}{d\phi_D} = -Z^*(Z^* - S) > 0$$

$$\frac{dG_S}{d\phi_1} = -(Z^*)^2 < 0.$$

These results are quite intuitive. A steeper demand curve in the delivery market induces a larger price depression in response to a given Z; this reduces the cost the short pays to repurchase his outstanding positions. Conversely, a steeper demand curve in the other market induces a larger price increase there in response to a given Z; this increases the cost the short incurs to obtain the supplies he dumps on the delivery market. This suggests that highly perishable goods may be acutely susceptible to short manipulation. All else equal, the lower the storage costs for a commodity, the more elastic its demand.[7] This is true because the demand curve for a storable commodity is a derived demand equal to the sum of the demand curve for immediate consumption and the demand curves for future consumption (net of future production and storage costs). The ability of consumers and producers to respond to sudden increases in supplies through storage and the adjustment of future consumption or production decisions (such as, increasing future consumption or reducing future shipments of the commodity to the delivery market) tends to dampen the price response to an increase in supply of a storable commodity. In contrast, any increase in stocks of a perishable (and thus non-storable) commodity in a particular location is likely to cause a substantial price decline in order to induce the additional consumption required to clear the market. That is, consumers and producers cannot respond to a sudden increase in supplies of a perishable good by adjusting future consumption, transportation, or production decisions. As a result, current consumption–and thus current prices–must bear the entire burden of adjustment to an increase in supplies. This result can explain why many of the few cases of alleged short manipulation have occurred in onions and potatoes. Both of these commodities–but especially the former–are far more perishable than grains or metals. Indeed, the congressional ban on onion futures trading is largely attributable to allegations of repeated short manipulation of this commodity. In at least one episode, the price of deliverable onions fell below the cost of the bags in which they were shipped.

A comparison of Results 17 and 20 to Results 8 and 9 reveals

Result 21. *The conditions that increase the profitability of long manipulation reduce the profitability of a short manipulation, and vice versa.*

A corner is more profitable the steeper the marginal cost of delivery curve and the less responsive the delivery market price to increased deliveries. These factors make short manipulation *less* profitable. A steep marginal cost of delivery curve increases the cost that a short manipulator must pay to bring supplies to the delivery point, while the lack of price response to additional supplies at that point mitigates the spot price depressing effect of deliveries from whence his profit derives. Thus, if the marginal cost and marginal benefit of delivery functions are fairly stable, one type of manipulation should predominate. This result may explain why major short manipulations are allegedly rare when compared to the number of long manipulations.

The foregoing model demonstrates that spatial factors can make short as well as long manipulation possible. Indeed, even though a large short bears the cost of transportation in this case (while in a long manipulation the manipulated rather than the manipulator bear this expense) transportation costs and geographic dispersion of consumers facilitate manipulation because the large short can distort the spatial distribution of consumption and impose a cost on holders of long futures positions.

2.6. Pure Monopoly Manipulation

The previous sections show how economic frictions (especially transportation costs) can make manipulation possible. This raises the question of whether such frictions are necessary for manipulation to occur. The model of this section implies that the answer to this question is no, but that very restrictive conditions must obtain for manipulation to occur in a market where transportation and transactions costs are trivial (such as the markets for precious metals, currencies, or securities).

Consider a market with negligible transportation and transactions costs. (For brevity I restrict my analysis to long manipulation, although there is a pure monopsony analog to the pure monopoly model I discuss here). Again assume that a single trader has an outstanding long position of X contracts and that all other traders are atomistic with net open positions of Y contracts. Also assume that the large long trader places no intrinsic value on the good.

In Section 2.3, I assumed that a long accepting delivery simply sells the stock thus received at a competitive auction. In contrast, here I assume that the long receiving delivery acts as a monopolist with respect to the residual demand curve he faces on completion of the delivery process. As in the previous section, the would-be manipulator must decide how many deliveries to take, and thus how many contracts to liquidate.

It should be noted that even if the market demand curve for the commodity is downward-sloping, the large long may not be able to restrict credibly his sales in order to raise the postdelivery spot market price due to the durable monopolist's problem first posed by Coase.[8] If the deliverable commodity is durable (such as, gold) the long can sell it at many times in the future. Coase's argument implies that a holder of a large position in the commodity cannot exploit market power because as long he retains some of the commodity he has an incentive to sell more. Anticipating this, demanders are only willing to pay the competitive price that they expect to prevail when he has sold off his entire stock. In this case the relevant liquidation demand curve is perfectly elastic, and the large trader cannot charge a supercompetitive price.

In contrast to Coase, Phlips argues that even if the good is durable, a monopolist can exercise market power if consumers differ in their time preferences for the good.[9] Phlips' analysis implies the holder of a large stock of the commodity faces a downward-sloping demand curve; the more impatient holders of the commodity only sell for a higher price than the more patient ones. This gives the long the market power in the commodity market required to make a pure monopoly manipulation profitable. Thus,

Result 22. *One of the following must be true in order for manipulation to occur in a frictionless market: (1) The deliverable commodity is non-durable or perishable, (2) the large trader can pre-commit to restraining spot market sales after delivery, or (3) the large trader can intertemporally price discriminate.*

I examine the situation when conditions (1) or (2) holds.[10] The demand curve for the product deliverable against the futures contract equals $P(q)$, where q is the stock outstanding, and $P'(q) < 0$. First consider the revenues earned from reselling the delivered commodity. Assume that the trader accepts q_M deliveries. Thus, $q - q_M$ units of the commodity remain in the hands of their original owners, and the manipulator faces a demand curve for this commodity equal to $P(q-q_M+q^*)$ where q^* is the number of units he resells.

The trader's objective function is

$$\max_{q^*} q^* P(q - q_M + q^*) + \eta[q_M - q^*], \tag{2.24}$$

where η is the Lagrangean multiplier on the constraint that the long's sales cannot exceed the number of deliveries he accepts. The first-order conditions for a maximum are:

$$q^* P'(q - q_M + q^*) + P(q - q_M + q^*) - \eta = 0. \tag{2.25}$$

Solution of this equation defines an implicit function $q^*(q_M)$, which relates the optimal number of sales to the number of deliveries the long takes. Note that a necessary condition for a profitable manipulation is $\eta = 0$, that is, $q^*(q_M) < q_M$, as otherwise the manipulator simply sells at the competitive price. I ignore that case, and assume that q_M (and therefore X) is sufficiently large to allow the manipulator to increase the spot price after receiving delivery.

Assuming perfect foresight, current owners of the commodity expect that if the manipulator accepts q_M deliveries, he will sell $q^*(q_M)$ on the spot market for a price of $P[q - q_M + q^*(q_M)]$ after the delivery period. They therefore supply q_M units to shorts to make delivery at a price of $P[q - q_M + q^*(q_M)]$, as this equals the expected postdelivery price. This also equals the price that shorts are willing to pay to liquidate $X - q_M$ contracts, as this equals the marginal cost of delivering another unit of the commodity. Thus, the monopolist's gross revenues from accepting q_M deliveries equal:

$$R(q_M) = P[q - q_M + q^*(q_M)][X - q_M + q^*(q_M)]. \tag{2.26}$$

Maximizing (2.26) with respect to q_M and substituting from (2.25) with $\eta = 0$ implies

$$\frac{dR}{dq_M} = (-1 + \frac{dq^*}{dq_M})[(X - q_M)P'(q - q_M + q^*)].$$

It is straightforward to show that $dq^*/dq_M < 1$, and since $P'(.) < 0$,

$$\frac{dR}{dq_M} > 0$$

for $q_M < X$. The the pure monopoly manipulator therefore chooses $q_M = X$. Thus

Result 23. *A pure monopoly manipulator accepts delivery on his entire position.*

This prediction contrasts starkly with that derived for a frictional manipulator. In a pure monopoly manipulation the ability to exploit market power in the spot market makes it profitable for the manipulator to amass as large a position as possible to maximize this power by taking delivery on his entire position. There is no incentive to trade off liquidations against delivery (as was found in the models of Section 3) because in a frictionless market the price the long receives when liquidating the marginal contract equals the price he receives when selling the marginal delivery.11

This difference between the behavior of a pure monopoly manipulator and a frictional may lead to differing price effects. In particular,

Result 24. *If either condition (1) or (2) from Result 22 is the source of the trader's market power, pure monopoly manipulation does not distort intertemporal price relationships.*

This result obtains because after delivery the manipulator sells the commodity on the spot market at the same price as shorts are willing to pay to liquidate the marginal futures contract. There is, therefore, no backwardation.

It is important to note that this result does *not* hold if condition (3) from Result 22 is the source of market power. This is true because to price discriminate intertemporally the large long initially sells at a high price but gradually decreases price over time to exploit differences in time preference among consumers. Such behavior may induce backwardation.[12] Even if this is the case, however, there is no burying the corpse effect in the pure monopoly manipulation. Instead of causing a precipitous collapse in price immediately following the end of the delivery period, a pure monopoly manipulation that results from the ability of a large trader to intertemporally price discriminate leads to a gradual decline in the spot price over time. If condition (1) or (2) is the source of market power, then no price decline occurs at all. Thus, a pure monopoly manipulation is observationally distinct from a frictional one.

In summary, the holder of a sufficiently large long futures position who can exert market power in the commodity market when transactions and transportation costs are negligible (such as, for precious metals, securities, or currencies) can manipulate profitably. Thus, frictions are not necessary for a manipulation to occur. Given the strict conditions (specified in Result 22) that must hold to make pure monopoly manipulation possible, however, its practical importance is doubtful. Moreover, it is arguable (due to the public nature of futures trading) whether it is less costly for a trader to acquire spot market power via the futures delivery process rather than via spot market transactions.

Nonetheless, since one of the most infamous instances of alleged manipulation, the Hunt silver episode of 1979 and 1980, involved a commodity for which transport costs and other frictions are presumably small, the results of this section are of interest.[13] They strongly suggest that it is extremely difficult, if not impossible, to exercise market power over a commodity like silver.

They also show, however, that the symptoms of a market-power manipulation for such a commodity are very different than the symptoms of a frictional manipulation. A pure monopoly manipulation does not necessarily distort relative prices. Specifically, this type of manipulation may not affect spatial or temporal price patterns. Most important, there is no burying the corpse effect in a pure monopoly manipulation. If conditions (1) or (2) hold, there is no price decline after the end of the delivery period. If condition (3) holds, there is only a gradual price decline after the delivery period.

This lack of a distinctive price trail makes pure monopoly manipulation more difficult to detect than frictional manipulation. Moreover, in a pure monopoly manipulation the long does not simultaneously buy and sell the same thing–claims on the commodity in the delivery market. This makes it easier for an accused manipulator to claim that his actions were motivated by a legitimate desire to acquire the physical commodity. It is true that the monopolist must sell the commodity at some later date, but he may be able to argue convincingly that this was merely due to a change in his opinion or financial position. Therefore, it is likely to be far more difficult to punish a pure monopoly manipulator than a frictional manipulator.

2.7. Summary, Conclusions, and Extensions

This chapter has examined the economics of market power during the delivery period of a futures contract (or other derivative claim). In essence, the analysis shows that economic frictions such as transport costs can make it profitable for a large long trader to exercise market power. Although frictions can make manipulations by short traders possible, and although manipulations can occur even in the absence of such frictions, it is most likely to be the case that long frictional manipulation is the most likely manifestation of market power in futures markets.

As with most examples of market power, frictional futures market manipulation distorts prices and creates deadweight losses. Manipulation causes shorts to utilize real resources to make excessive deliveries. Manipulation also distorts consumption, which forces shorts to pay higher prices to acquire the commodity. The size of these effects depends on the size of the manipulator's futures position as well as structural factors including supply conditions, the slope of demand curves, transportation and storage costs, time preferences, and seasonal factors.

The deadweight losses attributable to corners provides a reason to deter them. The next chapter demonstrates, moreover, that market-power manipulation causes other costly distortions. This creates an additional motive to reduce the frequency and severity of manipulation.

Fortunately, the price and effects of market-power manipulation analyzed in this chapter can be used to detect corners and squeezes. This, in turn, makes it possible to apprehend and punish manipulators. Chapters 5 and 6 examine in detail how the results of this chapter can be used to create an efficient method of manipulation deterrence.

Although this chapter has derived important results, it does not answer all of the interesting theoretical questions about manipulation. Most important, by focusing on the delivery period end game, this analysis begs the question: How can a trader accumulate a futures position that is large enough to permit him to manipulate the market? After all, shorts will not knowingly subject themselves to a squeeze. The next chapter provides an answer to this question.

Appendix

This appendix proves the assertions in the text that in the spatial model the marginal cost of delivery is increasing with the number of deliveries over n intervals and that there also may be intervals where the marginal cost of delivery is constant. The strategy of the proofs is as follows. Lemma 1 demonstrates that increasing deliveries come from progressively more distant locations. Lemma 2 shows that consumption at the source of marginal deliveries declines as Q increases. Proposition 1 combines these results to show that if the commodity is not backhauled after the completion of delivery, the marginal cost of delivery is increasing due to increases in transport costs or the prices that shorts must pay to acquire the commodity. Proposition 2 demonstrates that if the commodity is backhauled, prices in all markets are unchanged as Q increases, which implies that the marginal cost of delivery is constant in this case. Proposition 3 shows that prices in the delivery market move inversely with the marginal cost of delivery. Lemmas 3 through 7 demonstrate that consumption at non-deliverable locations fall by a smaller amount and consumption at D rises by a larger amount in odd-periods, than even-periods for a given Q. Proposition 4 combines this result, and the fact that transport costs are lower in the odd-periods to demonstrate that odd-period manipulations are less profitable.

In order to arrive at these results, it is first helpful to prove some simple facts. The theorem of the maximum implies that $y_i^*(Q)$ and $s_i^*(Q)$ are both nondecreasing and continuous in Q, so I omit the proofs here. The following lemmas are also useful in deriving the main results.

Lemma 1. *Assume that $C_k > C_i$, and that the initial distribution of the commodity is efficient. If $y_k^*(Q) > 0$ then $y_i^*(Q) > 0$.*

Proof. Assume the contrary. Then (2.6) and (2.7) imply

$$P_i(Q) + tC_i > P_D(Q) + \lambda$$

$$P_k(Q) + tC_k = P_D(Q) + \lambda.$$

Thus,

$$P_i(Q) > P_k(Q) + t(C_k - C_i) > P_k(Q). \tag{2.27}$$

Since by assumption the initial distribution of the commodity is efficient, by (2.2) $P_k(0) = P_i(0) + t(C_k - C_i)$. Given the assumption that $y_k^*(Q) > 0$ and $y_i^*(Q) = 0$, this and (2.27) imply that $s_k^*(Q) > 0$. This is true because price cannot have risen at i, as the quantity has not decreased there. Thus, for the price at i (given Q deliveries) to exceed the price at k, the price at the latter point must fall, and thus some output must be shipped back to k. Thus, (2.7) implies

$$P_k(Q) = P_D(Q) + tC_k.$$

This and (2.27) imply:

$$P_i(Q) > P_D(Q) + 2tC_k - tC_i > P_D(Q) + tC_i.$$

This violates (2.7) and thus by contradiction if $y_k^*(Q) > 0$ then $y_i^*(Q) > 0$ as well.

Lemma 1 implies that increased deliveries come from more distant locations. It also implies that there is always a Q' such that $y_j^*(Q') > 0$, and that $Q' \leq \sum_{i=0}^{j-1} q_i^*$.

Lemma 2. *Assume that the initial distribution of the commodity is efficient. If* $\mu_j^*(Q) = 0$ *then* $s_j^*(Q) > 0$ *implies* $y_j^*(Q) > s_j^*(Q)$.

Proof. Consider two locations i and j. By (2.2), the assumption that the initial distribution of the commodity is efficient implies that

$$P_j(0) = P_i(0) + t(C_j - C_i). \tag{2.28}$$

Assume that $s_j^*(Q) > 0$ and $y_j^*(Q) < s_j^*(Q)$. Thus, $P_j(Q) < P_j(0)$ as the quantity on hand there at the end of the delivery process exceeds the initial stocks. Similarly, for some location i it must be true that $P_i(Q) > P_i(0)$, as in order to increase stocks at j stocks must fall at some i. Moreover, (2.7) implies that for j and this i

$$P_i(Q) - tC_i \leq P_D(Q) = P_j(Q) - tC_j. \tag{2.29}$$

Subtracting (2.28) from (2.29) implies

$$P_j(Q) - P_j(0) \geq P_i(Q) - P_i(0)$$

This is a contradiction as the previous discussion implies that the right side of this expression is strictly positive, while the left side is strictly negative. Thus, $s_j^*(Q) > 0$ implies $y_j^*(Q) > s_j^*(Q)$.

Lemma 2 implies that a market that is the source of deliveries under the optimal plan, and is capable of making further deliveries (that is, a marginal source of deliveries) must deliver more than it receives after the end of the delivery process.

These results allow the proof of

Proposition 1. *Assume the distribution of the commodity is initially optimal. Then there are n intervals where the marginal cost of delivery increases with Q. That is, there are n intervals $[D_i, U_i]$ where the marginal cost of delivery is increasing in Q when $D_i \leq Q \leq U_i$.*

Proof. Since $y_j^*(Q)$ is nondecreasing and continuous, and since Lemma 1 implies that each location j must be the marginal source of delivery for some Q, there exists a Q^* s.t. $y_j^*(Q) > 0$ for $Q \geq Q^*$ and $y_j^*(Q) = 0$ for $Q < Q^*$. Thus, for some arbitrarily small $\epsilon > 0$

$$P_j(Q^* - \epsilon) + tC_j > P_{j-1}(Q^* - \epsilon) + tC_{j-1}.$$

Lemma 2 implies that $q_j^* - y_j^*(Q^*) + s_j^*(Q^*) < q_j^*$, thus

$$P_j(Q^*) + tC_j > P_{j-1}(Q^* - \epsilon) + tC_{j-1}.$$

The l.h.s. of this expression is the marginal cost of delivery when $Q = Q^*$, while the r.h.s. is the marginal cost of delivery for a Q arbitrarily below Q^*, thus the marginal cost of delivery must increase at that point.

The next lowest cost source of deliveries is $j+1$. The marginal cost of delivery from that point is $P_{j+1}(Q^*) + tC_{j+1}$. By (2.2), under the assumption that the distribution of the commodity is optimal $P_{j+1}(Q^*) = P_j(Q^*) + t(C_{j+1} - C_j)$. Thus,

$$P_{j+1}(Q^*) + tC_{j+1} = P_j(Q^*) + 2tC_{j+1} - tC_j > P_j(Q^*) + tC_j$$

Since the price functions are continuous and downward-sloping, there must be some interval $[Q^*, V_j]$ (with $V_j > Q^*$) such that j is the source of marginal deliveries. Moreover, by Lemma 2 $P_j(Q)$ must rise in some interval $[Q^*, U_j]$ with $U_j \leq V_j$.

Finally, Lemma 1 implies that each location must be the marginal source of deliveries for some Q. Thus, there must be such an interval for each $j \leq n$.

Proposition 2. *Assume $s_j^*(Q) > 0$ for $Q \geq Q'$, and $s_j^*(Q) = 0$ for $Q < Q'$. If $y_j^*(Q') < q_j^*$ (and thus $\mu_j^*(Q) = 0$) then there is an interval $[Q', Q' + q_j^* - y_j^*(Q')]$ such that the marginal cost of delivery is constant and equal to $P_j(Q') + tC_j$.*

Proof. Since $s_j^*(Q)$ is continuous and nondecreasing, if $s_j^*(Q) > 0$ for some Q, then there will be a Q' s.t. $s_j^*(Q) > 0$ for $Q \geq Q'$ while $s_j^*(Q) = 0$ for $Q < Q'$. Then (3.7) implies:

$$P_j(Q') = P_D(Q') + tC_j.$$

Thus, the marginal cost of delivery equals $P_D(Q') + 2tC_j$.

Now consider what happens when $Q = Q' + dQ$. Note $s_j^*(Q' + dQ) = s_j^*(Q') + dQ$ and $y_j^*(Q' + dQ) = y_j^*(Q') + dQ$. Condition (3.7) would be violated if either of these expressions did not hold, since strictly decreasing demand functions would then imply

$$P_j(Q' + dQ) > P_D(Q' + dQ) + tC_j.$$

Thus, any additional deliveries from j are shipped back there, and $dP_j(Q)/dQ = 0$ at this point. As Q increases beyond Q', deliveries can be made from j until supplies are exhausted there. This occurs when $Q = Q' + q_j^* - y_j^*$. Since the marginal cost of delivery must be at least as great for all other locations $k > j$ when $Q = Q'$, and since the marginal cost of delivery from j does not change in the interval $[Q', Q' + q_j^* - y_j^*]$, it must be true that j is the lowest cost source of delivery for all Q in this interval. Hence, the marginal cost of delivery is constant for these Q.

Note that it is possible that $y_j^*(Q) = q_j^*$ for all Q s.t. $s_j^*(Q) > 0$. Hence, it is not always the case that there is a constant marginal cost segment for each $j \leq n$.

Proposition 3. *Given the assumptions of Propositions 1 and 2, the postdelivery price is decreasing in Q when $D_i \leq Q \leq U_i$ and is constant when the marginal cost of delivery is constant.*

Proof. For each i, $s_i(Q) = 0$ when $Q \in [D_i, U_i]$. If $s_j(Q) = 0$ for all $j \leq i$, then the incremental delivery remains at D after delivery, and this depresses the price there. If $s_j(Q) > 0$ for some $j \leq i$, (2.7) implies that $P_D(Q) + tC_j = P_j(Q)$. This condition would be violated if none of the incremental delivery from i remained in D after delivery but was instead sent to markets where $s_j(Q) > 0$ as price would remain constant in the delivery market but fall in these other markets. This proves the first part of the proposition. As for the second part, note that when $\mu_i(Q) < 0$ at the marginal source of delivery Proposition 2 implies the incremental delivery is returned to i leaving prices in both markets unchanged.

Now consider the odd-period spatial manipulation model. It is straightforward to see that all terms in the cost function (2.3) are identical in this case except that

$$T_j = t[C_j s_j + (C_j - C_1)(q_j^* - y_j)].$$

and that one must add the following term (which equals the total cost of transport from the production area to the delivery point)

$$\int_{x^*}^{x^* + \frac{Q}{\rho}} tx dx.$$

Using $y_i^1(Q)$ and $s_i^1(Q)$ to distinguish this case from the even-period analysis, the relevant first-order conditions are

$$P_j[q_j^* - y_j^1(Q) + s_j^1(Q)] - t(C_j - C_1) + t[x^* + \frac{Q}{\rho}] \geq$$

$$P_D\{q_D^* + \sum_{i=1}^{n}[y_i^1(Q) - s_i^1(Q)]\} + \lambda, \tag{2.30}$$

where this must hold with equality if $y_j^1(Q) > 0$ and

$$P_D\{q_D^* + \sum_{i=1}^{n}[y_i^1(Q) - s_i^1(Q)]\} + tC_j \geq P_j[q_j^* - y_j^1(Q) + s_j^1(Q)], \tag{2.31}$$

where this holds with equality if $s_j^1(Q) > 0$. These first-order conditions imply the following lemmas and proposition.

Lemma 3. *$y_1^1(Q) < y_1^*(Q)$ for all Q.*

Proof. First observe that if $y_1^1(Q) > 0$ then $y_j^1(Q) > 0$ for all $j > 1$. By (2.2), the optimal distribution of the commodity implies $P_j(q_j^*) = P_1(q_1^*) + t(C_j - C_1)$. If $y_1^1(Q) > 0$ and $y_j^1(Q) = 0$, this expression implies a violation of (2.30). This implies that $y_1^1(Q) < Q$. Also note that either $y_1^*(Q) = Q$ or $y_1^*(Q)$ is such that

$$P_1[q_1^* - y_1^*(Q)] = P_2[q_2^* - y_2^*(Q)] + t(C_2 - C_1) \tag{2.32}$$

If $y_1^1(Q) = y_1^*(Q)$, (2.32) is inconsistent with (2.30).

Lemma 4. *Assume $s_1^*(Q) > 0$ for $Q \geq Q_e$ while $s_1^1(Q) > 0$ for $Q \geq Q_o$. Then $Q_o > Q_e$.*

Proof. Assume not. Then there would exist a $Q_e > Q > Q_o$ s.t.

$$P_D\{q_D^* + \sum_{i=1} n[y_i^1(Q) - s_i^1(Q)]\} + tC_{1j} = P_1[q_1^* - y_j^1(Q) + s_j^1(Q)]$$

and

$$P_D\{q_D^* + \sum_{i=1}^{n}[y_i^*(Q) - s_i^*(Q)]\} + tC_1 > P_1[q_1^* - y_1^*(Q) + s_1^*(Q)].$$

Since $y_1^1(Q) < y_1^*(Q)$ this implies

$$\begin{aligned} P_D(q_D^* + Q) + tC_1 > & P_1[q_1^* - y_1^*(Q)] > \\ & P_1[q_1^* - y_1^1(Q) + s_1^1(Q)] = \\ & P_D[q_D^* + Q - \sum_{i=1}^{n} s_i^1(Q)] + tC_1. \end{aligned}$$

Since $s_i^1(Q) \geq 0$ this is a contradiction.

Lemma 5. *If $s_i^1(Q) > 0$ then $d[s_i^1(Q) - y_i^1(Q)]/dQ = 0$.*

Proof. If $s_i^1(Q) > 0$ condition (2.31) holds as an equality. The equation $P_1(q_1^* + v) = P_D(q_D^* - z) + tC_1$ holds for a unique v and z, which implies the stated result.

Lemma 6. *The price shorts pay to acquire the deliverable commodity is always lower in the odd-period than in the even-period.*

Proof. Lemma 4 implies three cases are relevant. When $s_1^*(Q) = 0$ and $s_1^1(Q) = 0$ then Lemma 3 implies $P_1[q_1^* - y_1^*(Q)] > P_1[q_1^* - y_1^1(Q)]$. When $s_1^*(Q) > 0$ and $s_1^1(Q) = 0$ then the result is again immediate from Lemma 3. Thus, for all $Q_o \geq Q$ the odd-period price at location 1 exceeds the even-period price at this location. Lemma 5 implies that the highest price at location 1 equals $P_1[q_1^* - y_1^1(Q_o])$. Since by Propositions 1 and 2 the price that shorts pay delivered to location 1 (that is, the price at marginal source of delivery j plus $t[C_j - C_1]$) in the even-period is nondecreasing in Q, this implies that the price shorts pay in the even-period always exceeds $P_1[q_1^* - y_1^1(Q_o)]$ for $Q > Q_o$.

Finally, note that in the even-period shorts obtain the commodity at $x' = x^* + (Q/\rho) < C_1$, so the price they pay equals P_1 less the cost of transport from x' to C_1. Thus, the price the shorts pay in the odd-period to obtain the commodity equals $P_1[q_1^* - y_1^1(Q) + s_1^1(Q)] - t[C_1 - x^* - (Q/\rho)]$. The stated result follows immediately.

Lemma 7. $P_D[q_D^* + Q - \sum_{i=1}^n s_i^1(Q)] \leq P_D[q_D^* + Q - \sum_{i=1}^n s_i^*(Q)]$ *for* $Q_o \geq Q \geq Q_e$.

Proof. For Q s.t. $s_1^1(Q) = s_1^*(Q) = 0$ the price at D equals $P_D(q_D^* + Q)$ in both even and odd-periods. If $Q_o \geq Q \geq Q_e$ then the price at D in the odd-period equals $P_D(q_D^* + Q)$ while the price in the even-period is greater than or equal to $P_D[q_D^* + Q - s_1^*(Q)] > P_D(q_D^* + Q)$ since $P_D' < 0$.

Proposition 4. *A large long who owns X futures positions finds manipulation less profitable in the odd-period than in the even-period.*

Proof. It is evident that a profit-maximizing odd-period manipulator will choose $Q^* \leq Q_o$. For any Q the marginal cost of delivery is higher in the even period for two reasons. First, the marginal cost of transport is higher in the even period because shorts must transport it further. Second, Lemma 6 implies that they must pay a higher price to obtain the commodity in the even period than in the odd period. Thus, if the manipulator chooses to liquidate $X - Q^*$ contracts in the odd period, he must receive a smaller revenue from liquidations than if he chooses the same action in the even period. Lemma 7 implies that the long's receipts on sale of Q^* units are smaller in the odd period than in the even period. The long's revenues are thus smaller in the odd period than the even if he takes Q^* deliveries in each period. Since a $Q \neq Q^*$ may generate higher profits in the even period, manipulation then must be more profitable.

Endnotes

[1] The following results do not depend in any important way on the consumption and production locations. As long as consumers are spatially separated and transport is costly, the results derived here obtain. The main effect of changing the identity of the delivery point is that the marginal cost of delivery is higher when delivery occurs at a relatively low-price point (like D) rather than a low-price point (such as C_i, where i is large).

Note that there is no risk in this model. This is not to suggest that risk is unimportant in futures markets. The assumption of perfect certainty is simply intended to focus attention on the sources of market power conditional on supply and demand at contract expiration. That is, there may be uncertainty about supply and demand when traders initiate positions, but it is resolved by contract expiration when any manipulation occurs. Chapter 3 extends the analysis to include the possibility of uncertainty about supply and demand conditions prior to the delivery period.

[2] The assumption of competitive behavior in the postdelivery market is intended to emphasize how frictions facilitate manipulation. See Section 2.5 for an analysis of the effects of spot market power on a trader's actions. The analysis of that section implies that very strong conditions must hold for the long to exert spot market power, so the assumption of competition in the postdelivery market is quite plausible.

It should be noted that a manipulator who takes large deliveries may be able to exploit market power more effectively in the future because of his control over such large supplies. Thus, a manipulator may not dump his supplies on the market immediately following a corner, but may hold on to them to enhance his ability to squeeze the market in coming months. This would limit the severity of the spot price collapse after a manipulation. It could cause the deferred futures price to *rise* during a corner (although by less than the increase in the spot price) because a manipulation today increases the probability of a future manipulation. A manipulator is less likely to follow this strategy when squeezing an *old crop* agricultural futures contract (such as, May wheat in

Chicago) because retaining control of stocks will (1) not appreciably increase his ability to squeeze contracts after the new harvest and (2) force him to sell the stocks when supplies are more plentiful after the harvest rather than they are relatively scarce before the harvest. However, it may be profitable to squeeze repeatedly a futures contract for a good that is not seasonally produced, such as copper or silver. Similarly, it may be profitable to retain control of stocks acquired during a manipulation of a seasonally produced commodity with several futures contracts expiring prior to the new crop. For example, it may be profitable to retain deliverable stocks acquired in a May soybean manipulation to facilitate manipulation of the July and September contracts.

[3] To characterize the manipulator's wealth-maximizing choice it is sufficient to focus on his delivery end game gross revenues alone, as by that time the cost the long paid to acquire his position (the other determinant of his profit) is sunk. Only in deriving Result 11 do I need to examine predelivery prices.

[4] Since this analysis is restricted to the delivery end game, one must of course be careful when drawing conclusions that depend on events that occur prior to this game. There is no guarantee that a large trader will be able to purchase at competitive prices because his activities might tip off the possibility of a manipulation. Holding the informativeness of trading inside and outside the delivery market constant, however, Result 11 implies that a trader has a strong reason to purchase outside the delivery market because of the relative price and burying-the-body effects. Moreover, it is plausible that it is easier for a manipulator to acquire stocks of a commodity undetected outside the delivery market than inside it. Purchases of a commodity dispersed over a wide geographic area may not attract attention, whereas purchases concentrated in the delivery market are more likely to be noticed. If this is true, this provides a trader an even stronger motive to acquire stocks outside the delivery market than Result 11 suggests.

[5] Market participants have told me that seasonal factors affect manipulation in grain futures markets. Late in the crop year processors and consumers hold most grain inventories, while early

in the year they are held by producers and marketers. As a result, it is allegedly difficult to "pry the grain" out of the processors. This is consistent with the analysis of this article.

[6] Virtually identical results obtain a spatial-intertemporal model of the type discussed in Section 2.3.3. It is also possible to construct a model of pure monopsony manipulation analogous to the analysis of section 2.6. In such a manipulation an owner of a commodity sells off stocks and depresses the price if he can credibly commit to repurchase less than he sells.

[7] Jeffrey Williams and Brian Wright, Storage and Commodity Markets 116-120 (1991), and Angus Deaton and Guy Laroque, On the Behavior of Commodity Prices, 59 Rev. of Econ. Stud. 1 (1992) demonstrate that storage increases the elasticity of demand for a commodity. Williams and Wright show that demand for a commodity is more elastic (1) the lower the cost of storage, (2) the less perishable the commodity, and (3) the more elastic future supply.

[8] Ronald Coase, Durability and Monopoly, 15 Journal of Law & Econ. 143, (1972).

[9] Louis Phlips, The Economics of Price Discrimination ch. 2 (1983).

[10] All results but Result 18 hold in the context of a model where condition (3) is the source of the long's market power. The intertemporal price discrimination model is considerably more complicated, so I analyze the simpler case and state the reasons for any differences between the models where relevant.

[11] One can also demonstrate this result in the context of a model where the ability to intertemporally price discriminate is the source of the trader's spot market power. Assume that the price-discriminating trader's maximal revenues from spot sales when he owns q units of the commodity equal $M(q)$. The price he is willing to pay for the qth unit therefore equals $M'(q)$. This equals the futures price when he liquidates $X-q$ contracts, as current owners recognize that this is the value of the marginal unit after delivery and so sell the commodity to shorts at this price. The long's combined revenues from liquidating $X-q$ contracts and selling

q deliveries over time thus equal $R(q) = M'(q)(X - q) + M(q)$. Therefore, $R'(q) = -M'(q) + (X - q)M''(q) + M'(q) = (X - q)M''(q)$. Note that the price the manipulator receives on the sale of the marginal unit must rise with q, that is, $M''(q) > 0$. Thus, $R'(q) > 0$ for all $q < X$. Again the manipulator takes delivery on his entire position.

[12] It is also possible to derive comparative statics results in the pure monopoly model. In particular, the long's profit is increasing in X. Moreover, a steeper demand curve increases manipulative profit.

[13] The Fisk-Gould gold corner discussed in Chapter 1 also involved a precious metal but is properly considered a frictional manipulation. Due to the relatively inefficient transport technology of that era, traders incurred transactions costs to bring additional gold to New York. For example, there were large stocks of gold in California, but it was very costly to ship that gold to New York. Kenneth Ackerman, The Gold Ring (1988). Thus, the nineteenth century gold market was a spatial one, and the analysis of section 2.3 is relevant. In contrast, although the cost of transporting silver today is not zero, it is trivial relative to the value of the commodity. The spatial analysis is consequently inappropriate for the Hunt silver episode. Instead, the pure monopoly model is apposite.

CHAPTER 3
THE ACQUISITION OF MARKET POWER: RANDOM TRADING STRATEGIES AND PRICE DYNAMICS

3.1 Introduction

The preceding chapter examines how a trader would exercise market power during the delivery period, and derives the empirical and welfare effects of such conduct. That analysis begs a very important question. Namely, how can a trader *acquire* a futures position large enough to confer market power on him from shorts alive to the possibility of a squeeze? Put differently, why would shorts sell the rope by which they are hanged? Moreover, although the analysis of Chapter 2 describes the effects of market power on prices and quantities, it alone is not sufficient to determine how frequently market power is exercised. It also fails to show how market participants form expectations concerning the frequency and severity of manipulation and how these expectations affect prices prior to the delivery period. A complete analysis of the causes and effects of market power manipulation requires a thorough study of these issues. The present chapter undertakes this analysis.

A completely new examination of these issues is required because the existing literature on manipulation fails to address them in a satisfactory manner. Section 3.2 analyzes this literature in detail. Some papers present sufficient conditions for the existence of manipulation in equilibrium that are so restrictive that it is implausible that they could ever be observed in practice. Others present conditions that are so weak that they imply that corners and squeezes should be ubiquitous. Thus, the existing literature either proves too much or too little. Moreover, this literature employs very crude models of the delivery market end game. As a result, it cannot shed light on how the profitability and frequency of manipulation depend on the factors that determine the marginal cost of delivery or the nature of demand in the delivery market or on how prices behave prior to the delivery period.

Sections 3.3, 3.4, and 3.5 of this chapter present formal models that address these issues in detail. The models demonstrate that two conditions are sufficient for manipulation to occur in equilibrium. First, trading volume is unpredictable and trading is anonymous. Second, the marginal cost of delivery is increasing. Given these conditions, a would-be manipulator can choose a randomized trading strategy that earns a positive expected profit. Moreover, with positive probability this trader buys enough contracts to manipulate the market. This strategy is profitable on average because the random variations in order flow make it impossible for shorts to detect perfectly when a trader is attempting to accumulate a large futures position. Put another way, variations in the order flow provide camouflage for manipulators.

This model has several important implications. First, a simulation analysis demonstrates that the profitability and frequency of manipulation both increase as (1) the order flow becomes more variable, (2) the marginal cost of delivery function becomes less elastic, and (3) the demand curve in the delivery market becomes more elastic. Results (2) and (3) reinforce the arguments made in Chapter 2 concerning the determinants of the profitability of market power manipulations. Second, randomized manipulation reduces the informativeness of the futures price. Third, the randomized exercise of market power affects the variance of the futures price and the hedging effectiveness of a futures contract. Indeed, the most plausible result is that randomized manipulation increases futures price volatility and reduces hedging effectiveness for out-of-position hedgers. Since the primary functions of futures markets are to aggregate information and to facilitate the efficient transfer of risk through hedging, these effects are costly. They cause additional deadweight losses. This provides another reason to prevent or deter manipulation.

The remainder of this chapter is organized as follows. The next section reviews the previous literature on this subject. Section 3.3 outlines a model of the futures market. Sections 3.4 and

3.5 show that in this model, randomized manipulative trading strategies are profitable in equilibrium when the flow of orders to the futures market is unpredictable. These sections also derive the effects of randomized trading strategies on the informativeness and variability of prices, and the variability of the basis between the futures price and cash prices at non-deliverable locations. Section 3.6 uses simulation techniques to study how the profitability of manipulation (and therefore its frequency and severity) varies with supply and demand conditions, and the variability of the order flow. Section 3.7 examines how factors not formally modeled affect the results and their interpretation. Section 3.8 summarizes the chapter.

3.2. Previous Research on the Acquisition of Market Power

The fundamental problem confronting any would-be manipulator is how can he induce other traders (who are alive to the prospect of a potential corner) to sell contracts to him at a price low enough to allow him to squeeze the market and earn a profit in the process. Three models have attempted to answer this question. For a variety of reasons, however, each of these models fails to explain some important stylized facts about manipulation.

Kyle's theory represents the most rigorous attempt to date to show how manipulation can occur in equilibrium.[1] In Kyle's model a trader with superior information about the futures market order flow from hedgers exploits this advantage by amassing a large long position (which allows him to squeeze the market at delivery) when hedgers sell large numbers of contracts. Hedgers and other traders, who can observe only the combined hedger-informed trader order flow, cannot detect his presence in the market. They therefore sell at a price that on average is below the spot price that prevails at expiration in the event of a squeeze. Thus, the informed trader earns a profit, and manipulation occurs in equilibrium in Kyle's model.

Although the model is quite elegant, the sufficient condition for manipulation that drives this result is very restrictive; a trader must have superior information on hedger order flow. It is quite doubtful whether this condition obtains in practice, given the great lengths to which traders go to conceal their activities, and the large numbers of hedgers and speculators present in most markets. Thus, this model cannot explain how the historical manipulations in the grain and cotton markets chronicled by Taylor, Andreas, and Bouilly occurred.[2] Moreover, the very stylized model of the costs of delivery makes it difficult to determine how the susceptibility of a market to manipulation varies with cash market characteristics.

Jarrow also presents a model in which manipulation occurs in equilibrium.[3] He argues that a large trader that acquires a long position in a derivative security and the security deliverable against the derivative that is larger than the total deliverable supply can profitably squeeze shorts by forcing them to settle their positions at an arbitrarily high price. Jarrow proves that if the large long can indeed specify any settlement price he chooses, he can always profitably corner and squeeze the market (with no risk of a financial loss) *regardless of the price generating process prior to the delivery period.*

This theory presents some rather serious problems. Most important, it explains too much; if a large trader can always manipulate the market by simply buying a large position and then charging an arbitrarily high price to ensure that he can liquidate this position at a profit, why doesn't manipulation occur more frequently? Thus, the Jarrow theory cannot explain the relative rarity of corners, even during their heyday in the late nineteenth century.

The reason manipulations do not always occur (even in the absence of regulatory or legal impediments to this practice) is clear: Jarrow's assumption that a large long trader can force shorts to settle at an arbitrarily high price is clearly wrong. In the context of a physical commodity market, in almost all circumstances additional supplies can be brought to the delivery market at finite cost, and as demonstrated in Chapter 2, this cost places an upper bound on the price a manipulator can and will extract. Even if a trader accumulates claims that exceed the total supply of a commodity or security, however, the price he can squeeze from shorts is limited by their ability to default against their obligations to deliver. At most, the manipulator can extract all their (finite) wealth. As long as such an upper bound exists on the price a manipulator can set, Jarrow's result no longer holds for an arbitrary equilibrium price process even if this upper bound is very large.

Moreover, although Jarrow abstracts from the determination of the equilibrium price process, consideration of this issue throws further doubt on the validity of his model. Recall that it implies corners should always occur, and the equilibrium price in the delivery period is arbitrarily large. Call this price $\bar{P}$. Anticipating that this price will obtain during the delivery period with probability one, traders will only sell at $\bar{P}$ prior to the delivery period. That is, using an arbitrage argument to determine the implications of Jarrow's model for the equilibrium price prior to the delivery period shows that the large trader must pay the arbitrarily high price that will prevail at delivery to acquire his position. Since (according to the analysis of Chapter 2) the large long cannot sell his entire position at this high price, he necessarily loses money. For instance, if the large trader owns N contracts, he can sell only $N - k$, $k > 0$, at $\bar{P}$, and must sell the remaining k at no more than (and probably less than) the competitive price $P_c < \bar{P}$. As a result, his profits are less than $(N-k)\bar{P}+kP_c-N\bar{P} < 0$. Thus, in addition to the difficulties described in the previous paragraph, the conclusion of the Jarrow model that corners and squeezes should be ubiquitous is inconsistent with rational behavior by market participants.

Finally, in the context of a structural noise trader model in the spirit of Kyle, Kumar and Seppi demonstrate that manipulation can occur in a cash-settled futures contract.[4] This theory does not specify a model of market clearing via delivery, and therefore it cannot explain how squeezes and corners occur in equilibrium. It does contain a key insight, however, that can be used to construct a model in which a delivery settled contract is manipulated. Specifically, Kumar and Seppi show that if order flow in the futures and cash markets is unpredictable, randomized trading may allow an individual to obtain a futures position that permits him to manipulate the cash market profitably at the expiration date of the futures contract. This sort of trading is especially profitable if the manipulator's wealth is unpredictable, as this adds an additional element of noise to the problem facing market makers.

Although the Kumar-Seppi theory is not directly applicable to delivery settled markets, the models in Section 3.4 and 3.5 demonstrate that a different sort of randomization strategy is profitable in this case as well. In order to demonstrate this result, it is first necessary to specify a models of (1) the price determination process during the delivery period, and (2) the futures trading process prior to the delivery period. This is the subject of the next section.

3.3. A Model of Pre-Delivery Period Futures Trading

Consider the following simple model of a futures market. At time t traders can negotiate futures contracts that expire at $T > t$. The futures contract is delivery settled. Traders may therefore exit their positions at T either via delivery, or by taking an offsetting position in the futures market.

As in the insider-trading model of Kyle[5] both noise traders and market makers participate in the t period futures market. Noise traders are either hedgers or speculators, and are uninformed and atomistic. They trade by submitting market orders to the floor of the exchange at t. The net order flow from the noise traders equals η, where η is a random variable with probability density $\phi(\eta)$. Market makers observe the order flow, act as perfect competitors, and absorb the net order flow at a price equal to the price expected to prevail at T, where the expectation is conditional on the order flow. In addition to the noise traders and market makers, there is a large risk-neutral trader—trader 1—who can buy or sell an arbitrarily large quantity of contracts at his discretion.

Conditions in the market at T are as follows. Stocks of the commodity at the delivery point equal $q_D^*(\tilde{\Theta})$, where $\tilde{\Theta}$ is a vector of parameters that affect supply and demand conditions. At time t traders do not necessarily observe $\tilde{\Theta}$, although they do observe these parameters at T.[6] Thus, at t there may be some uncertainty about supply and demand conditions at T.

The demand curve in the delivery market at T is $P_D(q, \tilde{\Theta})$ where q is the quantity of stocks on hand there and

$$\partial P_D(q, \tilde{\Theta})/\partial q < 0.$$

The marginal cost of increasing deliverable stocks to $Q \geq q_D^*(\tilde{\Theta})$ equals $MC(Q, \tilde{\Theta})$, where

$$MC(Q, \tilde{\Theta}) > P_D(q_D^*, \tilde{\Theta})$$

and

$$\partial MC(Q, \tilde{\Theta})/\partial Q > 0.$$

The delivery market conditions at T satisfy the necessary conditions for a long manipulation derived in Chapter 2.[7] In particular, the increasing marginal cost of delivery implies that if trader 1 acquires a futures position of size $X > q_D^*(\tilde{\Theta})$ and demands delivery of $Q \geq q_D^*(\tilde{\Theta})$ contracts, atomistic shorts are willing to pay a price in equal to $MC(Q, \tilde{\Theta}) > P_D(q_D^*, \tilde{\Theta})$ to liquidate their remaining $X - Q$ positions. This is true because any short that does not liquidate must pay the marginal cost of delivery to satisfy his contractual obligations and is therefore willing to pay any price less than or equal to that marginal cost to close his position by offset. These considerations imply that the large trader can force an artificially high liquidation price at contract expiration and may therefore be able to manipulate profitably.

It is important to note that $X > q_D^*(\tilde{\Theta})$ is *not* a sufficient condition for manipulation to occur due to the burying the corpse effect analyzed in detail in the previous chapter. When a trader takes delivery of $Q > q_D^*(\tilde{\Theta})$ units of the commodity, stocks in the delivery market rise and postdelivery spot price (that is, the price at $T + dt$) in that market falls due to the inflation in stocks. The manipulator sells the units delivered to him at this depressed price. Thus, the large long sells these units at a price lower than the competitive price in the market, $P_D(q_D^*, \tilde{\Theta})$. Unless the long liquidates enough contracts at the elevated price $MC(Q, \tilde{\Theta})$ the losses he incurs when burying the corpse exceed the profits he realizes on the contracts he sells to shorts. Trader 1 must own, therefore, some minimum futures position $X_{min}(\tilde{\Theta}) > q_D^*(\tilde{\Theta})$ to make manipulation profitable. For any such X, the revenues from restricting liquidations exceed $XP_D(q_D^*, \tilde{\Theta})$ because a trader can earn this revenue by liquidating his entire position at the competitive price. (The simulation analysis in Section 3.6 provides a simple example of the determination of X_{min}, and how it depends on supply and demand conditions.)

Formally, when trader 1 buys X futures contracts at t, at T he chooses Q to maximize:

$$R(Q, \tilde{\Theta}) \equiv (X - Q)MC(Q, \tilde{\Theta}) + QP_D(Q, \tilde{\Theta}) < XMC(Q, \tilde{\Theta}). \tag{3.1}$$

The first term on the right side equals the long's revenues from liquidating $X - Q$ contracts. The second term equals the long's receipts from sale of the Q units delivered to him. The inequality holds because $MC(Q, \tilde{\Theta}) > P_D(Q, \tilde{\Theta})$ due to the burying the corpse effect. Maximization of this expression defines an implicit function $Q(X, \tilde{\Theta})$, where $Q(X, \tilde{\Theta}) > q_D^*(\tilde{\Theta})$ for all $X > X_{min}(\tilde{\Theta})$, and $Q(X, \tilde{\Theta}) = 0$ otherwise. This function reports the number of deliveries the manipulator accepts to maximize his profit, given the size of his position.[8]

The foregoing implies that the delivery-market price at contract expiration and the futures price then equal $P_D[q_D^*(\tilde{\Theta}), \tilde{\Theta}]$ if trader 1 has acquired less than $X_{min}(\tilde{\Theta})$ units of the commodity. Conversely, if he purchases $X > X_{min}(\tilde{\Theta})$ units at t, the price at T equals $MC[Q(X, \tilde{\Theta}), \tilde{\Theta}] \equiv MC(X, \tilde{\Theta}) > P_D[q_D^*(\tilde{\Theta}), \tilde{\Theta}]$.

Recall that at t, traders may not know $\tilde{\Theta}$. Thus, at this time they must make decisions on the basis of expectations about these supply and demand parameters. Let $MC^*(X) = E_{\tilde{\Theta}} MC(X, \tilde{\Theta})$ conditional on information available at t. Similarly, $R^*(X) = E_{\tilde{\Theta}} R(X, \tilde{\Theta})$, and $P_D^*(X) = E_{\tilde{\Theta}} P_D^*(X, \tilde{\Theta})$; both expectations are conditional on information available at t. For simplicity, assume that all parties have access to the same information about $\tilde{\Theta}$ as of t.

Since the price at T varies with the size of trader 1's position, the price at t must depend on the market makers' information concerning the size of trader 1's order. The order flow may communicate some information about his trading activity, and since market makers observe the order flow, they charge a price equal to the expected price at T conditional on the realization of this variable. The following sections show that if the order flow varies randomly, market makers are unable to detect reliably the presence of a large trader. Therefore, an agent employing a randomized trading strategy may be able to acquire a large position and earn a positive expected profit by squeezing the market.

3.4. A Simultaneous Move Manipulation Model

It is clear that if trader 1 chooses a pure trading strategy, he earns a negative profit with certainty. To see why, assume he purchases $X^* > X_{min}(\tilde{\Theta}_1)$ contracts with probability 1 by entering market orders, where $\tilde{\Theta}_1$ is some value of $\tilde{\Theta}$ that is realized with positive probability at T. Although market makers cannot identify his particular order, if it is known that he is following this strategy the equilibrium futures price equals $MC^*(X^*)$. This is true because market makers know with certainty that this is the price that will prevail at T. The cost of buying X^* contracts therefore equals $X^* MC^*(X^*) > R^*(X^*)$. The inequality follows from taking expectations over $\tilde{\Theta}$ on both sides of (1). Therefore, trader 1 expects to lose money if he employs a pure strategy of buying contracts; he can do better by staying out of the market altogether. (This argument is closely related to the criticism of Jarrow's model made in Section 3.2.)

Since pure strategies are unprofitable, a manipulator must use mixed strategies. This section and the one following shows that under certain conditions such mixed strategies are profitable on average, and result in corners with positive probability.

The model in this section assumes that trader 1 and the market makers choose their strategies simultaneously. The primary difference between this simultaneous-move model and the sequential model discussed in Section 3.5 is that in the latter, trader 1 recognizes how the market makers' price function responds to his choice of trading probabilities and incorporates this response into his maximization problem; in the simultaneous-move model, in contrast, trader 1 takes the market makers' price function as given. Thus, the essential distinction between simultaneous and sequential models is the information possessed by the market makers; the labeling of the models is standard terminology from game theory. The models are complementary in that some results are easier to demonstrate within the context of the simultaneous model, while others are best shown in the sequential one.

In the simultaneous model, trader 1 chooses a function $h(x)$, which gives the probability that he will trade x contracts at t, with $h(x) \geq 0$ for all x, and $\int_{-\infty}^{\infty} h(x)dx = 1$. The trader can sell contracts; $x < 0$ represents such a sale. Simultaneously with trader 1's choice of $h(.)$, market makers choose a pricing function $P(y)$, which gives the price they charge as a function of the net order flow at t.

The functions $h^*(x)$ and $P^*(y)$ are Nash equilibrium strategies if and only if

1. Given $P^*(y)$, $h^*(x)$ is the choice of $h(x)$ that maximizes trader 1's expected profit, which is given by the function:

$$E(\Pi) = \int_{-\infty}^{\infty} [R^*(x) - x \int_{-\infty}^{\infty} P^*(x+\eta)\phi(\eta)d\eta]h(x)dx,$$

and

2. Given $h^*(x)$, $P^*(y)$ satisfies:

$$P^*(y) = E_x[MC^*(x)|y = x+\eta] = \int_{-\infty}^{\infty} MC^*(x)g(x|y)dx, \quad (3.2)$$

where by Bayes' rule the probability of x conditional on y equals:

$$g(x|y) = \frac{\phi(y-x)h^*(x)}{\phi(y-x)h^*(x) + \int_{z\neq x}\phi(y-z)h^*(z)dz}.$$

Condition 1 states that given the pricing function the market makers choose, trader 1 chooses his probability function to maximize expected profit. Condition 2 states that given trader

1's choice of $h^*(x)$, competition among market makers ensures that the futures price equals the expected spot price at expiration, where the expectation is conditional on the order flow and on the information about $\tilde{\Theta}$ available at t.

The following propositions demonstrate that manipulation occurs with positive probability in the simultaneous move model and that the manipulator earns a positive expected profit by employing a mixed strategy.

Proposition 1. *Assume that the distribution of η is continuous with infinite support. In equilibrium, $h^*(x) > 0$ for some $x > X_{min}(\tilde{\Theta}_1)$, where $\tilde{\Theta} = \tilde{\Theta}_1$ at T with positive probability.*

Proof. The proof is by contradiction. Assume that $h^*(x) = 0$ for all $x > X_{min}(\tilde{\Theta})$ for all realizations of $\tilde{\Theta}$. Given such an $h^*(.)$ function, by (3.2) $P^*(y) = P^*_D(0)$ for all y, where $P^*_D(0)$ is the expected price at T if no manipulation occurs. Given such a choice of $P^*(y)$, however, trader 1 chooses an arbitrarily large $x > X_{min}(\tilde{\Theta}_1)$ with probability 1. This is true because he can purchase as much as he wants at the expected competitive price, and still profitably squeeze the market with positive probability. Thus, by contradiction, $h^*(x) = 0$ for all $x > X_{min}(\Theta)$ for all Θ cannot be an equilibrium.

The foregoing result demonstrates that manipulation must occur in equilibrium of the simultaneous move game. That is, $h^*(x) > 0$ for some $x > X_{min}(\tilde{\Theta}_1)$ is a necessary condition of an equilibrium. Thus, corners and squeezes must occur with positive probability in equilibrium. The following proposition demonstrates, moreover, that trader 1 earns a strictly positive expected profit in this equilibrium.

Proposition 2. *In equilibrium, $E(\Pi) = k > 0$.*

Proof. In a mixed strategy equilibrium trader 1 earns the same profit for any x such that $h^*(x) > 0$. That is, for all such x, trader 1 earns a profit equal to k. Thus,

$$k = R^*(x) - x \int_{-\infty}^{\infty} P^*(x + \eta)\phi(\eta)d\eta$$

for all such x. For any x'' such that $h^*(x'') = 0$,

$$k > R^*(x'') - x\int_{-\infty}^{\infty} P^*(x'' + \eta)\phi(\eta)d\eta.$$

Thus, if $\pi(x)$ equals the large long's profit when he chooses x, $k \geq \pi(x)$ for all x.

Note that for some $x' < 0$, $k \geq \pi(x')$ and $R^*(x') = x'P_D^*(0) < 0$. Moreover, since by Proposition 1 $h^*(x) > 0$ for some $x > X_{min}(\tilde{\Theta}_1)$, $P^*(y) > P_D^*(0)$ for all y. Therefore, $\bar{P} \equiv \int_{-\infty}^{\infty} P^*(x' + \eta)\phi(\eta)d\eta > P_D^*(0)$. Consequently,

$$k \geq R^*(x') - x'\int_{-\infty}^{\infty} P^*(x' + \eta)\phi(\eta)d\eta = x'[P_D^*(0) - \bar{P}] > 0.$$

for $x' < 0$. Since the manipulator earns this profit for all x such that $h^*(x) > 0$, his expected profit equals k and is therefore positive.

Together these propositions demonstrate that mixed manipulative trading is profitable *on average,* and corners and squeezes occur in equilibrium. This does not imply that trader 1 earns a positive profit regardless of the value of η; if η is a large positive number, $R^*(x)$ may be smaller that $xP^*(x + \eta)$. For such a realization of η, which occurs with positive probability, the large long loses money. Similarly, for a given η, trader 1 may experience an unfavorable draw of $\tilde{\Theta}$ at T. Given such an unfavorable draw, $R(x, \tilde{\Theta}) < xP^*(x + \eta)$. The manipulator does earn a positive profit on average, however; thus, the profitable manipulative episodes more than offset the unprofitable ones.

It should be noted that Proposition 1 continues to hold even if there are several large traders acting strategically. That is, the validity of these propositions is not limited to the case where there is a single manipulator. This can be demonstrated easily by using the logic of the proof of Proposition 1. Specifically, if there are several large traders, it cannot be an equilibrium for all of them to choose $h(x) = 0$ for $x > X_{min}(\tilde{\Theta})$, for all possible $\tilde{\Theta}$, as a profit opportunity would be present in this case. Thus, although entry of large traders may dissipate the rents earned by manipulators, this does not imply that entry eliminates corners altogether.

Several results flow from this basic model. The first result characterizes the manipulator's trading activities. Specifically

Result 1. *Trader 1 sells contracts with positive probability in equilibrium.*

To prove this result by contradiction, assume that for all $x > 0$ such that $h(x) > 0$,

$$k = R^*(x) - x \int_{-\infty}^{\infty} P^*(x+\eta)\phi(\eta)d\eta,$$

while for all $x' < 0$, $h(x') = 0$. Therefore, for such x',

$$k > R^*(x') - x \int_{-\infty}^{\infty} P^*(x'+\eta)\phi(\eta)d\eta.$$

Assume that $\hat{x}$ is the smallest x such that $h(x) > 0$. Therefore, in equilibrium, $P^*(y) \geq MC^*(\hat{x}) \geq P_D^*(0)$ for all y, with $P^*(y) > MC^*(\hat{x})$ for some y. Given such a $P^*(y)$, however, trader 1 can earn an expected profit greater than k by *selling* $\hat{x}$, contracts, that is, by choosing $x = -\hat{x} < 0$. To see why, note that by doing so he earns a profit equal to

$$\begin{aligned} \hat{x}EP_\eta^*(\eta - \hat{x}) - P_D^*(q_D^*)\hat{x} >& \hat{x}MC^*(\hat{x}) - \hat{x}P_D^*(q_D^*) > \\ & \hat{x}MC^*(\hat{x}) - \hat{x}E_\eta P^*(\eta + \hat{x}) > \\ & R^*(\hat{x}) - \hat{x}EP^*(\eta + \hat{x}) = k. \end{aligned}$$

Thus, $h(-\hat{x}) = 0$ cannot be an equilibrium strategy. By contradiction, this implies that in equilibrium the trader 1 must *sell* contracts with positive probability.

The foregoing result implies that manipulators should both buy and sell futures contracts and do so in an unpredictable fashion. Historical descriptions of the activities of famous manipulators (such as Thomas "Old Hutch" Hutchinson at the Chicago Board of Trade and Arthur Patten on that exchange and the New York Cotton Exchange) are consistent with the behavior predicted by the model. In particular, as Taylor and Kolb and Spiller note, these men traded erratically and unpredictably.[8] Sometimes they bought contracts, and sometimes they sold them. Other traders tried to ascertain the activities of these "plungers," but their ability to trade actively and secretly in the tumult of the grain and cotton pits allowed them to change direction and manipulate successfully with some frequency. Similarly, noted cornerers in the nineteenth century stock market such as Jay Gould and Daniel Drew frequently switched undetected between long and short positions.

The other two results pertain to the effects of mixed manipulative strategies on the depth of the futures market and the informativeness of futures prices.

Result 2. *Mixed manipulative strategies reduce market depth.*

In the absence of manipulation and asymmetrically informed trading in the model, the futures market is infinitely deep. That is, the price in the futures market does not depend on the size of the order flow. If traders can employ mixed manipulative strategies, however, this is no longer true. To see why, take the derivative of the first-order condition

$$k = R^*(x) - x\int_{-\infty}^{\infty} P^*(x+\eta)\phi(\eta)d\eta$$

with respect to x. This produces

$$0 = MC^*(x) - \int_{-\infty}^{\infty} P^*(x+\eta)\phi(\eta)d\eta - x\int_{-\infty}^{\infty} \frac{dP^*(x+\eta)}{dx}\phi(\eta)d\eta.$$

This equation holds because the envelope theorem applied to (3.1) implies $R_x(x,\tilde{\Theta}) = MC(x,\tilde{\Theta})$ for all realizations of $\tilde{\Theta}$. Thus for all x

$$x\int_{-\infty}^{\infty} \frac{dP^*(x+\eta)}{dx}\phi(\eta)d\eta = MC(x) - \int_{-\infty}^{\infty} P^*(x+\eta)\phi(\eta)d\eta.$$

Take $x > 0$. (A similar argument holds for $x < 0$.) The right hand side of this expression is strictly positive because $xMC^*(x) >$

$R^*(x) = k + xEP(\eta + x) > 0$. Thus, the left hand side is positive as well. For positive x, this implies:

$$\int_{-\infty}^{\infty} \frac{dP^*(x+\eta)}{dx}\phi(\eta)d\eta > 0 \tag{3.3}$$

This must be true for all x. Expression (3) can be rewritten as

$$\int_{-\infty}^{\infty} \frac{dP^*(y)}{dy}\phi(y-x)dy > 0 \tag{3.4}$$

Since $\phi(y - x) > 0$ for all y and x, (4) states that the expected change in the futures price at t that results from a small, positive (dy) increase in the observed order flow is positive for all x. Since noise traders and the manipulator do not know what the actual order flow will be when they submit their orders for execution at t, this means that they pay a higher price on average, the larger the net order flow. Thus, buyers anticipate that they will lose if order flow is an unusually large positive number, while sellers anticipate that they will lose if order flow is an unusually large negative number. Put another way, the market is no longer infinitely deep when a trader employs a mixed manipulation strategy.

Result 3. *Mixed manipulative strategies reduce the informativeness of the futures price.*

In the absence of manipulation, the futures price at t equals $E_{\tilde{\Theta}}P_D(\tilde{\Theta})$. Thus, uninformed individuals can infer information about $\tilde{\Theta}$ (that is, about fundamental supply and demand conditions) by observing the futures price. When manipulation can occur, however, the futures price equals $E_{\tilde{\Theta},\eta,x}[P_D(\tilde{\Theta}) + \epsilon(\tilde{\Theta}, \eta, X)]$, where $\epsilon(.,.,.)$ is the manipulative price premium at t. Since η and X are random variables, the distribution of $\tilde{\Theta}$ conditional on $E_{\tilde{\Theta},\eta,x}[P_D(\tilde{\Theta}) + \epsilon(\tilde{\Theta}, \eta, x)]$ and $E_{\tilde{\Theta}}P_D(\tilde{\Theta})$ does not depend on $E_{\tilde{\Theta},\eta,x}[P_D(\tilde{\Theta}) + \epsilon(\tilde{\Theta}, \eta, x)]$. That is, the manipulable futures price is noisier than the nonmanipulable futures price. Therefore, the futures price is a less informative signal of $\tilde{\Theta}$ when manipulation can occur than when it cannot.

Mixed manipulation strategies also affect the volatility and hedging effectiveness of a futures contract. First consider the effect of randomized manipulation on price variances.

When manipulation is completely prevented or deterred, the variance of the price change between t and T equals

$$V_0 = E_{\tilde{\Theta}}[P_D(\tilde{\Theta}) - E_{\tilde{\Theta}} P_D(\tilde{\Theta})]^2, \tag{3.5}$$

where as before the expectation is taken conditional on information available at t. This expression holds because when market makers are risk-neutral, the futures price at t equals the expected spot price at T (conditional on information available at t). When randomized manipulation is possible, the variance in the futures price change between t and T equals

$$V_M = E_{\tilde{\Theta},y}[P_D(\tilde{\Theta}) - E_{\tilde{\Theta}} P_D(\tilde{\Theta}) + \epsilon(\tilde{\Theta}, \eta, X) - E_{\tilde{\Theta},y}\epsilon(\tilde{\Theta}, \eta, X)]^2, \tag{3.6}$$

where $y = \eta + X$.

Define $\Delta P_D(\tilde{\Theta}) = P_D(\tilde{\Theta}) - E_{\tilde{\Theta}} P_D(\tilde{\Theta})$ and $\Delta\epsilon(\tilde{\Theta}, \eta, X) = \epsilon(\tilde{\Theta}, \eta, X) - E_{\tilde{\Theta},y}\epsilon(\tilde{\Theta}, \eta, X)$. Then

$$V_M - V_0 = 2cov[\Delta P_D(\tilde{\Theta}), \Delta\epsilon(\tilde{\Theta}, \eta, X)] + var[\Delta\epsilon(\tilde{\Theta}, \eta, X)]. \tag{3.7}$$

where $cov(.,.)$ and $var(.)$ are the covariance and variance functions, respectively.

An examination of (3.7) reveals that one effect of mixed manipulation unambiguously tends to increase the volatility of futures prices. Specifically, the $var[\Delta\epsilon(\tilde{\Theta}, \eta, X)]$ term contributes to a higher futures price change variance. That is, price changes resulting from random variations in the premium caused by random variations in y lead to an increased variance when randomized manipulation can occur. It is not possible to determine whether futures price volatility rises in total, however, because the covariance between the change in the competitive price and the change in the manipulative price premium could be negative. Determination of this covariance requires the construction of a model that (1) relates fundamentals to prices and price premia, (2) specifies the information available about fundamental supply and demand parameters, and (3) solves for the optimal manipulative trading strategy. This problem is intractable in general, so it is not possible to establish definitively that mixed manipulation increases price volatility.

It is unlikely, however, that this covariance effect is sufficient to offset the effect of the variance of the change of the price premium. This is true for two reasons. First, the change in the manipulative price premium is driven in part by random differences between the realized values of noise trader order flow and the manipulator's trading and the values of these variables expected by market makers conditional on their noisy information. These factors are orthogonal to the changes in fundamental factors that cause changes in the competitive price. This orthogonality tends to drive the covariance between competitive price changes and changes in the manipulative premium toward zero. Second, certain parameter changes will have the similar effects on the competitive price and the manipulative price premium. For example, a steepening of the marginal cost of delivery curve tends to increase the competitive price. It also increases the manipulative price premium. That is, for a given steepening of the marginal cost of delivery curve, the manipulative price rises by a greater amount than the competitive price. Changes in other fundamental factors (such as the elasticity of the delivery-market demand curve) have similar effects. The appendix to this chapter proves this result in the special case of linear supply and demand. This suggests that the covariance between changes in the competitive price and changes in the manipulation premium is positive, as positive (negative) values of $\Delta P_D(.)$ are associated with positive (negative) values of $\Delta\epsilon(.,.,.)$.

Given that (1) the $var[\Delta\epsilon(\tilde{\Theta},\eta,X)]$ term unambiguously inflates manipulative price volatility relative to competitive price volatility and (2) the covariance term is likely to be positive, and is small in any event, there is very strong reason to believe that mixed manipulation strategies increase the volatility of futures prices. This is an important result.

A similar argument suggests that mixed manipulation reduces the value of a futures contract as a hedge for out-of-position producers, consumers, storers, and processors. Hedgers benefit when the basis is stable. (The basis is the difference between the futures price and the price of the commodity being hedged. Formally, $B_i = P_D - P_i$, where B_i is the basis and P_i is the price at some location $i \neq D$.) When the basis is very stable, changes in the price of the hedging instrument (the futures contract) and changes in the price of the hedged commodity are highly correlated. This high correlation implies a high hedging effectiveness. That is, the variance of a hedger's wealth is very small if the variance of the basis is small.

Recall from Chapter 2 that a long market power manipulation causes the futures price to rise relative to cash prices outside the delivery market. That is, a manipulation causes the basis to increase at T. Moreover, the basis will vary at t as the information embedded in the order flow causes traders to revise their estimates of the probability of a manipulation. This in turn causes them to revise their expectations concerning the value of the basis at T. Changes in these expectations cause the basis at t to adjust. Thus, the mere possibility of manipulation affects the volatility of the basis just as it affects the volatility of the futures price.

Formally, when manipulation cannot occur, the variance of the change in the basis between t and T is

$$VB_0 = E_{\tilde{\Theta}}[B_i(\tilde{\Theta}) - E_{\tilde{\Theta}}B_i(\tilde{\Theta})]^2.$$

When mixed manipulation strategies are allowed, the variance of the change in the basis between t and T is

$$VB_M = E_{\tilde{\Theta},y}[B_i(\tilde{\Theta}) - E_{\tilde{\Theta}}B_i(\tilde{\Theta}) + b_i(\tilde{\Theta},\eta,X) - E_{\tilde{\Theta},y}b_i(\tilde{\Theta},\eta,X)]^2,$$

where $b_i(\tilde{\Theta},\eta,X)$ is the distortion in the basis caused by a manipulation. Thus,

$$VB_M - VB_0 = 2cov[\Delta B(\tilde{\Theta}), \Delta b(\tilde{\Theta},\eta,X)] + var[\Delta b(\tilde{\Theta},\eta,X)] \qquad (3.8)$$

where

$$\Delta B(\tilde{\Theta}) = B_i(\tilde{\Theta}) - E_{\tilde{\Theta}} B_i(\tilde{\Theta})$$

and

$$\Delta b(\tilde{\Theta}, \eta, X) = b_i(\tilde{\Theta}, \eta, X) - E_{\tilde{\Theta}, y} b_i(\tilde{\Theta}, \eta, X).$$

Again, the variance of the change in the manipulative distortion of the basis tends to cause the manipulated basis to be more variable than the change in the competitive basis. Moreover, although as before it is impossible to sign the covariance term, it is likely that this covariance is small and positive. Much of the variability of $b(.,.,.)$ is due to factors that are orthogonal to the fundamental factors that cause variations in $B(.)$. Furthermore, factors that cause a widening of the basis in the competitive market are likely to have an even larger effect on $b(.,.,.)$. This would induce positive covariance between $b(.,.,.)$ and $B(.)$. As is the case with price volatility, manipulation therefore most plausibly increases the variance of the basis.

An increase in basis variability due to manipulation reduces the effectiveness of the futures contract as a hedging instrument. That is, out-of-position hedgers bear more risk when traders employ mixed manipulation strategies than when randomized manipulation cannot occur. Thus, it is likely that randomized manipulation impairs the ability of risk-averse parties to reduce the amount of risk they bear. Manipulation therefore impairs the ability of the futures market to perform its primary function of insuring risk-averse producers, consumers, storers, and processors against price changes.

The results in this section are important. They imply that manipulation reduces the social benefits of futures markets. Futures prices are more volatile, less informative, and less effective hedges against the risks borne by out-of-position hedgers. These represent additional sources of deadweight loss attributable to manipulation over and above the losses due to consumption, production, transportation, and storage distortions analyzed in Chapter 2. Thus, the mere prospect of manipulation can reduce the efficiency of futures markets.

3.5. A Sequential Move Manipulation Model

This section demonstrates that mixed-manipulative strategies are profitable even if market makers choose their pricing strategies *after* observing trader 1's trading strategy as long as they do not observe his actual trade. This alternative model is useful for two reasons. First, it demonstrates that mixed manipulative equilibria are robust to assumptions about the information possessed by market makers. Second, given some simplifying assumptions, it is possible to simulate the optimal strategy in the sequential model, whereas this is not feasible in the simultaneous move setup. This permits an analysis of the comparative statics results. This exercise is carried out in the following section.

In this model, trader 1's strategy specifies a function $f(x)$, where he purchases x contracts at t with probability $f(x)$. As before, $x < 0$ represents a sale of contracts. Since $f(x)$ is a probability function, $f(x) \geq 0$ for all x, and $\int_{-\infty}^{\infty} f(x)dx = 1$. In the sequential model, trader 1 chooses $f(x)$ first. Competitive Bayesian market makers know this function and observe a net order flow of y. Given this information, they choose a price equal to

$$P_F(y) = E_x[MC^*(x)|y = x + \eta] = \int_{-\infty}^{\infty} MC^*(x)g(x|y)dx, \quad (3.9)$$

where by Bayes' rule

$$g(x|y) = \frac{\phi(y-x)f(x)}{\phi(y-x)f(x) + \int_{z \neq x} \phi(y-z)f(z)dz}.$$

Given this response by market makers, trader 1 earns the following expected profit when he selects strategy $f(x)$:

$$E(\Pi) \equiv \int_{-\infty}^{\infty} \{R^*(x) - xE_\eta[P_F(x+\eta)]\}f(x)dx.$$

The first term inside the brackets equals trader 1's expected revenues at T given that he acquires x contracts at t. The second term gives the cost he expects to pay for these x positions. This cost is uncertain because by (3.9) the price market makers actually charge depends on the realization of η, which occurs after trader 1 submits his market order.

An examination of (3.9) reveals that it is possible that the market makers may underestimate the true probability of a manipulation and charge trader 1 a price below $MC[Q(X)]$ when he purchases X contracts. Proposition 3 proves that this allows him to squeeze the market profitably.

Proposition 3. *Assume the distribution of η is continuous with infinite support. Then there exists a function $f(.)$, where trader 1 purchases x contracts with probability $f(x)$, such that he manipulates at T with positive probability. That is,*

$$\int_{X_{min}(\tilde{\Theta}_1)}^{\infty} f(x)dx > 0$$

for some value of $\tilde{\Theta}_1$ that is realized with positive probability. Moreover, given this $f(.)$ he earns a positive expected profit. That is, $E(\Pi) > 0$.

Proof. Assume that trader 1 submits a market order equal to $X^* > X_{min}(\tilde{\Theta}_1)$ with probability p and submits no order with probability $1-p$. Thus $f(X^*) = p$ while $f(x) = 0$ for $x \neq X^*$. If the noise trader order flow equals η, the price trader 1 pays when he trades X contracts equals the expected price at T conditional on $y = X + \eta$. Given this $f(x)$ and y, the futures price equals

$$P_F(y) = \frac{MC^*(X^*)p\phi(y - X^*)}{p\phi(y - X^*) + (1-p)\int_{-\infty}^{\infty}\phi(y - x)dx} + P_D^*(0)[1 - \frac{p\phi(y - X^*)}{p\phi(y - X^*) + (1-p)\int_{-\infty}^{\infty}\phi(y - x)dx}]. \quad (3.10)$$

Given this extremely naive strategy, trader 1's expected profit equals:

$$E[\Pi(X^*, p)] = (1-p)\cdot 0 + p\int_{-\infty}^{\infty}[R^*(X^*) - X^* P_F(\eta + X^*)]\phi(\eta)d\eta.$$

Consider the bracketed term $[R(X^*) - X^*P_F(\eta + X^*)]$. In the sequential game, trader 1 recognizes that his choice of p affects the $P_F(.)$ function. Note that $P_F(y)$ is continuous and increasing in p and that given the restrictions on the order flow

$$\lim_{p \to 0} P_F(y) = P_D^*(0).$$

Moreover, $R^*(X^*) > P_D^*(0)X^*$ since $X^* > X_{min}(\tilde{\Theta})$ with positive probability. Thus, for all η there exists a $p > 0$ such that $R^*(X^*) - X^*P_F(\eta + X^*) > 0$. This implies that there exists a $p > 0$ such that $E[\Pi(X^*, p)] > 0$. This strategy dominates any trading plan in which $X \leq X_{min}(\tilde{\Theta})$ for all possible realizations of $\tilde{\Theta}$, as the latter strategy generates zero profits. This implies that there exists at least one mixed strategy such that manipulation occurs in equilibrium.

It is possible to show that the results relating to market depth, price informativeness, price volatility, and hedging effectiveness derived in the previous section hold in this model as well. Therefore, regardless of the assumptions made concerning the order of moves (and thus the information available to market makers), randomized manipulation strategies reduce the social value of futures markets.

3.6. A Simulation Analysis of Comparative Statics

The comparative statics of the mixed strategy manipulation model are of considerable importance, as they identify the factors that determine a contract's susceptibility to corners. Unfortunately, because of the complexity of the problem, it is intractable to determine these results in closed form. However, given some simplifying assumptions, a simulation analysis of the sequential choice model shows how the profitability and frequency of manipulation depend on underlying structural parameters. These include the variance of the net order flow and the elasticities of supply and demand at the delivery point.

In this simulation, for simplicity it is assumed that there is no uncertainty at t; all traders know $\tilde{\Theta}$ at that time. Moreover, the marginal cost of delivery and demand functions are assumed linear. Formally,

$$MC(Q) = \theta + \delta Q,$$

and

$$P_D(Q) = \alpha - \beta Q.$$

Given these functions, the optimal competitive quantity in the delivery market equates the marginal cost of delivery to the marginal value of the commodity. Thus, q_D^* solves

$$P_D(q_D^*) = \alpha - \beta q_D^* = \theta + \delta q_D^* = MC(q_D^*).$$

This implies

$$q_D^* = \frac{\alpha - \theta}{\beta + \delta}.$$

The marginal cost and demand parameters also determine the potential manipulator's optimal strategy at time T. Assume that this trader has amassed X long futures contracts. Applying (1), at T he chooses Q to maximize

$$[\theta + \delta Q][X - Q] + Q[\alpha - \beta Q].$$

Solving the relevant first-order conditions implies

$$Q = \frac{\delta X + \alpha - \theta}{2(\beta + \delta)}. \tag{3.11}$$

In order for manipulation to be profitable, it must be the case that $Q \geq q_D^*$; if the large trader accepts fewer than q_D^* deliveries, he cannot elevate the price above the competitive level $P_D(q_D^*)$. Since (3.11) implies that Q is increasing in X, profitable manipulation at T therefore requires

$$\frac{\delta X + \alpha - \theta}{2(\beta + \delta)} \geq \frac{\alpha - \theta}{\beta + \delta}. \tag{3.12}$$

The smallest X that satisfies this condition is X_{min}. Solving (11) implies that

$$X_{min} = \frac{\alpha - \theta}{\delta} = q_D^* \frac{\beta + \delta}{\delta}.$$

Thus, X_{min} increases relative to q_D^* as demand becomes less elastic (that is, as β increases) or as the marginal cost of delivery becomes more elastic (that is, as δ decreases). In the simulations, these parameters are varied in order to determine how the profitability and frequency of manipulation depend on the supply and demand conditions in the delivery market.

It is assumed that the net noise-trader order flow is normal. The standard deviation of the distribution equals σ. This parameter is varied in the simulations in order to determine how the profitability and frequency of manipulation depends on the variability of the order flow.

The most important simplifying assumption in the simulation analysis is that at t the manipulator can trade n different quantities of contracts X_i, where n is finite. That is, in contrast to the theoretical analysis of the preceding sections, where the manipulator has an infinite number of possible choices at t, in this section it is assumed that the number of possible trades is finite. This assumption is necessary to make simulation feasible. Simulations have been executed for values of n ranging between 6 and 20; the upper bound is dictated by computational costs. The comparative statics results reported here are robust to changes in n.

Formally, at t trader 1 chooses $\{p_i\}_{i=1}^{i=n}$ in order to maximize his expected profit, where p_i is the probability that he trades X_i contracts at t, and where $\sum_{i=1}^{n} p_i = 1$. The X_i are both positive and negative, and are distributed at equal intervals along a line segment $[u, l]$. The parameters u and l are determined by experimentation so that the simulated profit maximizing strategy puts zero weight on these extreme points for all values of σ used. This is intended to ensure that the range of feasible choices available to the simulated manipulator is not artificially bounded.

Given the choices of u, l, σ, α, β, θ, δ, and the X_i, the nonlinear programming software MINOS 5.0 and a SUN workstation are used to solve for the $\{p_i\}_{i=1}^{i=n}$ that maximizes

$$E(\Pi) = \sum_{i=1}^{n} p_i[R(X_i) - E_\eta P_F(X_i + \eta)], \tag{3.13}$$

where

$$P_F(X_i + \eta) = \sum_{j=1}^{n} \frac{MC(X_j) p_j \phi(X_i + \eta - X_j)}{p_j \phi(X_i + \eta - X_j) + \sum_{k \neq j} p_k \phi(X_i + \eta - X_k)} \tag{3.14}$$

and the expectation in (3.14) is taken over the normal density $\phi(\eta)$, where η is of mean zero and variance σ^2. Fifteen point Gauss-Legendre quadrature is used to calculate the price expectation integral.

Given a FORTRAN program to estimate $E(\Pi)$ and its gradients, and initial values for the probabilities, MINOS uses quasi-Newton, reduced-gradient, and projected Lagrangian methods to determine the solution to constrained nonlinear optimization problems. In order to ensure that the program is locating global optima, rather than local ones, for each set of parameters the simulations were started from a variety of initial values of $\{p_i\}_{i=1}^{i=n}$. In each case, the optimal solution provided by MINOS was the same regardless of these starting probability values. Thus, it appears that the reported solutions are globally optimal.

The baseline case in the simulation analysis is $\alpha = 20$, $\beta = 5$, $\theta = 10$, $\delta = 10$, and $\sigma = 1$. In this case, $q_D^* = .667$, $P_D(q_D^*) = 16.667$, and $X_{min} = 1.00$. The effects of changes in δ, β, and σ are simulated. When varying the slopes of the supply and demand curves, the intercepts are varied as well in order to keep the competitive price and q_D^* unchanged. This is necessary to avoid confusing the effects of changing slopes on the profitability of manipulation t per se with their effect on the value of long positions under competitive conditions. Formally, when δ is changed, θ is also changed according to the following formula:

$$\theta = P_D(q_D^*) - \delta q_D^* = 16.67 - .667\delta.$$

The supply curve intercept therefore falls as its slope increases. Similarly, when β is changed, α is determined as follows:

$$\alpha = P_D(q_D^*) + \beta q_D^* = 16.67 + .667\beta.$$

Given these adjustments, the simulations estimate the effects of rotating the supply and demand curves around the original equilibrium point; this is equivalent to changing the elasticities of these curves without changing the competitive equilibrium price or quantity.

Table 3.1 presents the simulated values of $E(\Pi)$ for a variety of choices of σ and δ, and for $n = 20$. Reading across any row of the table shows how expected manipulative profit increases as δ increases, that is, as the delivery-market supply curve becomes less elastic. These results show that reducing supply elasticity increases manipulative profit. Reading down any column of the table shows how manipulative profit increases as σ increases, that is, as the net order flow becomes more variable. The results demonstrate clearly that the manipulator's expected profit increases as the net order flow becomes more volatile. Part of these profits is attributable to short selling. In the simulations, the manipulator short sells frequently (50 percent of the time or better) at a price that exceeds the competitive price.

Table 3.2 illustrates how the frequency and severity of manipulation changes with δ and σ. This table reports the average price at T as a function of these parameters. This average equals $\sum_{i=1}^{n} p_i MC(X_i)$. The average price at T increases as the manipulator chooses large, positive X_i with greater frequency. Thus, this number measures the average price distortion attributable to manipulation. The table shows that the expected price at T is increasing in both σ and δ. The severity and frequency of manipulation therefore increase as the order flow becomes more volatile and as the elasticity of supply to the delivery market declines.

Tables 3.3 and 3.4 depict the effect of changes in β on $E(\Pi)$ and the expected price at T. The simulations show that given the levels of σ and δ, manipulation becomes more profitable, more frequent, and more severe, as β *declines.* That is, the manipulator benefits from an increase in the elasticity of demand at the delivery point.

TABLE 3.1

MANIPULATOR'S PROFITS

δ

σ	10	12	14	16	18
1.0	..0148	.0202	.0267	.0333	.0406
1.5	.0722	.1014	.1334	.1664	.2010
2.0	.2084	.3030	.3881	.4797	.5747
2.5	.4500	.6112	.7812	.9867	1.1727
3.0	.8192	1.0992	1.3909	1.6917	1.9991

TABLE 3.2

AVERAGE PRICE AT *T*

δ

σ	10	12	14	16	18
1.0	16.70	16.73	16.75	16.77	16.79
1.5	16.83	16.90	19.97	17.05	17.13
2.0	16.99	17.14	17.28	17.42	17.57
2.5	17.26	17.38	17.69	17.83	18.05
3.0	17.31	17.78	18.07	18.37	18.66

TABLE 3.3

MANIPULATOR'S PROFITS

	β				
σ	1	2	3	4	5
1.0	.0401	.0311	.0239	.0187	.0148
1.5	.1607	.1330	.1081	.08856	.0722
2.0	.4456	.3682	.3076	.2584	.2084
2.5	.8795	.7432	.6336	.5407	.4500
3.0	1.4480	1.2439	1.0769	.9377	.8192

TABLE 3.4

AVERAGE PRICE AT *T*

	β				
σ	1	2	3	4	5
1.0	16.78	16.76	16.73	16.71	16.70
1.5	17.04	16.97	16.90	16.86	16.83
2.0	17.35	17.24	17.14	17.07	16.99
2.5	17.69	17.54	17.41	17.31	17.26
3.0	18.11	17.91	17.75	17.62	17.31

These various results are intuitive and related. First consider the effect of an increase in σ. When the variance of the order flow increases, market makers have less reliable information about the activities of the would-be manipulator. As a result of this reduced precision, they are less likely to attribute a large, positive order flow to an attempt by trader 1 to accumulate a position larger than X_{min}. Therefore, he can buy large numbers of contracts at a lower average price when the variability of the order flow is large than when it is small. This increases his profit and induces him to trade more aggressively.

Next consider the effect of an increase in δ. *Ceteris paribus,* for any given X_i, as δ rises both the revenues at T and the price paid at t increase; these effects have opposing effects on $E(\Pi)$. What is decisive, however, is that the increase in δ causes X_{min} to decline. This creates new manipulative opportunities for the large trader. Thus, for any given σ, market makers cannot reliably detect levels of trading that would not have allowed trader 1 to manipulate prior to the change in supply elasticity but that are now profitable given the decline in δ.

Put another way, when supply to the delivery market is very elastic, trader 1 must buy a huge quantity of contracts in order to manipulate the market. Market makers are almost certain to detect such large purchases and charge the would-be manipulator a price that is quite close to the realized marginal cost of delivery at T. This induces trader 1 to buy and sell cautiously and manipulate only infrequently. When supply is inelastic, however, trader 1 can manipulate even if he accumulates a relatively small number of contracts. Such relatively small purchases are more readily camouflaged in the normal variations of the net order flow. This allows the trader to escape undetected with greater frequency. As a result, he trades more aggressively and manipulates more frequently given these circumstances.

The intuition behind the relation between β and the profitability and intensity of manipulation is similar. As demand in the delivery market becomes more elastic, X_{min} declines. This allows trader 1 to manipulate with a smaller position. Since smaller trades are more difficult to detect, trader 1 can increase the frequency and intensity of his manipulations without greatly increasing the cost of acquiring positions. This makes manipulation more attractive and therefore he does so more frequently and more intensively.

This simulation analysis implies that categorical statements to the effect that futures markets "are susceptible to manipulation and control" are inappropriate. The degree of vulnerability of a market to manipulation is contingent on the characteristics of order flow and delivery-market supply and demand elasticities. A futures contract with very stable net order flow and very elastic delivery-market supply can be manipulated only very infrequently. In contrast, a contract with extremely volatile order flow and very inelastic supply may be very vulnerable to corners.

The analysis also implies that the susceptibility of a contract to manipulation can vary over time as order flow variability changes or as delivery-market supply and demand conditions change.

In this vein, one potentially important conclusion is that improved transportation efficiency (such as, the deregulation of rail transport or the creation of unit trains discussed in Chapter 2) should reduce the frequency and intensity of manipulation. Thus, *ceteris paribus,* at present manipulation should be a less serious concern than was the case in eras past (such as, the 1880s in the grain market) when transportation systems were far less efficient than is currently the case.

Other factors may lead to the opposite result. Specifically, increases in wealth and the development of hedge funds and managed futures funds make it easier for traders to accumulate the resources required to manipulate a market. Moreover, these factors have led to an increase in the volume of futures trading. (Volume would be even larger if positions limits were not in place.) This volume increase is due to increases in (1) the size of orders flowing to the trading floor and (2) the rate of orders flowing to the market. Together, these factors can increase the variability of the order flow. The simulation results imply that these increases the probability of market power manipulation. Thus, the theory suggests that various developments in American futures markets over the past decades have had countervailing effects on their vulnerability to market power. Therefore, it is impossible to determine a priori whether manipulation would have increased or decreased in frequency and intensity in the absence of preventative regulatory measures.

Given these results, the prototypical example of a manipulable contract may be the New York Cotton Exchange contract in the late-nineteenth and early-twentieth centuries. Secular changes in consumption patterns caused the stock of cotton held at the contract's delivery point (New York) to fall from over 9.9 percent of United States production in 1870-1880 to under 1.3 percent of United States production in 1900-1907.[9] This decline in stocks in New York reflected a change in cotton shipping patterns away from Northern ports and toward Southern ones. The models in Chapter 2 imply that such a change in shipping patterns would have made cotton supply in New York less elastic because it made it necessary to reverse the natural direction of commodity flows in order to attract additional supplies to New York. At the same time, improvements in telegraphic communication and a growth in the world wide trade of cotton led to substantial growth in hedging and speculative trading activity. This almost certainly increased the variability of order flow.[10] The model predicts that these developments should have led to an increase in the frequency and intensity of manipulation and the historical record suggests that this was indeed the case.[11]

These conditions are by no means the rule in futures markets, however. Thus, although the formal model implies that absent regulation, corners should occur with positive probability in all futures markets, it does *not* imply that manipulation should be a chronic problem in all markets. Instead, the vulnerability of a contract to manipulation is highly dependent on the market environment. This conclusion is strengthened when one examines some practical considerations not explicitly incorporated into the formal model. The next section discusses these considerations.

3.7. Other Factors that Influence the Manipulability of a Futures Contract

The foregoing has presented a simple theoretical model of manipulation in delivery settled futures markets. The model's results are potentially important, inasmuch as they reveal (1) that randomized manipulative trading is profitable when anonymity provides some camouflage to traders that desire to create large positions and (2) the susceptibility of a market to manipulation depends on the variability of order flow and supply and demand elasticities. In the interest of enhancing the practical contribution of this chapter, however, it is worthwhile to discuss other features of futures markets that may affect their susceptibility to the type of trading modeled here.

First, it is necessary to note that since a lack of information by market makers is the source of manipulative profit in this model, any information (in addition to that embodied in the net order flow) that allows market makers and other market participants to better detect impending manipulations will reduce the profitability and frequency of corners and squeezes.

In general, although a manipulator will attempt to conceal his activity by using many brokers (or other means), experienced local traders may be able to identify and detect trading patterns that distinguish the manipulator's buy and sell orders from those entered by noise traders. Locals may not be able to identify each of the manipulator's orders with certainty. However, to the extent that market makers have sufficient information so that their priors concerning the source of any order are not diffuse, they can raise the manipulator's costs by trading at a high (low) price when their information leads them to believe the manipulator is buying (selling). This increase in the manipulator's costs reduces the frequency and intensity of manipulation. Thus, experienced and observant locals can deter manipulation to some degree. It is important to note, however, that the model implies that they cannot eliminate it altogether unless they can identify a manipulative order with certainty.

Information can be valuable even if it is obtained *after* a would-be manipulator has acquired a large, long futures position. Given sufficient warning of an impending manipulation, commercial firms can make arrangements to ship additional supplies to the delivery market. Since supply curves are more elastic in the long run, the more warning time commercials have to make such shipments, the more elastic the delivery-market supply curve becomes. Recall that the profitability and intensity of manipulation vary inversely with supply elasticity. Thus, if commercials learn through their myriad sources of an impending manipulation well before the delivery period, the would-be manipulator may face a very elastic supply curve at delivery. This makes cornering far less profitable than would be the case if commercials were ignorant of his activities.

Commercial traders in grains, metals, petroleum products, and other goods potentially vulnerable to manipulation have very well developed commercial intelligence systems. Even though they may not be able to detect a would-be manipulator's trading when it occurs, they may learn of it in time to make arrangements that increase delivery-market supply elasticity. This reduces the profitability of mixed-manipulative strategies and therefore deters manipulation to some degree.

Second, the formal model assumes that shorts are atomistic. In reality, some shorts may be large traders who may be able to exert market power themselves. In this case, the large long faces a classical bargaining problem. His profits in this situation are smaller than when all shorts are atomistic. Indeed, if there is a single short pitted against the single long, it is possible that the large long trader could lose money. This reduction in the profitability of manipulation attributable to the bilateral bargaining problem tends to deter manipulation.

This possibility is especially important if large shorts plan to participate in the futures market for a considerable time to come and thus have a vested interest in deterring future manipulations. This plausibly characterizes large commercial hedgers. In this case, a large short may be willing to incur a loss today in order to undermine a manipulation attempt in the expectation that this action will serve to reduce the frequency of manipulation in the future. That is, a large short may be willing to incur costs in the short term in order to gain a reputation for crushing manipulators, in the expectation that this will deter would-be cornerers.

The heroic actions of P.D. Armour in getting wheat to market in 1897 in order to ruin Alfred Leiter during the latter's attempt to corner the CBT wheat contract may represent an example of such reputation building. Armour used specially converted ships to transport wheat from Duluth to Chicago through the ice of the frozen Great Lakes. It is quite possible that Armour could have settled with Leiter at a lower cost than he incurred to complete this mammoth undertaking. Nonetheless, the salutary effect of his actions on the calculations of other potential manipulators may have justified this additional cost.

It should be noted that the various considerations just discussed serve to reduce the frequency and intensity of manipulation. They do not necessarily eliminate it altogether. Thus, as long as market makers cannot *always* identify manipulative trades, or commercial traders cannot *always* make delivery-market supply infinitely elastic, or the short side of the market is not *always* concentrated, mixed manipulation strategies will still be profitable. To the extent that better information and short-side concentration serve to reduce the profitability of manipulation, however, it will be a less severe problem than the formal model suggests.

It also deserves mention, however, that efforts to collect information and create reputations are costly. These expenditures must be included in any evaluation of the costs of manipulation. They must also be included in the calculation of the benefits of alternative forms of manipulation deterrence, including self-policing measures by exchanges and market oversight by government agencies. The following chapters discuss this issue in detail.

3.8. Summary and Conclusions

This chapter constructs models that explain two stylized facts about corners and squeezes in unregulated futures markets. First, corners sometimes occur in futures markets. Second, not all markets are cornered all the time. The models presented herein show that corners and squeezes will occur with a probability strictly between 0 and 1 in markets where (1) noise traders cause unpredictable variations in order flow and (2) the supply curve in the delivery-market is less than perfectly elastic. Since these are quite plausible conditions in physical commodity futures markets settled by delivery (such as, grains and industrial metals), the model suggests that absent exchange or government intervention, *some* manipulation will occur in delivery settled futures markets. (This statement should not be taken to imply that regulation necessarily eliminates corners or that the benefits of antimanipulation regulations exceed their costs.)

The analysis also shows that the frequency and severity of corners that occur in a particular market depend on the magnitude of order-flow variability and the elasticities of supply and demand in the delivery market. Markets with very volatile order flows, very inelastic delivery-market supply curves and/or elastic delivery-market demand curves may be acutely vulnerable to corners, whereas other markets with stable order flows, elastic supplies, and inelastic demands should experience very little manipulation. This information is necessary to determine the susceptibility of a market to corners and squeezes.

Finally, the models have important implications concerning the effects of market power manipulation on prices and quantities. First, the analysis implies that the mere threat of manipulation makes prices less informative. Second, manipulation can increase the volatility of futures prices. Third, and perhaps most important, randomized manipulation can reduce the hedging effectiveness of a futures contract. Thus, manipulation impairs the ability of futures markets to achieve their primary social functions.

Existing models of market manipulation cannot credibly explain the two stylized facts concerning manipulation. Moreover, they specify neither the factors that determine a market's vulnerability to manipulation nor the effects of manipulation on the behavior of prices prior to the delivery period. Thus, this chapter sheds some new light on a subject that has vexed market participants and policy makers since the birth of futures trading in the United States. This information is essential to an analysis of the efficient deterrence or prevention of market manipulation. The succeeding chapters address this subject in detail.

Appendix

Chapter 3 demonstrates that the effect of manipulation on the variances of the futures price and the basis between the futures price and spot prices in other markets depends on the covariance between the manipulation premium and the no-manipulation competitive price. It is highly likely that this covariance is positive, thereby ensuring that manipulation increases futures price variability and reduces hedging effectiveness for out-of-position hedgers. The analysis in this appendix demonstrates this result rigorously for linear supply and demand structures.

Continue to assume (as in the text) that the delivery-market supply curve is $\theta + \delta Q$ and the delivery-market demand curve is $\alpha - \beta Q$. In this case, the competitive price is

$$P_D(q_D^*) = \theta + \delta \frac{\alpha - \theta}{\beta + \delta} = \alpha - \beta q_D^*$$

and the manipulation price is

$$P_M = \theta + \delta \frac{\delta X + \alpha - \theta}{2(\beta + \delta)}$$

First consider how P_D and P_M vary with δ. It is straightforward to show that $dP_D/d\delta > 0$. Similarly,

$$\frac{d(P_M - P_D)}{d\delta} = \frac{d\epsilon}{d\delta} = \frac{1}{2(\beta + \delta)}\{\delta X + \frac{\delta \beta X}{\beta + \delta} - (\alpha - \theta)[1 - \frac{1}{\delta + \beta}\beta]\} =$$
$$\delta X + \frac{\beta(\delta X - \alpha + \theta)}{\beta + \delta}.$$

The first term of the second line is positive. The second term is positive by (3.12), a necessary condition for profitable manipulation. Therefore, shocks to the slope of the supply curve affect the competitive price and the manipulation premium in the same way.

Next consider how P_D and ϵ vary with β. Again, it is straightforward to show that $dP_D/d\beta < 0$. Similarly, after some algebra it is possible to show that

$$\frac{d(P_M - P_D)}{d\beta} = \frac{d\epsilon}{d\beta} = \frac{\delta}{2(\beta + \delta)^2}[\alpha - \theta - \delta X].$$

Expression (3.12) implies that the bracketed term is negative. Therefore, P_D and $P_M - P_D = \epsilon$ covary positively in response to shocks to the slope of the demand curve.

It is easy to show that the competitive price and the manipulative price premium also covary positively in response to shocks to θ and α. Thus, for each possible structural shock, P_D and $P_M - P_D$ move in the same direction. According to (3.6) and (3.7), this implies that manipulation unambiguously increases the volatility of the futures price and the volatility of the futures-spot basis.

Endnotes

[1] Albert Kyle, A Theory of Futures Market Manipulation, in The Industrial Organization of Futures Markets (Ronald Anderson ed. 1984).

[2] Charles Taylor, A History of the Chicago Board of Trade (1917); Arthur Andreas, A History of Chicago (1887); Robert W. Bouilly, The Development of American Cotton Exchanges, 1870-1916 (Ph.D. dissertation, University of Missouri, 1975).

[3] Robert Jarrow, Market Manipulation, Bubbles, Corners, and Short Squeezes, 27 J. of Fin. & Quant. Anal. 311 (1992).

[4] Albert Kyle, Continuous Auctions and Insider Trading, 53 Econometrica 1315 (1985). Praveen Kumar and Duane Seppi, The Manipulation of Cash-Settled Futures Contracts, 47 J. of Fin. 1485 (1992).

[5] Kyle, supra note 4.

[6]The analysis in Section 2.5 of Chapter 2 also shows that short manipulation may also occur in spatial commodity markets. In a short manipulation, a trader sells a large number of futures contracts, and then brings excessive supplies to the delivery point. This depresses the price there, which allows the manipulator to repurchase his futures position at an artificially low price.

In order to simplify the analysis, in what follows I assume that traders cannot employ such short manipulation strategies to force the delivery-market price at T below the competitive price, $P_D(q_D^*)$. Ruling out short manipulations does not alter dramatically the implications of the analysis. Giving trader 1 more options to distort the market must make him better off; thus, since the model shows that he earns a positive profit when only long manipulations are permitted, his profit would-be even larger if short manipulation were possible as well. Moreover, Section 2.5 of Chapter 2 shows that the conditions that increase the profitability of long manipulation reduce the profitability of short manipulation. One form of manipulation is therefore likely to dominate in practice. Casual empiricism strongly suggests that long manipulation is far more common than its short cousin, so I restrict my attention to the more important form of conduct.

[7] It may be the case that the manipulator does not know $\tilde{\Theta}$ at T. In this case, he maximizes his expected revenue, conditional on his information about the supply and demand parameters. Uncertainty about $\tilde{\Theta}$ at T can explain a phenomenon sometimes observed in actual corner attempts; the collapse of a manipulation caused by an unexpected avalanche of deliveries. If the large long underestimates the elasticity of supply in the delivery market, and demands too high a price to liquidate, shorts may deliver far more than he expects. This can impose ruinous losses on the long. The spectacular failure of the Lyon wheat and Chandler oats corners attempted in 1872 may represent prominent examples of this phenomenon; see 2 Taylor (1917), supra note 2, at 451-455, 458. The results of the models derived in sections 3.5 and 3.6 still hold even in the case where trader 1 does not know $\tilde{\Theta}$ for certain at T.

[8] Taylor, supra note 2. Robert Kolb and Pablo Spiller, The Manipulation of Futures Markets (manuscript, 1990).

[9] 2 United States Commissioner of Corporations, Report of the Commissioner of Corporations on Cotton Exchanges 50 (1908).

[10] A simple model shows how an increase in the *level* of trading activity can increase the variability of the order flow. Assume that noise traders submit N orders to the market. The probability that any order is a buy (sell) order is .5. This implies that the number of buy (sell) orders has a binomial distribution. Call S the number of sell orders submitted, and B the number of buy orders. Then $N = S + B$. Due to the properties of the binomial distribution, the expected number of buy (sell) orders is $.5N$, and the variance in the number of buy (sell) orders is $.25N$. The order imbalance is $\eta = B - S = 2B - N = 2(B - .5N)$. The expected order imbalance therefore equals 0. The variance in the order imbalance equals $4E(B - .5N)^2 = N$. Note that the variance in the order imbalance increases linearly with N. Thus, as the level of trading activity (as measured by the number of orders submitted to the market) increases, the variance of the order imbalance also increases. (Also note that expected noise trader trading volume in this model equals $E \max[S, B]$ and that the value of this expectation increases as S and B become more variable. Thus, higher

noise trading volume facilitates manipulation.) Although the distribution of the order flow generated by this trading process is not identical to the normal distribution assumed in the simulation (though it does converge to the normal as N approaches ∞), this analysis demonstrates how increasing the flow of noise trader orders to the market can increase the volatility of the order imbalance. This, in turn, increases the vulnerability of the market to manipulation. Thus, *ceteris paribus* manipulation should be more likely in markets with large trading activity.

[11] See Bouilly, supra note 2, for a detailed account of cotton manipulations in this period.

CHAPTER 4
THE DETERRENCE OF MANIPULATION

4.1. Introduction

The foregoing chapters demonstrate that manipulation may have very deleterious effects on futures markets. Specifically, manipulations distort prices, consumption, and commodity flows during the delivery period; jeopardize the credit arrangements required for commodity markets to function (with the potential for spillovers into other areas that utilize the same credit institutions); reduce market liquidity and depth, causing excessive price volatility and compromising futures markets as a price discovery mechanism; and impair futures contract hedging effectiveness.

These effects are not merely theoretical possibilities. An examination of the historical record reveals that market-power manipulation has occurred with some frequency, particularly in the unregulated American commodity markets of the pre-1922 period. The evidence is most clearcut for the Chicago Board of Trade, the New York Cotton Exchange, and the New Orleans Cotton Exchange. In the period 1867 through 1921, on the order of 124 corner attempts occurred on the Chicago exchange.[1] Some of these corner attempts fizzled and some failed dismally. Other succeeded spectacularly, however. Both the successful and some of the failed corners had dramatic effects on prices, the pattern of commodity flows, and the production and consumption of commodities. The documented effects include exceptionally large flows of grain into Chicago; artificial shortages of rolling stock and congestion in Chicago freight yards, flows of grain and provisions from markets that Chicago normally shipped to, the failure of banks that had lent to traders bankrupted in a corner attempt, excessive basis volatility and poor hedging performance, and the idling of processing facilities due to the abnormally high prices caused by corners. As an illustration of the last effect, during a large wheat corner in 1879, 75 percent of United States milling capacity was idled due to the price distortions and the exceptional demand to ship wheat to Chicago for delivery against futures.

The New York and New Orleans Cotton Exchanges also suffered from frequent manipulation. Historical evidence documents twenty-seven corners in these markets over the 1870 through 1910 period.[2] These cotton corners also had pronounced effects on prices, shipments, production, and consumption. During some corners, cotton grown in the United States was shipped back to the states from Great Britain for delivery against cornered futures contracts. The British cotton spinning industry shut down for twelve days in October, 1901 because it was more profitable to ship cotton to the United States for delivery than to spin it. Hedgers also suffered from the corners in this market. The Federal Trade Commission opined that the New York Cotton Exchange was so "frequently cornered" that it was "a truism to state that for some years the New York futures market has failed to perform satisfactorily its chief function" of furnishing "a safe hedge for cotton merchants."[3]

The nation's most important financial market--the New York Stock Exchange--was also cornered often in the late nineteenth and early twentieth centuries. Outstanding examples include manipulations in the stocks of the Harlem Railway (1863, 1864), the Hudson River Railroad (1855), the Prairie du Chien Railroad (1865), the Rock Island Railroad (1866, 1868, 1871), the Michigan Southern Railroad (1866), Cumberland Coal (1866), Chicago and Northwestern Railroad (1965, 1872 (twice), 1873), the Erie Railroad (1865, 1867, 1868, 1872), the Hannibal and St. Joseph Railroad (1881), the Delaware, Lackawana and Western Railroad (1884), the Northern Pacific Railroad (1901), United Copper (1907), and Stutz Motors (1920). These corners caused violent fluctuations in stock prices. For example, in the Hannibal and St. Joe corner, prices rose from 135 to 200 over a three-day period and then collapsed to below 120 after the deal was settled. In the Michigan Southern corner, the price for immediate delivery of stock equaled $106 per share at the same time that the stock for delivery two days hence sold for only $84 per share. In some cases, the corners caused panics in the entire stock market. In the Northern Pacific corner, the stock market collapsed as desperate shorts sold off other stocks to raise money to purchase the cornered stock. The failure of the United Copper corner led to the failure of the Knickerbocker Trust. This in turn led directly to the Panic of 1907, which was ended only when J. P. Morgan intervened to support the financial system.[4]

Although the Chicago grain and provision markets, the New York and New Orleans cotton markets and the New York Stock Exchange in the late nineteenth and early twentieth centuries furnish the most complete evidence of the prevalence of market-power manipulation, there are numerous references to manipulations in other less prominent, markets. For example, corners occurred in contracts traded on the Liverpool Corn Trade Association, the Liverpool Cotton Association, the London Metal Exchange, the New York Gold Exchange, the Winnipeg Grain Exchange, the Calcutta Cotton Exchange, the St. Louis Merchants' Exchange, the New York Produce Exchange, the New York Coffee Exchange, the New York Petroleum Exchange, the Oil City Oil Exchange, the Titusville Oil Exchange, the Pittsburg Oil Exchange, the Milwaukee Chamber of Commerce, and the San Francisco Chamber of Commerce.

Some may argue that this historical evidence is of limited relevance to the modern futures marketplace. In particular, as noted in Chapters 2 and 3, economic frictions such as transportation costs are a primary determinant of the susceptibility of a futures market to manipulation. Over the past century, the efficiency of transportation has improved dramatically. The benefits attributable to the deregulation of railroad transport in the late 1970s are especially important in this regard for agricultural commodities. As a result of this reduction in transport cost-related frictions, it is possible that modern American futures markets are less manipulable than was the case in the late nineteenth or early twentieth centuries.

Other developments undercut this argument, however. Most important, there have been other changes that have direct implications for the susceptibility of modern futures markets to manipulation--the growth of wealth, the maturation of capital markets and the development of managed futures funds. In the heyday of manipulation in the late nineteenth and early twentieth centuries, the value of products traded on futures exchanges--primarily agricultural products--represented a relatively high fraction of the total liquid wealth of Americans. Although agricultural production has risen dramatically over the past century, the total income and wealth have increased even more rapidly. For example, in 1890, production of wheat, corn, oats, cotton, and hogs (five important goods on which futures contracts were traded) accounted for 3.05 percent, 6.29 percent, 1.95 percent, 5.67 percent, and 1.6 percent of United States GNP, respectively. In 1992, production of wheat, corn, soybeans, cotton, and hogs accounted for .15 percent, .37 percent, .22 percent, .08 percent, and .007 percent of United States GNP, respectively. (Soybeans are included instead of oats because the former is now far more important in both production and futures trading.) Therefore, given this expansion in income and wealth relative to the output of many products traded on futures exchanges there is now a greater potential for traders to amass a futures and cash position large enough to permit manipulation. Moreover, the improved efficiency of capital markets--especially the ability to borrow vast sums of money--facilitates the concentration of sufficient financial resources to carry out a manipulation than was the case in earlier times when only the very wealthy--men like Vanderbilt, Gould, Gates and Patten--could finance a corner. Relatedly, the development of hedge funds and managed futures funds also allows the pooling of modest amounts of money from numerous individuals to create vast sums sufficient to acquire market power in a variety of commodities. In addition, the growth in futures trading volume attributable in large part to the rapid development of institutional futures trading could make it more difficult for market participants to determine when a manipulation is in progress.[5] As noted in Chapter 3, this would tend to increase the profitability of manipulation and thus would tend to make it more common.

One therefore cannot be confident that manipulation is a historical curiosity. Some forces at work would tend to make manipulation less prevalent. Other forces have the opposite effect. We cannot know definitively which effect is stronger because since 1922 the United States government has taken a variety of measures to deter manipulation. As a result, it is impossible to state with confidence that manipulation would be substantially less frequent today than it was 100 years ago if all restrictions against manipulation were lifted. Manipulation is less frequent today than in the past, but this could well be due to numerous restrictions placed on futures markets in an effort to curb this activity.

In sum, historical experience reveals that corners have occurred with some frequency and that they have had severe adverse effects on important commodity markets. Given (1) the substantial costs attributable to the exercise of market power on commodity exchanges in an unfettered environment and (2) the very real possibility that absent regulation, market-power manipulation could occur frequently in modern futures markets, there are strong reasons to consider the desirability and feasibility of deterring market-power manipulations. That is, it is necessary to answer the question: Are there legal or regulatory remedies for market-power manipulation that generate benefits (arising from a reduced frequency of corners) that exceed the costs of implementation and enforcement?

The remainder of this book examines this question in great detail. My short answer to it is yes. There are compelling reasons to deter market manipulation. Moreover, the characteristics of corners make it possible to deter them at relatively low cost. Unfortunately, however, for a variety of reasons the myriad legal and regulatory means that have been adopted in the United States over the past seventy-odd years to achieve this end are excessively costly or ineffective. Thus, it is both possible and desirable to overhaul the regulation of manipulation in commodity markets in order to improve their efficiency.

Chapters 5 and 6 provide my long answer to the question. The balance of this chapter describes the evolution of antimanipulation law and regulation in the United States in the period commencing with the passage of the Grain Futures Act in 1922. It then proceeds to provide a taxonomy of the different types of deterrence methods embodied in American commodity law. Subsequent chapters contain an analysis of each of the different types of deterrence methods. Chapter 5 examines the enforcement of antimanipulation laws by the courts and regulatory agencies and finds recent precedents troubling because they are based on a complete misunderstanding of the economics of manipulation. That chapter then proceeds to show how to use economic evidence properly to detect and punish manipulation. Chapter 6 compares and contrasts the costs and benefits of alternative forms of manipulation deterrence. It concludes that the punishment of manipulation after the fact through the imposition of monetary sanctions is almost certainly more efficient than regulatory measures intended to prevent manipulation.

4.2. A Brief History of Antimanipulation Regulation

The history of legislative efforts to deter manipulation dates back to the very early days of futures trading in the United States. In 1874 the Illinois General Assembly passed a statute banning corners. The law was never enforced, however. In the late nineteenth century, discontent arising from corners contributed to several attempts to ban or impose punitive taxes on tax futures trading. In the 1890s several "anti-option" (that is, anti-futures) bills were introduced before Congress. These attempts proved abortive. As a result, the only institutional bulwark against corners prior to 1922 was the exchanges themselves. The exchanges were, however, largely unsuccessful in their efforts to curb market-power manipulations. Some exchanges passed rules proscribing corners but seldom enforced them. Many exchanges did not even bother to pass rules or to take measures (such as expanding deliverable supplies) that would have made them less likely and severe. Indeed, some exchanges actively fought the adoption of measures to reduce their vulnerability to manipulation.

Not until 1921 did the federal government pass a law pertaining to market manipulation. In that year Congress passed the Futures Trading Act. This Act was declared unconstitutional soon after its passage because of its inappropriate use of the taxing power, but in 1922 Congress passed a nearly identical bill stripped of its offending tax features. Renamed the Grain Futures Act (GFA), this law as amended provides the basis for the existing regulation of United States futures markets in general and of market manipulation in particular.

Although the main impetus behind the movement to pass this law regulating commodity futures trading in the United States was the pronounced decline in grain prices following the end of World War I, corners were the subject of considerable complaint both in testimony before Congress and statements and speeches by the legislators themselves. In essence, corners were considered an exemplar of the speculative excess that plagued commodity markets and caused unreasonable and unwarranted fluctuations in the prices of grain. Many Congressmen considered other forms of speculative activity to be even more destructive. Most important, farm state legislators were convinced that "bear speculation"--that is, massive short selling by speculators--systematically depressed farm prices. It is clear that many representatives and senators considered such short selling just as manipulative as corners. These legislators clung to these beliefs despite the nearly unanimous testimony of grain market participants that although corners and squeezes could and did occur in grain markets, "downward manipulation" was a near impossibility.[6]

As a result of this widespread conviction that much speculative activity perverted the pricing process for agricultural products, the GFA required exchanges to take actions to prevent manipulation. Exchanges that failed to do so would not be registered to trade futures contracts; this was a costly penalty because the Act allowed futures trading only on registered exchanges.

Unfortunately, Congress proved incapable of defining exactly what it meant by manipulation. In particular, it could not specify precisely the difference between legitimate short selling and manipulative short selling that "artificially" depressed prices. Although some witnesses and Congressmen advocated the abolition of short selling altogether, cooler heads recognized that such a prohibition was overly broad because much (and perhaps all) short selling contributes to the efficient functioning of a futures market.

As a result of this inability to define the term manipulation in more detail, the clear efforts of the creators of the Grain Futures Act to sharply circumscribe speculative short selling have gone for naught. This is almost certainly for the best, as there is little respectable theory and even less empirical evidence that speculative short selling of the type decried by populists and their elected representatives is detrimental, as corners quite clearly are. However, although the GFA did not specify what it meant by the broader term manipulation, it also explicitly required exchanges (called "contract markets" in the law) to take actions to prevent corners in order to maintain their necessary registration. Indeed, a "corner" was the only specific form of "manipulation" explicitly mentioned in the Act. Moreover, the Act stated that futures transactions are "susceptible to . . . control . . . and may generate sudden and unreasonable price fluctuations." It also stated that an objective of the legislation of futures markets was to prevent the distortion of commodity flows. Both "sudden and unreasonable price fluctuations" and the distortion of commodity flows are symptomatic of market-power manipulations. Taken together, this evidence shows that the GFA was clearly intended in large part to deter market-power manipulation.

The Supreme Court decision that established the constitutionality of the GFA also reveals that the deterrence of corners was the primary practical effect of the Act's purpose to curb manipulation. Indeed, in his opinion in this case--Chicago Board of Trade v. Olsen[7]--Justice Taft relied heavily on evidence concerning the prevalence of manipulation and the detrimental effects thereof, to determine that the GFA was a legitimate exercise of Congress' power to regulate interstate commerce. Taft noted that corners caused substantial distortions of prices of and in the pattern of shipments of, commodities that flowed in interstate commerce. He stated: "The effect of such a 'deal' as that of May, 1922 . . . illustrates in a striking way the direct of such manipulation in disturbing the normal flow of grain in interstate commerce most injuriously."[8] He consequently concluded that there is a "direct relation" between futures and interstate commerce in grain and affirmed the GFA's constitutionality.[9] This decision placed the Supreme Court's imprimatur on government efforts to act against corners.

The GFA relied mainly on exchanges themselves to deter manipulation. The Act required all futures trading to take place on an exchange. All exchanges were required to obtain a designation as a "contract market" from the Secretary of Agriculture. In order to obtain designation, the law required an exchange to take measures to "provide for the prevention of manipulation or prices or cornering of any grain by the dealers or operators."[10] Section 6(a) of the Act allowed a commission consisting of the Secretary of Agriculture, the Secretary of Commerce, and the Attorney General to revoke or suspend the designation of any contract market that failed to comply with this requirement.

The powers of the government authority charged with enforcing the Act--the Grain Futures Administration, an agency of the Department of Agriculture--were quite limited, especially after the Supreme Court decision in the case of Wallace v. Cutten.[11] In that decision, the Court stated that the Grain Futures Administration could not punish those who had manipulated in the past because the GFA merely specified that manipulation was to be prevented rather than punished *ex post*. Reacting to this decision as well as to discontent over large price moves, Congress amended the GFA. The new statute, titled the Commodity Exchange Act (CEA), extended regulation of futures markets to include cotton and other fibers, butter, eggs, potatoes, fats and oils, and meats in addition to grains. Moreover, the CEA closed the loophole revealed by Wallace v. Cutten and allowed the new regulator of the markets--the Commodity Exchange Administration--to sanction manipulators after the fact. The Act made manipulation a misdemeanor punishable by a fine of $10,000 and imprisonment of not more than one year. Finally, the CEA empowered the government to limit the size of positions that traders could hold. Again, although concern over corners motivated much of this legislation, it also reflected the persistent belief that speculative short selling was detrimental to the purposes of the markets as well. The position limit clause is especially revealing in this regard because it allows the limitation of (1) both short and long positions and (2) positions held prior to the delivery month. Prevention of corners alone would require limits on long positions in the delivery month only.

Under the CEA, the Commodity Exchange Administration took many actions against alleged manipulators. Virtually all of these cases (thirty-one out of thirty-four) involved market-power manipulation. For the most part, those found guilty of violating the CEA lost their futures trading privileges for varying time periods or paid relatively modest monetary penalties.

The Commodity Exchange Administration also took various measures to strengthen contractual deterrence. For example, after the Cargill corn case of 1938, the agency required exchanges to terminate trading of a future at least seven business days prior to the last delivery day of the future. This was intended to give shorts additional time and flexibility to obtain deliverable supplies, thereby reducing the marginal costs of delivery and constraining a would-be cornerer's market power.

The CEA remained unchanged until 1974. During the interim period, however, charges of repeated manipulation of the onion futures market led Congress to ban futures trading in this commodity (PL 85-839, enacted in August 1958).

In 1974, Congress amended the Commodity Exchange Act and passed the Commodity Futures Trading Commission Act. This established a new regulatory body, the Commodity Futures Trading Commission (CFTC) independent of the Agriculture Department. Moreover, the Act allowed the CFTC to award damages to individuals by a violation of the Commodity Exchange Act--including the prohibition of corners and manipulations--by a person registered with the CFTC. The 1974 amendments to the CEA also gave the CFTC emergency authority to intervene into a market during "threatened or actual market manipulation and corners." This authority allowed the CFTC to direct exchanges to take actions believed necessary to ensure orderly trading of, or liquidation of, a contract. The amendments also gave exchanges the power to declare a market emergency. The CFTC was also given other powers clearly intended to reduce the frequency and severity of corners. Most important, the Act allowed the CFTC to change or supplemented delivery specifications in order to prevent price distortions and the disruption of commodity flows. Specifically, the CFTC was empowered to designate additional delivery points and to change price differentials for different deliverable grades and locations, in order to make a futures contract less vulnerable to the exercise of market power. The Act also made manipulation a felony and increased the penalty for manipulation from $10,000 to $100,000. Finally, the CFTC was granted the power to specify position limits.

4.3. A Taxonomy of Deterrence Methods

An examination of the foregoing overview of the evolution of United States antimanipulation law reveals that Congress has employed a variety of methods to deter corners. It is convenient to classify these methods into four categories: (1) outright prohibition of futures trading, (2) modification of the contractual rights of futures market participants, (3) intervention into the market in order to prevent the consummation of a corner, and (4) the imposition of sanctions on traders who exercise market power after the completion of a corner. For simplicity, I will refer to these methods as: (1) prohibition, (2) contractual deterrence, (3) *ex ante* deterrence (because it occurs before the completion of a corner), and (4) *ex post* deterrence (because it is imposed after the completion of a corner).

Two facets of the law employ prohibition. First, and most obviously, the unconditional ban on onion trading clearly falls within this category. Second, the contract designation process implicitly invokes the threat of prohibition. A particular contract cannot be traded until the exchange listing the contract demonstrates that it has taken measures to prevent its manipulation. (These deterrence measures may be contractual, *ex ante*, or *ex post*.) Moreover, a contract's designation can be revoked--that is, trading can be banned, at least temporarily--if the listing exchange fails to prevent manipulation. Prohibition is a form of preventative deterrence because it attempts to eliminate manipulation by eliminating the opportunity for the exercise of market power.

Position limits and the statutory power of the CFTC to alter delivery specifications are contractual deterrence methods. Position limits circumscribe the contractual rights of traders; they do not have the ability to enter into as many contracts as they would like. This is a clear limitation of their rights of contract. Delivery specification changes limit the rights of exchanges to choose contract terms. Moreover, the addition of delivery points and the adjustment of delivery differentials deter corners by expanding the contractual rights of shorts. Put another way, they impose additional contractual obligations on longs so as to limit their market power. Contractual methods are preventative because they attempt to reduce the frequency of corners by raising the costs and/or reducing the benefits of executing a manipulation.

The ability of the CFTC to declare a market emergency is a form of *ex ante* deterrence. It allows the market regulator to intervene to prevent the completion of a manipulation. *Ex ante* deterrence is analogous to civil code law systems. Like a civil code justice system, this anti-corner measure attempts to foresee every eventuality, to define clearly the boundary between allowed and disallowed behavior before any case has arisen and to intervene while a transgression is in progress. Because of the ability to intervene (1) while a corner is in progress, or (2) simply because the conditions are favorable for a corner, *ex ante* deterrence is preventative; the regulator can intervene before a harm occurs in order to prevent it.

Finally, the criminal and civil penalties for manipulation serve as an *ex post* deterrent. After a corner has been completed, the government or parties harmed by the manipulation can bring a legal case against the alleged perpetrator. If the accused trader loses this case (that is, if she is convicted of the felony of manipulation or is found liable for damages due to manipulation), she is subject to fine and imprisonment. *Ex post* deterrence is analogous to a common law system of justice. Like such a system, under *ex post* deterrence the legal rules that apply in any factual setting are not defined until a case arises under those facts. That is, it is harm based because there is no case--and thus no sanction--without a harm.

In sum, it is clear that Congress has enacted a variety of deterrence methods. These methods rely on very different mechanisms to deter manipulation. These mechanisms entail very different costs and benefits. Thus, they will necessarily differ in their efficiency and effectiveness. This raises the questions: Which method, or combination of methods, is the most efficient way to deter market-power manipulation? Does the current regulatory structure more or less correspond to this optimal deterrence system? If not, how can the regulatory structure be changed in order to improve the efficiency of futures markets by deterring market-power manipulation in the most cost effective manner? The remaining chapters of this book explore the answers to these questions in detail.

Endnotes

[1] A variety of sources present evidence on the prevalence of corners on the Chicago Board of Trade. Charles Taylor, History of the Chicago Board of Trade (1917); William Ferris, The Grain Traders (1988). Arthur Andreas, History of Chicago (1887); Holbrook Working, Price Relations Between May and New Crop Wheat Futures Between May and New-Crop Wheat Futures at Chicago Since 1885, 10 Wheat Studies 183 (1934); Holbrook Working, Price Relations Between July and September Wheat Futures at Chicago Since 1885, 9 Wheat Studies 187 (1933); 7 Federal Trade Commission Report on the Grain Trade (1926).

[2] Robert Bouilly, The Development of American Cotton Exchanges, 1870-1916 373 (Ph.D. dissertation, University of Missouri, 1975).

[3] Federal Trade Commission, 1 The Cotton Trade 20 (Senate Document 100, 68th Cong., 1st Sess., 1924).

[4] For details on corners on the NYSE, see Charles A. Dice, The Stock Market 440-450 (1926). Also see generally Henry Clews, Fifty Years on Wall Street (1908), and William Worthington, Ten Years on Wall Street (1870). These episodes are extremely well documented due to their connection with historical figures such as Cornelius Vanderbilt, Daniel Drew, and Jay Gould. For information on the Northern Pacific and United Copper corners and their connection to major financial dislocations, see Robert Sobel, Panic on Wall Street 273-296, 308-313 (1988).

[5] Recall from note 10 of Chapter 3 that under quite plausible conditions the variability of the order flow increases with the volume of trading. In turn, the profitability increases with the variability of the order flow. Thus, the profitability of manipulation (and hence its frequency) almost certainly increases with the volume of trading.

[6] Senate Hearings on the Futures Trading Act. See especially the testimony of: B. L. Hargis, the President of the Kansas City Board of Trade at 240; grain dealer S. P. Arnot at 315; and L. F. Gates at 329. Gates considered the allegations of downward manipulation unprecedented and seemed somewhat nonplused at how to respond to them. The exchange between Arnot and Senator Capper (the sponsor of the bill in the Senate) reveals, however, that the anti-futures Congressmen were not easily persuaded. Arnot stated that although it was possible to manipulate a market upward (that is, corner it), it is impossible to manipulate it downward. Undeterred, immediately after Arnot made this statement, Capper asked "The manipulation is usually on a bear market, is it not?" Arnot replied, "I understand it differently." Id. at 315. Capper's questioning of subsequent witnesses continued to focus on bear manipulations, however. Nonetheless, there was no testimony from industry representatives that admitted the possibility of this form of manipulation, even though virtually all such witnesses testified that corners could occur in grain futures markets if undeterred.

The analysis of Chapter 3 does imply that short selling is a component of a randomized manipulative trading strategy and that futures prices fall in response to this short selling. It is necessary to note, however, that (1) this activity is profitable only because corners are feasible and (2) this short selling does not depress the futures price below the competitive price. The opponents of futures trading argued that "bear raids" force the futures price below the level justified by supply and demand fundamentals. Thus, the theory derived earlier does not support the view advanced by the critics of short selling.

[7] 262 United States 1 (1921).

[8] Id. at 478.

[9] Id.

[10] Section 5(d) of the Grain Futures Act.

[11] 298 United States 229 (1936). Section 6(b) of the GFA allowed the Secretary of Agriculture to suspend the trading privileges of any individual suspected of manipulating prices after a hearing. The Court overturned this section.

CHAPTER 5
THE *EX POST* DETERRENCE OF MANIPULATION: A CRITICAL ANALYSIS OF EXISTING LAW AND A PROPOSED ALTERNATIVE

5.1. Introduction

Levying harm-based sanctions on convicted manipulators is one way to deter corners and squeezes. Unfortunately, evidence abounds that commodity market manipulation law in the United States is extraordinarily confused.[1] For example, court and administrative law judges have violently attacked the reasoning underlying precedent-setting cases.[2] Commodity market regulators have publicly lamented the acute difficulty of determining whether a manipulation has occurred.[3] Legal scholars have argued that the existing law borders on the chaotic. In the extreme, some have claimed that judicial action is incapable of deterring manipulation and that more thoroughgoing regulatory restrictions on trader conduct are thus necessary.[4]

In order to determine whether these conclusions concerning the state of antimanipulation law are correct and whether the prescriptions intended to address this alleged failure are justified, it is necessary to examine the economics of *ex post* deterrence using the tools derived in the previous chapters. To achieve this objective, this chapter utilizes the implications of the formal model of the economic effects of manipulation examined in Chapter 2 to analyze critically (1) the legal precedents on the subject of market-power manipulation and (2) the legal literature on the subject. This analysis demonstrates that the existing state of *ex post* deterrence is indeed disreputable. In short, many of the existing decisions--and especially the most recent judgments--are based on a thorough misunderstanding of the economics of manipulation. I then proceed to show that this failure is not irredeemable. That is, manipulation is *not* an "unprosecutable crime," as some have argued. In fact, the combination of a sound understanding of the economic effects of manipulation and classical statistical hypothesis-testing methodology in market-power manipulation cases allows the detection of a corner or squeeze with high probability and with little probability of erroneous conviction. As a result, judicial confusion is not inevitable. Therefore, a reform of *ex post* deterrence can make more intrusive regulations unnecessary.

The basic approach that I present below is as follows. Economic theory predicts how prices and quantities behave during a market-power manipulation. In particular, as noted in Chapter 2, it demonstrates that prices and quantities behave very differently during a manipulation than they do when no traders exercise market power. Thus, it is possible to use data on prices and data and classical statistical techniques to test the hypothesis: "A manipulation did not occur in market *X* at time *T*." Rejection of this hypothesis creates a presumption that some trader(s) exercised market power in *X* at date *T*. Economic theory also describes how traders must behave in order to corner a commodity market. Thus, by comparing the observed behavior of traders to this predicted behavior, it is possible to identify who exercised market power. In sum, I show that since manipulation is essentially an economic offense, standard economic tools can be reliably employed to detect and deter it. Such a rigorous approach avoids the numerous pitfalls inherent in the existing legal tests for manipulation.

The remainder of this chapter is organized as follows. Section 5.2 provides a brief summary of the economic analysis of long manipulation and lists several testable implications of this conduct. Section 5.3 uses the insights derived from the economic analysis to critically examine manipulation case decisions and the scholarly legal literature on manipulation. Section 5.4 builds on the economic analysis to construct an alternative set of tests for manipulation that avoids the glaring errors and logical inconsistencies inherent in the existing precedents. Section 5.5 provides a brief summary of the work.

5.2. A Brief Review of the Economics of Commodity Market Manipulation

Chapter 2 derives several implications of a market power manipulation of a futures market. Specifically, recall that if a trader exercises market power during the delivery period,

1. The futures price and the cash price at the delivery market is abnormally high relative to prices at other, nondeliverable locations, prices of nondeliverable grades of the same commodity and prices of related commodities (such as, in a corn manipulation, the corn

price should rise relative to the price of soybeans, which is affected by similar weather and demand factors). Again, these distortions may manifest themselves gradually and are largest immediately prior to the time that the manipulator liquidates. Moreover, sometime prior to contract expiration the futures and deliverable spot prices rise abnormally relative to prices of comparable commodities.

2. Large shipments of the commodity flow to the delivery point immediately prior to and during the delivery period. Moreover, shipments *from* the delivery point are abnormally small during the delivery period as traders amass stocks to make delivery.

3. The price of the manipulated contract is abnormally high relative to the price of the next expiring contracts (that is, the price of the "front month" contract is artificially high relative to the deferred or "back month" contracts). This elevation should become evident sometime prior to the end of trading and may become manifest only gradually as traders become progressively more aware of the possibility of a manipulation. The magnitude of the distortion is largest immediately prior to the time that the manipulator liquidates his position, as then other traders are most fully aware of the prospects for a squeeze. For a given value of the spot-futures differential (adjusted for the costs of carrying inventory between the current date and the expiration of the deferred futures contract), there is an abnormally large amount of the deliverable commodity in store in the delivery market. That is, the amount of the commodity in store at the delivery market is significantly larger than implied by the so-called supply of storage curve.[5]

4. The spot price in the delivery market declines precipitously relative to deferred month futures prices and spot prices at other locations around the end of futures trading or the delivery period. (This is the burying-the-body effect.) The timing of this decline may vary, depending on when the manipulator liquidates and the time required to move stocks to the delivery point.

5. Delivery point receipts are abnormally small *after* the delivery period because of the glut of the commodity that results from the artificially large shipments. Shipments from the delivery point

increase after the end of a corner as some of the excess shipments are returned to their original sources and delayed shipments are released.

The intuition behind these results is straightforward. A manipulation may be profitable when (1) the incremental cost of augmenting deliverable supplies increases as shorts make more deliveries and (2) a trader owns enough futures positions.[6] Under these circumstances, a large long who stands for an excessive number of deliveries and drives up the costs shorts must incur to deliver even more of the commodity. Shorts are willing to pay the long a price equal to this artificially inflated cost of delivering against another contract in order to settle the remainder of their positions. Submitting to the long's "extortion" in this fashion allows shorts to avoid incurring the high cost of delivering even more. Thus, by calling for too many deliveries of the commodity (that is, by liquidating too few contracts) the large long induces shorts to repurchase their remaining positions at artificially high prices. The large long profits when he sells contracts at these high prices.

This description shows that a cornerer artificially increases demand for the commodity at a the delivery point during the delivery period in order to earn a supercompetitive profit. This artificial demand stimulus explains the five enumerated effects of manipulation. Since the demand increase is confined to the delivery market, the price in that market rises relative to the prices in other markets (implication (1). Moreover, this relative price increase in the delivery market (1) attracts additional supplies to that point and (2) induces some traders to hold stocks at that point that they would have shipped elsewhere but for the manipulation (implication (2). Together these actions inflate stocks in the delivery market. The demand increase is also confined to a narrow time interval--the delivery period. This raises the price in the delivery market during the delivery period relative to the prices for deferred delivery (implication 3). This distortion in temporal pricing patterns is even more evident when one controls for the size of the stocks in the delivery market. In a competitive market, the spot price is high relative to the deferred futures price only when deliverable stocks are unusually small. Therefore, if the current spot price is high relative to the deferred futures price at the same time deliverable stocks are very large, it is unlikely that all traders were acting competitively at contract expiration. Finally, the cornerer abruptly terminates the artificial demand stimulus at the end of the delivery period. This sudden decrease in demand, combined with the artificial inflation in stocks causes the spot price to plunge in the delivery market (implication 4). The spot price declines relative to (1) prices in other markets, (2) the deferred futures price and (3) the but-for-manipulation competitive spot price.[7] Market participants refer to this post-delivery price collapse as the burying-the-body (or corpse) effect.[8] The decline in demand at the end of the delivery period demand also leads to an increase in shipments from and a reduction in shipments to, the delivery market (implication 5).

It is important to note that these price and quantity effects are quite distinct from the price and quantity effects of other "unusual" events in futures markets.[9] Most important, the effects of manipulation are readily distinguishable from systemic demand or supply shocks.[10] For example, it is sometimes argued that an export boom or a crop failure could produce the same economic symptoms as a manipulation. It is indeed true that shocks of this sort can lead to a large increase in prices and changes in commodity flows, but the pattern of these price and quantity changes is substantially different from those resulting from a manipulation.

Take, for instance, the case of an export boom in soybeans. During the typical boom, demand increases at the major export points, including the Gulf of Mexico, Toledo, the East Coast of the United States, as well as Chicago, the primary delivery point for the Chicago Board of Trade soybean futures contract. This increase in demand cause prices to vary at all of these points and at the points tributary to them (such as, the growing regions of Iowa). Although prices rise at all locations, relative prices between the various export ports should not change much because demand is rising at all points. In particular, the relative price at the futures delivery point does not *necessarily* rise during an export boom. Indeed, it may fall. During a squeeze, in contrast, demand increases only at the delivery point and thus the price in Chicago should rise significantly relative to the prices in the other important soybean markets. Put another way, during an export boom the relative price in Chicago would increase dramatically only if the boom were confined to that point. This would be peculiar, to say the least.

Manipulation has other tell-tale signs that distinguish it from systemic shocks. For example, the burying-the-body effect is unique to manipulation.[11] Moreover, export booms do not lead to an unusual relationship between stocks of the commodity and the spread between spot and futures prices. Furthermore, during an export boom shipments from the delivery market should increase, whereas during a manipulation shipments from the delivery market should decline. Similar arguments hold for other systemic shocks. In sum, therefore, one can distinguish a large manipulation from other unusual events that affect commodity prices and flows. Only a large surge in demand confined to the delivery market during the delivery period can explain the price and quantity effects of manipulation; absent a squeeze such a demand shock is highly unusual and hence should be readily identifiable.

One should not interpret the foregoing to mean that unusual events cannot make a manipulation more likely. For example, a drought that reduces supplies of a commodity can make a manipulation more profitable and hence more likely. It is inappropriate to conclude, however, that the drought *causes* the corner. A trader (or traders) have to take positive actions to complete a corner and their actions cause prices to deviate noticeably from those that would prevail if there is a drought, but no squeeze.[12]

The economic theory derived in Chapter 2 also describes how a manipulator behaves in order to maximize her profits. I will argue below that these implications are important because they allow a fact finder to determine whether a large long acted with manipulative intent. Specifically,

- The manipulator takes an abnormally large number of deliveries, but also liquidates a substantial portion of her position.

- The manipulator may sell large quantities of the commodity immediately after the expiration of the cornered contract, but a competitive trader would not.

The first implication holds because the cornerer must take delivery of a large quantity of the commodity in order to drive up the marginal cost of delivery.[13] These deliveries are "large" relative to (1) the amount of that deliveries normally occur in the market and (2) the number of deliveries taken by other traders during a manipulation. The second implication is true because competitive traders would rather liquidate their futures positions at the artificially high price rather than take delivery of a good they know is going to decline in value imminently. Put another way, the manipulator bears the burden of burying the body and she must take the lion's share (and perhaps all) of the deliveries. Although she takes substantial deliveries the manipulator must sell some futures contracts prior to expiration in order to earn a profit; due to the burying-the-body effect, if she took delivery on the entire position she would actually incur a loss when reselling the goods delivered to her.

These implications distinguish a manipulator's conduct from a competitive trader's actions. A trader that takes delivery because he actually wants the commodity (rather than to corner the market) would not simultaneously sell futures contracts. Moreover, a cornerer knows that the price of the commodity will decline at the end of the delivery period but takes deliveries nonetheless because she knows that she must do so in order to inflate the price at which she sells futures contracts. Once the manipulated contract expires, she has no use for what was delivered to her, so she is likely to sell. The sale of the commodity in the face of a price decline on contract expiration is not consistent, however, with competitive motivations. In the absence of new information about the value of the commodity, a competitive trader that takes a large number of deliveries for legitimate reasons (such as, to fill an export order) would want to *buy* more of the commodity if the price were to decline precipitously immediately after he had just taken delivery of the good at the expiration of a futures contract.

It should be noted that the trader may hold on to the commodity to facilitate a manipulation of later-expiring contracts. In this case, the holding of large stocks may be questioned if the term structure of futures prices does not make it profitable to store until the expiration of these deferred contracts. Similarly, if an alleged manipulator simply consumes the units delivered to him to preclude them from being delivered in a future manipulation, competitive motivations may be ruled out if the long could have obtained other sources of supply cheaper than by taking delivery against futures contracts.

In conclusion, market-power manipulation has distinctive effects on price and quantity relations. In the sections that follow, I use the criteria identified by this economic analysis of manipulation to (1) analyze the manipulation case law and (2) construct an antimanipulation doctrine that addresses the shortcomings of the existing doctrine implicit in these cases.

5.3. An Analysis of Manipulation Law and Commentary

5.3.1. An Overview

There is a substantial, though not overwhelming, body of case law on manipulation. This case law derives from various authorities, including the federal and state courts in criminal and private suits and administrative law judges and commissioners of federal regulatory agencies including (in chronological order) the Grain Futures Administration, the Commodity Exchange Authority, and the Commodity Futures Trading Commission. Unfortunately, these examples of *ex post* adjudication of manipulation (as noted by one commentator) "have become an embarrassment--confusing, contradictory, complex, and unsophisticated."[14] In particular, the current precedents make it extremely difficult to find a trader guilty of manipulation even in cases where the economic analysis suggests that he has indeed manipulated. Given this state of affairs, *ex post* deterrence is currently a weak bulwark against future manipulations. This raises the question of whether it is possible to construct a set of legal rules applicable *ex post* that would provide a superior deterrence mechanism.

The remainder of this section documents the failings of the received law and constructs an economically and legally defensible set of alternative legal criteria. Section 5.3.2 examines this law critically, using the economic analysis of the previous section as a benchmark. Section 5.3.3 analyzes some alternative tests for manipulation that have been advanced in the legal literature.

5.3.2. The Existing Law on Manipulation

The existing law on manipulation derives from a relative handful of Federal judicial and regulatory agency decisions. The landmark court cases include Great Western Food Distributors v. Brannan (Great Western),[15] Cargill, Inc. v. Hardin (Cargill),[16] and Volkart Brothers, Inc. v. Freeman (Volkart).[17] Important regulatory decisions include *In re* Hohenberg Bros.[18] (Hohenberg), *In re* Indiana

Farm Bureau Cooperative Association[19] (Indiana Farm Bureau), *In re* Cox[20] ("Cox"), and *In re* Abrams[21] (Abrams).

These cases have defined a basic three part test for determining whether a manipulation has occurred.[22] Specifically, to prove a trader manipulated the market at a particular time it is necessary to demonstrate that: (1) an artificial price existed at that time, (2) the accused trader caused the artificial price, and (3) the accused trader intended to cause the artificial price. This set of conditions is eminently defensible. Unfortunately, the burden of proof concerning each that has evolved is not. I discuss each part in turn.

5.3.2.1. Price Artificiality

The analysis of Section 5.2 demonstrates clearly that manipulation has pronounced effects on prices. Specifically, it elevates the futures price and the price of the deliverable commodity both absolutely and relative to the prices for other grades, locations, and delivery dates. Thus, price artificiality is the sine qua non of manipulation.

By making price artificiality a necessary (but not sufficient) condition for a finding of manipulation, the courts have recognized the central importance of prices in determining whether a corner or squeeze occurred. Unfortunately, however, the relevant decisions have not established firm or defensible criteria for determining whether a particular price is or is not artificial. Indeed, recent decisions may have the effect of excluding the evidence most valuable for establishing price distortion. Specifically, these cases (and some scholarly commentary) discount the use of historical price comparisons as a means of determining price artificiality.

Cargill and Great Western both illustrate the use of historical price comparisons. Cargill involved the actions of this large grain merchant during the liquidation of the May 1963 wheat future traded on the Chicago Board of Trade. Cargill owned all the deliverable supply of wheat, and in the days leading up to contract expiration purchased a speculative long futures position. Fifteen minutes before the close of trading on the contract's expiration date, Cargill entered limit orders to sell contracts at a price of $2.29 per bushel, $.14 per bushel higher than the price prevailing only forty minutes prior.[23] In finding the firm guilty of manipulation, the court relied on four types of price evidence: (1) the price rise in the last hour of trading was larger than any observed in the prior nine years, (2) the May-July spread change was larger than any observed in the prior nine years, (3) the spread between Chicago and Kansas City wheat was far larger than had been observed previously, and (4) the futures price at the trade of closing exceeded the price other traders were bidding for wheat in the Chicago cash market by a very large margin.[24]

In Great Western the court conducted a similar analysis of the defendant's conduct in the December 1947 refrigerated egg contract traded on the Chicago Mercantile Exchange. It found that at the close of trading was abnormally high (relative to past values) when compared to the January 1948 egg futures price.[25] Moreover, even though refrigerated eggs typically sold at a discount to fresh eggs, during the period of interest the opposite was true.[26]

According to the analysis of Section 5.2, the reasoning in both cases is solid. The courts relied on the appropriate relative prices. The only grounds for criticism is that the court did not establish a standard for determining how large a deviation from typical price relations is sufficient for a finding of artificiality. Prices can deviate from historical relations for reasons unrelated to manipulation. For example, the Chicago-Kansas City spread varies with local supply, demand, and transport conditions. It would have been desirable, therefore, for the court to have examined explicitly the variability of past price relations (such as, adjust the Chicago-Kansas City spread by its mean and standard deviation). If the observed deviations from the mean were far larger than those likely to appear by chance given the observed past variability, the court could have established artificiality more authoritatively.

The failure to adjust the deviations from normal price relations for their observed variability opened the door for later decisions to ignore historical price data altogether. Specifically, the decisions of the CFTC commissioners in the Indiana Farm Bureau and Cox cases discounted extremely strong evidence of price distortions resulting from the behavior of the Indiana Farm Bureau on the last trading day of the July, 1973 CBT corn contract and the actions of brokers Cox and Frey on the last trading day of the May, 1971 CBT wheat contract. In both cases, on the basis of historical price comparisons similar to those employed in Cargill and Great Western, administrative law judges (ALJ) found strong evidence of price distortions.[27] The distortion in Indiana Farm Bureau was particularly extreme; the price of corn rose 30 percent on the last trading day, an unprecedented rise in such a short period of time.[28] Relative prices were similarly out of line with previous experience. Although not as spectacular as those observed in July 1973 corn, the price distortions in May 1971 wheat were pronounced nonetheless. As had been observed in the Cargill case, the closing futures price was high (when compared to historical levels) in comparison to prices in other markets, prices of deferred contracts, and contemporaneous and deferred cash prices in Chicago.[29]

In later hearings, however, this kind of evidence did not persuade the commissioners of the CFTC. Although commissioners Johnson and West found prices artificial in Indiana Farm Bureau, a majority of the commissioners did not.[30] Indeed, the majority decision asserted cash-futures price comparisons were useless.[31] The commissioners argued that instead of examining prices alone, "one must look at aggregate forces of demand and supply and search for those factors that are extraneous to the pricing system."[32] The outcome in Cox was similar. In the majority opinion, the commissioners argued that the "prospective behavior of a 'normal' market is not bounded by the market's historical experiences."[33] In sum, the CFTC explicitly rejected the use of historical price comparisons and suggested that a complete analysis of overall supply and demand conditions was necessary to find price artificiality.

Some academic commentators have concurred with this reasoning.[34] Along with the commissioners, they argue that an anomalous price relation is not a sufficient condition for a finding of price artificiality because it is *possible* that such a relation could arise in the absence of manipulation due to the occurrence of unprecedented supply, demand, or transport considerations. In essence, these critics assert that since historical data cannot prove with metaphysical certainty that the price observed in a particular instance was not the result of unusual conditions in a competitive market, a court cannot use these data to determine whether this price was in fact the result of non-competitive conduct by some trader. Although it is certainly logically correct that divine revelation is more certain than historical comparisons, this is untenable as a principle of jurisprudence. One can never be absolutely certain of any "fact"; any decision based on any evidence involves some probability of error. The relevant questions are (1) how likely is a particular inference to be wrong, and (2) what level of confidence is required to establish guilt? If the answer to the latter question is 100 percent, a judicial system is superfluous, since certainty is impossible. Conversely, if a more practical standard (95 percent, say) is adopted, historical data analysis is extraordinarily useful.

Fortunately, statistical analysis of historical data allows a very precise answer to question (1). Given the variability observed in historical price relations (either spreads of various sorts, or changes in a single price, or changes in spreads), one can calculate measures of variability such as the standard deviation. Now consider a price relation that allegedly results from manipulative conduct. Given some assumptions about the probability distribution of the price relation, under the null (maintained) hypotheses that (1) the market was in fact competitive and (2) the structural conditions prevailing at the time of the manipulation were in the universe of possibilities that generated the historical data set, one can calculate the probability that the observed relation was actually consistent with competitive behavior by the accused and merely resulted from a chance combination of exogenous conditions. Thus, one can calculate exactly the likelihood of a wrongful conviction. To the extent that these various relative prices are independent, this probability may be extremely small.

Some still object to the use of historical data for a variety of reasons. Perdue claims that the historical prices may themselves be artificial, that cash prices are unreliable, and that the artificial price test is too vague, complex, and rigid.[35] She also asserts that price standards cannot detect attempted but failed manipulations and may provide a legal justification for regulators to intervene to prevent unusual price movements. McDermott claims any use of historical data assumes constant supply and demand conditions and that "a test of manipulation based on a price comparison has very limited utility."[36] These statements echo claims made in Indiana Farm Bureau and Cox. In addition, Lower claims that "because futures contracts are artificial in the sense that they are stylized and divorced from the actual commodities to which they relate, the concept of price artificiality as a measure of manipulation is elusive and, perhaps illusory."[37] Fischel and Ross argue that unusual supply and demand conditions create unusual prices and that it is therefore difficult to distinguish noncompetitive prices from competitive prices resulting from unusual scarcity.[38]

Fortunately, none of these objections is fatal nor even particularly damaging. If historical prices are themselves artificial, it is indeed true that given a standard of proof more, but not all, manipulators may escape conviction than if the historical data set is unblemished; the accused are the beneficiaries of past artificialities.

Note, however, that if these artificialities may themselves be identified, they can be excluded from comparisons. This costs degrees of freedom and therefore statistical precision but allows more exact comparisons. In any event, only borderline cases are affected. Extreme distortions (as sometimes occur) still stand out. Put another way, someone found guilty of manipulation on the basis of historical comparisons cannot claim that past artificialities in the data led to a wrongful verdict; only a disappointed plaintiff or prosecutor can do so. Inasmuch as it is most beneficial to deter the most egregious offenses, reduced precision in marginal ones is no reason to discard historical price analysis altogether.[39]

Nor are unreliable cash price data an insuperable obstacle. Like past artificialities, measurement errors simply add noise to the historical data; they are less precise as a result. As before, the lower precision favors the accused but mainly in borderline cases. Moreover, as a practical matter cash price data, though much maligned, are frequently quite precise. As an example, my analysis (in conjunction with Kormendi and Haddock) of grain futures markets in the 1980s demonstrates that grain cash bids (which are belittled by some industry participants) actually perform quite well when evaluated by objective standards.[40]

Insofar as vagueness, complexity, and rigidity are concerned, it should be noted that these tests are anything but vague; there is a huge literature describing the proper way to execute these tests. Moreover, courts have shown an ability to interpret statistical evidence in securities fraud, merger, antitrust, and affirmative action cases. Since the tests proposed here are typically more straightforward and more readily motivated and explained than those employed in these other settings, it is clear that they are not beyond the capacity of a court to utilize. Nor is rigidity a problem unless artificial rules are established limiting their use.

The alleged inability to detect failed manipulations is not especially damaging either. First, there are numerous historical examples of severe price distortions prior to and contemporaneous with the collapse of manipulations.[41] Second, if an attempted manipulation has no pronounced price effects, it is not particularly costly and therefore is not worth the expense of prosecution. Put another way, it is wasteful to prosecute those who act with malicious intent but who inflict no harm.

Given past criticisms of futures markets, the elastic use of the word manipulation, and the frequent overreaching of self-appointed guardians of market integrity, one can imagine that some overly aggressive regulator could use a statistical test to declare certain large price shocks resulting from large fundamental changes as the product of manipulation to justify an intervention into the price determination process. Since the existing manipulation standard also requires findings of causation and intent, however, it is unlikely that a price change alone is sufficient cover for such an action. Moreover, one should not discard a useful tool because it may be misused. Finally, manipulation causes large changes in (1) *relative* prices, while most fundamental driven price shocks (such as, weather announcements during the 1988 drought) do not alter relative prices drastically and (2) relations between relative prices and deliverable stocks, whereas fundamental shocks should not have the same effect in a competitive market.[42] A famous scholar of commodity markets, Holbrook Working, demonstrates the importance of this point. Working examined the relations between relative prices (that is, spreads) and deliverable wheat stocks in Chicago and declared

> Our first attempts at accounting for unusual spreads between old- and new-crop futures were directed toward finding explanations in prospects for late or early harvest and movement of the new crop; or explanations in the balance between immediate supply and demand for cash wheat, as affected by changes in market receipts and in rates of exportation. These attempts proved wholly fruitless. On the other hand, such information as we have since obtained on technical conditions of the general nature of corners and squeezes has uniformly proved highly pertinent in accounting for peculiar spread relationships that defied explanation otherwise. There arises, in consequence, a presumption that notably abnormal spread relationships have rested usually if not always on interference. . . with the normal operation of futures markets.[43]

Therefore, if applied correctly by focusing on relative price changes, it is a legitimate tool and unlikely to be vulnerable to opportunistic exploitation.

It is patently false, moreover, to claim that statistical comparisons assume constant supply and demand conditions. In fact, the proposed statistical tests recognize and explicitly correct for fundamental variability. In reality, the key assumption underlying the analysis is that the conditions prevailing at the time of the alleged manipulation were in the bounds of the experience that generated the observed data set. Larger data sets can therefore reduce the severity of this problem. Moreover, truly remarkable conditions should be readily identified. It is unlikely that an event that would cause an extreme price change would go unnoticed; if no one noticed the unique shock, how could it cause the price change? Finally, since manipulation distorts relative prices, any condition (other than manipulation) causing an observed price change must obtain in a fairly circumscribed market--the delivery market. Again, it is unlikely that any event that would cause such a noticeable distortion in such a narrow region would pass unobserved.

This discussion relates to the CFTC's assertion in Indiana Farm Bureau that it is necessary to examine "aggregate forces of supply and demand" in order to determine whether a price is artificial. This is an invitation to obfuscation. In particular, it ignores the main virtue of prices; their ability to summarize immense quantities of information dispersed among millions of individuals, information that would be impossible for any individual or group to collect, organize, or articulate coherently.[44] The alternative is to rely on ad hoc theorizing and incomplete information. Moreover, discarding the explicit use of historical price data does not eliminate the need to rely on some set of historical facts. Any analysis of "aggregate forces of supply and demand" presumes some underlying model of how these forces interact to determine price. Such a model is almost certainly based on some basic theory calibrated to some set of historical observations. Unfortunately, these historical observations are almost certainly imperfectly remembered and haphazardly interpreted and therefore vulnerable to criticism by the accused of subjectivity and incompleteness. It is also clear that these judgments are still based at least implicitly on historical data, but such data are not tested rigorously. Furthermore, such a standard provides the perfect opportunity for the accused to construct an elaborate theory and provide superfluous and misleading evidence with no purpose other than to sow confusion. As a result, an expansive review of more basic supply and demand factors should at most supplement, and not supplant, a rigorous analysis of price data.

The criticism that futures prices are inherently artificial is also far off-base. Futures prices are not, as Lower claims, "divorced from the actual supply and demand" situation specific to any time and place. In fact, the delivery requirement ensures that they are determined by the anticipated supply and demand situation at a very specific place and a very specific time--the delivery point during the delivery period.

Finally, the analysis in Section 5.2 demonstrates clearly that the exercise of market power has far different effects on prices than "unusual," but competitive, supply and demand conditions. In particular, the burying-the-body effect is unique to a corner.

In sum, although some seminal court cases have relied on historical data of price artificiality to determine whether a corner or squeeze in fact occurred, recent regulatory decisions and scholarly analysis discount the validity of historical price comparisons. This skepticism is entirely unwarranted and undermines one of the main means of detecting and proving manipulation. As the discussion here suggests historical, price data can provide a highly reliable (although not infallible) way to establish that someone has exerted market power. Indeed, it is difficult to see how one could prosecute manipulators without some reliance on historical data. As one commissioner (Fowler West) noted in his dissent in Cox, the interpretation of historical data implicit in recent manipulation cases suggests that *ex post* adjudicators cannot rely on *any* data in manipulation cases.[45] If this is true, there is a very high probability that anyone attempting a manipulation could escape punishment, as the main evidence of his conduct would be inadmissible. This is one reason why manipulation is unprosecutable under current law. Unfortunately, it is not the only one. As the following discussions show, the prevailing interpretations of causation and intent also benefit would be Pattens.

5.3.2.2. Causation

Assuming that a price artificiality has been proven, courts and regulatory agencies have established that a finding of manipulation against a particular trader requires a demonstration that he had the power to cause the artificiality. Demonstration of this power to cause price changes is analogous to the demonstration of market power in an antitrust case.[46] Parallel to the structure of an antitrust case, the demonstration of causation in manipulation cases has proceeded in two steps: (1) definition of the relevant market, and (2) presentation of evidence that the accused manipulator had the ability to affect price in the market as defined. Although theoretically appropriate in certain circumstances, in practice this two step test has produced some extraordinarily convoluted reasoning and created some dangerous precedents as a result.

The analysis of Section 5.2 suggests that a trader can exert market power if he holds claims granting ownership to the deliverable grade in the delivery market in excess of the quantity in store there at contract expiration. These claims can consist of either long futures positions or direct ownership of the physical commodity. In all of the relevant cases the courts and commissions have used some variant on this criterion to determine whether traders possess market power. Unfortunately, too often they have stumbled in the seemingly straightforward task of defining the deliverable stock.

The two most damaging cases are Indiana Farm Bureau and Cox. In the former, there were a total of 4.6 million bushels of corn in store in Chicago (the delivery point), while the Indiana Farm Bureau's position was only 2.5 million bushels.[47] At first blush, it appears that the Bureau's position was too small to confer market power. However, inquiries revealed that the vast bulk of the stocks in Chicago were committed to firm export sales.[48] According to CFTC Division of Enforcement investigations, only 511,000 bushels of free stocks of corn were readily accessible for delivery; that is, 4.1 million bushels were committed to firm export sales.[49]

This disparity resulted in considerable confusion. The ALJ and the CFTC commissioners both declared the deliverable supply to be 4.6 million bushels and therefore doubted whether any actions by the Bureau could have inflated prices artificially.[50] That is, they discounted the importance of committed stocks.

This interpretation is subject to dispute. The model of Section 2 did not address the issue of commitment explicitly, but it is readily modified to do so in order to reveal the defect in the reasoning in Indiana Farm Bureau. Specifically, delivering committed stocks may impose transactions costs on the short. Moreover, the model in that section implicitly *assumed* that the large long sold the commodity delivered to him in a competitive market immediately after the delivery period. If this assumption is changed and the long acts as a postdelivery monopolist instead, commitment of stocks may become a very important factor.

A grain merchandising firm that has committed to supply a customer with a given quantity of grain at a given time may incur very severe costs if he is unable to fulfill this contractual obligation. There may be explicit penalties for default. They may also be forced to pay demurrage on ship or rail transport committed to move the stocks. More importantly, a firm that earns a reputation for poor contractual performance is likely to operate at a disadvantage in this extremely competitive business. In order to avoid defaulting, a firm may have to make costly logistical adjustments in order to accommodate the disruptions that occur when it delivers committed stocks against futures.

These factors influence the willingness of merchants to supply stocks committed to fulfill obligations to shorts for delivery during a potential manipulation and thus they affect the marginal cost of delivery. The transactions costs of making delivery arising from defaulting on an export commitment or logistical adjustment are a form of economic friction that can make market-power manipulation profitable.

Moreover, owners of committed stocks in the delivery market realize that if control of these stocks falls into the hand of a single party, they are faced with several unpalatable options. They may (1) fail to meet their contractual obligations and bear the explicit penalties and the costs arising from reputational loss, (2) attempt to acquire replacement stocks outside the delivery market and transport them to an export point, or (3) repurchase the stocks from the trader who took delivery.

If the latter can act as a monopolist instead of a competitor, he recognizes that he can charge the merchants a high price for the stocks. This true because he recognizes that options (1) and (2) are very costly. Moreover, it is quite likely that the manipulator *can* indeed act as a monopolist in the spot market because the source of his market power is the ability to intertemporally price discriminate. He can intertemporally price discriminate because the necessity of timely delivery on export commitments makes the merchants willing to pay more for immediate return of the stocks than their return at some time in even the near future. Current owners of the stocks--the grain merchants with export commitments--recognize that if they sell their stocks to shorts to permit them to satisfy delivery obligations, they are likely to pay a monopoly price to reacquire them. As a result, they are willing to sell their stocks only at the high, monopoly price. This analysis implies that it is inappropriate to ignore commitment of stocks.

A similar issue arose in Cox. In that case there was dispute over the willingness of millers to make their stock of wheat available to shorts. Another delivery stock definition matter also caused contention in that case. Specifically, the accused argued that stocks of wheat outside the delivery point (Chicago) should be included when calculating the deliverable supply; these stocks included wheat owned by the principal short (Cook Industries) contained in barges on the Missouri River near Kansas City.[51] Cook intended to sell this wheat for export at New Orleans. The commissioners accepted this broad definition of deliverable supply and calculated that 26 million bushels of wheat were available for delivery.[52] Since this was far larger than the position owned by the alleged manipulators, this implied that they could not have caused any artificial price movement.

The argument supporting this position defies logic. For example, the commissioners argued that shipment of the wheat in Kansas City to Chicago was economic since Cook intended to ship it to New Orleans and New Orleans is farther (as the barge floats) from Kansas City than is Chicago.[53] This statement is consistent with the physical geography of the case but ignores the relevant economic geography. It was of course physically possible to ship the grain to Chicago; the appropriate question is, however, whether this was an economic transaction. If it was not, the short would have rationally paid a noncompetitive price to liquidate his futures positions in Chicago rather than deliver his Kansas City wheat.

The economics of manipulation demonstrate that the necessity of distorting the direction and timing of commodity flows in order to enhance delivery market stocks is just what allows the manipulator to inflate prices.[54] It is clear that the diversion of the Kansas City wheat to Chicago would have caused such a distortion; if Chicago was the most valuable destination for Kansas City wheat, why did Cook plan to ship it to New Orleans instead? The reasoning in Cox--namely, that the physical ability to move stocks into deliverable position makes them part of the deliverable supply--therefore makes it virtually impossible to prove causation, as the quantity of stocks that could be moved to the delivery market is quite large. Since many of the stocks that *could be* moved *should not be* shipped there, however, it is clear that situations will arise in which a large trader effectively exploits market power but can plausibly claim that the precedent of Cox implies that he is blameless. The Cox decision, therefore, is a strong card a manipulator can play in his defense.

There are other problems with Indiana Farm Bureau and Cox. Most important, they beg the following question: If deliverable supplies were indeed so large, why (in the absence of any new fundamental information) did shorts bid up the price so dramatically? This is most clearly evident in Indiana Farm Bureau because the price rise was so huge and because in Cox there is some dispute concerning whether shorts would have had the time to deliver the supplies in Kansas City and elsewhere.[55]

Recall that in the Indiana Farm Bureau case there was considerable disagreement concerning the size of the deliverable stock of corn; estimates varied from about 500,000 bushels to over 4 million bushels. If the latter estimate was correct, shorts would have been able to acquire more than enough corn to cover their outstanding futures commitments at prices far lower than the $3.90 per bushel that they willingly paid to liquidate their futures positions. Thus, if one presumes shorts were rational and acting in their own self interest, the decision in Indiana Farm Bureau cannot adequately explain how the price change resulted, as the commissioners advanced no other plausible explanation for it. Put another way, the price data strongly suggest that deliverable supplies were far smaller than 4 million bushels, but an expansive definition of the deliverable stock essentially removes the fact of the price change from the debate. This conflict is especially apparent in the concurring opinion of Commissioner Johnson, who found the price artificial but claimed that the Bureau had no power to affect the price because deliverable supply was so large.[56] Since Johnson advanced no other cause of the artificial price, it is impossible to reconcile these competing claims.

Other decisions (including Cargill and Great Western) do not include such egregious errors but rely on similar reasoning. That is, they compare some estimate of deliverable stock with the size of the accused's position to determine whether he had market power. In each case, the fact finders used a priori considerations to include or exclude certain stocks from the deliverable supply. In Cargill, for instance, the court excluded hard wheat,[57] while in Great Western it excluded fresh eggs; in each case the court decided these alternative sources were excessively expensive.[58]

Although these decisions are more defensible that those made in Indiana Farm Bureau or Cox (because the findings are consistent with the observed price pattern, which is not true in the two later cases), they are still fundamentally ad hoc and leave open the possibility of future errors. Unlike Volkart, Indiana Farm Bureau, Cox, and Abrams, they explicitly recognize that the cost of obtaining supplies for delivery are relevant. Because the courts and commissions are ill equipped to determine these costs, however, it is by no means clear that they will be able to evaluate accurately an accused manipulator's market power; that is, they will be unable to adequately assess his ability to "cause" an artificial price. Indeed, the market price at contract expiration implies a *lower bound* on these costs and provides the most reliable estimate of them. Thus, the deliverable supply test essentially collapses into a price artificiality test.[59]

In many respects, the analysis of deliverable supplies resembles the vacuous debates over market definition that occur in antitrust cases. In antitrust cases, the existence of a variety of substitutes in consumption and production makes it impossible to demarcate firm divisions between different markets. As a result, the accused attempt to define the market as broadly as possible, while the accusers attempt to define it as narrowly as possible. Similarly, in manipulation cases, issues of commitment and economic geography make it difficult to establish definitively what the deliverable stock is and therefore what the relevant marginal cost of delivery is. If manipulation cases turn on definitions of deliverable supplies, therefore, they may simply decay into struggles to draw firm boundaries where none naturally exist. Establishing the quantity of a commodity available at the competitive price requires information on the value of the alternative uses of the various stocks and this information is held by many individuals and may be extremely difficult to articulate. The history of antitrust analysis suggests that given the vagaries inherent in such a situation, confusing debates and incoherent outcomes are inevitable.[60] Put another way, deliverable supply estimates provide little information not already contained in prices and making a manipulation conviction turn on inevitably artificial estimates of supplies invites confusion and contradiction. Indiana Farm Bureau and Cox are two examples of how this can happen in manipulation cases.

There are other problems with the received view on causation. Most important, the precedents in Volkart, Indiana Farm Bureau, and Cox may allow a long manipulator to escape unscathed by arguing that behavior of the shorts was responsible for any price artificiality; that is, the shorts, rather than a large long, "caused" the artificial price. For example, in Volkart the court found that there was substantial uncertificated cotton (cotton not regular for delivery) that the shorts could have made deliverable through some effort, but did not:

> Unless shorts are to be excused from the performance of their contracts and from the *exercise of due diligence to that end*, the ample supply of uncertificated cotton must be considered as available to them [emphasis added].[61]

In the eyes of the court, therefore, the shorts were responsible for their own predicament. This reasoning, like that in Indiana Farm Bureau and Cox, implicitly assumes that the cost of making the uncertificated cotton deliverable was trivial; this is difficult to reconcile with the behavior of the shorts in bidding up the futures price. In Indiana Farm Bureau, the majority decision declared:

> That shorts with no delivery capacity chose to bid up the price rather than seek cash corn is not evidence on manipulative activity on the part of the long.[62]

The shorts were irresponsible, therefore, and thus the price change was largely attributable to them; they had no business staying short that late in the delivery month. In Cox, the commissioners also substantially blamed the shorts keeping their positions open without preparing for delivery for any resulting price increase.[63]

These decisions conflict sharply with the decisions in the Cargill and Great Western cases. Those decisions imply that shorts are not obligated to purchase fancy grades or to go outside the delivery market in order to acquire deliverable supplies.[64] The court's decision in Cargill is especially instructive in this regard. In that case, the defendant argued that

> it is clear that if the long is not permitted to ask, in his judgment, a price reflecting the cost of bringing wheat from outside, the futures market is no longer reflecting the real supply-demand situation, but is artificially low and prices are therefore useless to the trade and nation.[65]

In a stinging rebuke, the court replied: "It is this price [the price that reflected the cost of out-of-town wheat] that was artificially high, and therefore useless to the trade and nation."[66]

Indiana Farm Bureau, Cox, and Volkart contain no such limits on the actions shorts must take in order to satisfy the demands of a large long. These cases can be read to mean that if shorts can acquire supplies for delivery, no matter how uneconomical the source, a large long can be found innocent of a manipulation if they fail to do so, but instead consent to liquidate at high prices. The economic analysis of manipulation reveals that such an interpretation would render any antimanipulation statute meaningless.

Although there is some merit in giving shorts an incentive to take actions (such as preparing for delivery) that mitigate a long's market power, the wording in Indiana Farm Bureau, Cox, and Volkart is so broad that it could provide considerable legal cover for a would-be manipulator. Note that shorts with positions equal in total size to the manipulator's position must remain in the market at the latter's sufferance. Even if shorts *desire* to close their positions prior to the expiration of the contract, they cannot do so unless the long sells to them. Thus, although the wording in Indiana Farm Bureau, Cox and Volkart suggests that shorts have the option to leave the market unilaterally, this is not the case.

Moreover, if the failure of shorts to make delivery is considered evidence of their culpability for a corner--and a fair reading of Indiana Farm Bureau, Cox, and Volkart would clearly support such a position--it is nearly impossible to find a long guilty of market-power manipulation. Recall that a profit-maximizing manipulator liquidates some contracts at a price that exceeds the competitive price but that is low enough to make it rational for some shorts to liquidate rather than deliver. That is, he exploits the fact that it is costly for them to deliver in order to "blackmail" them into liquidating at high prices. Since a successful manipulation always involves substantial numbers of liquidations, if the failure of shorts to deliver is in itself considered sufficient to absolve a large long from any responsibility for an artificial price, by definition manipulation cannot occur.

It may be objected that the causation theory advanced in Indiana Farm Bureau (which I will call the "Indiana Farm Bureau rule") is desirable because it gives shorts an incentive to take actions that make manipulation less likely. It is indeed the case that under this rule, shorts have a strong motive to take such precautions and that this will reduce the vulnerability of futures markets to manipulation. The relevant question, however, is whether it is efficient to rely primarily on the efforts of shorts to prevent manipulation or whether it is better instead to impose sanctions on longs who exercise market power regardless of whether shorts take precautions or not.

In order to answer this question it is necessary to analyze how the behavior of market participants changes when the different rules are implemented. Under the Indiana Farm Bureau rule, shorts have no recourse against a corner unless they take actions to secure deliverable supplies As interpreted in Cox, such actions may include the distortion of normal commodity flows in order to enhance deliverable stocks.[67] Alternatively, they may attempt to liquidate their futures positions far before the end of the delivery period. Shorts possess greater flexibility in acquiring deliverable stocks the more time they have to make delivery. This flexibility reduces the marginal cost of delivery and therefore a large long possesses less market power when shorts attempt to liquidate early; the large long's market power is not necessarily eliminated, however.

Acting rationally under the Indiana Farm Bureau rule, shorts will take precautions until the marginal cost thereof equals the marginal benefit. The marginal benefit of precautions equals the expected savings to shorts attributable to a lower probability and a reduced severity of corners. In this legal regime, shorts will rationally take precautions that lead to increases in deliverable stocks, premature termination of futures positions, and excessive searching to obtain deliverable supplies relative to what would occur in a legal regime where the exercise of market power by long traders is effectively deterred. All of these actions are costly. For example, continuously holding large deliverable stocks of corn in Chicago may well reduce the probability of manipulation, but it also leads to the construction and use of more storage space in Chicago, the reduction of corn consumption outside of Chicago and the use of more railroad, barge, and trucking resources to transport the extra corn to that city. Similarly, early liquidation of futures positions may reduce hedging effectiveness. That is, just as the possibility of burglary induces homeowners to expend real resources on locks, alarms, and guard dogs in order to reduce the likelihood of theft, the possibility of manipulation induces shorts to expend real resources to reduce its likelihood and severity. These are the deadweight costs of the Indiana Farm Bureau regime.[68]

These costs are likely to be large. This conclusion is strengthened when one recognizes that when deciding on the amount of precautions to take, shorts have very poor information. The amount of precautions taken by an individual short depends on both the size of positions held by long traders and the amount of precautions taken by other shorts. Individual shorts are likely to know little about either. As a consequence of this poor information, the level of precautions taken will differ dramatically from those that would be appropriate under the Indiana Farm Bureau rule if knowledge were perfect. Therefore, given the vagaries of information, under this rule shorts will sometimes take too many precautions. Sometimes they will take too few.[69] When they take too many precautions, deadweight losses result in the form of excessive storage and transportation costs. When they take too few precautions, corners with their attendant deadweight losses will occur. Corners will occur because under the Indiana Farm Bureau rule longs know that they are immune from sanction for manipulation when shorts take few precautions.[70] Thus, substantial deadweight costs are inevitable if the Indiana Farm Bureau rule becomes the recognized standard for deciding guilt in a manipulation case.

There are no analogous incentive distortions in a legal regime that sanctions the exercise of market power by longs regardless of short precautions. Deterring longs from exercising market power during the delivery period does not confer market power on shorts.[71] Thus, this form of deterrence makes the market competitive during the delivery period. In such a competitive market, if shorts are subject to severe penalties if they default their contractual obligations, they have the incentives to bring the socially optimal supplies to the delivery point, liquidate their contracts in an efficient fashion, and search the right amount for cash supplies. As a result, the only cost of sanctioning longs for the exercise of market power is the administrative cost of enforcing antimanipulation rules.[72] There are no deadweight distortions analogous to those inherent in the Indiana Farm Bureau regime.[73]

The foregoing implies that the Indiana Farm Bureau rule is more efficient than an alternative rule that punishes manipulators even if shorts fail to take these precautions if and only if the costs of precaution and corners are less than the costs of detecting and punishing traders that exercise market power during the delivery period. Since (as I argue in more detail below) it is possible to detect and punish market-power manipulators with high probability, it is therefore possible to deter the exercise of market power at very low cost through the use of an alternative legal rule that bans market-power manipulation regardless of the actions of shorts. As a result, it is highly unlikely that it is cheaper to deter manipulation by inducing shorts to secure deliverable supplies that are larger than would be optimal if all traders act competitively than it is to deter it by sanctioning longs that exercise market power.[74] The Indiana Farm Bureau rule that imposes the primary manipulation deterrence burden on shorts is therefore objectionable.

The foregoing difficulties presented by Indiana Farm Bureau, Abrams, and Cox do not exhaust the problems with the current doctrine of causation. Two remaining problems stand out. First, the use of market shares to establish the market dominance of a large trader can be misleading. Second, the case law suggests that ownership of the deliverable commodity is essential to the completion of a manipulation. Since a futures contract and possession of deliverable supplies are perfect substitutes during the delivery period, this is incorrect.

Consider the use of market share. In all of the major cases, the decision makers have determined the fraction of the open positions owned by the large trader. Although (as I discuss in Section 5.4.3) market share and changes in market share can reveal important information, ownership of a large fraction of the open interest is neither necessary nor sufficient for a successful manipulation. A trader can own 100 percent of the outstanding positions, but this is of little importance if the marginal cost of delivery is constant over the range of his position. Alternatively, a trader may own a relatively small share but still exercise market power if the marginal cost of delivery is increasing, or if there are enough other large traders.

Finally, the case law attaches considerable importance to the alleged manipulator's ownership of the deliverable supply. In Volkart, for instance, the court averred:

> In most, if not all, of the cases in which a trader has been adjudged guilty of manipulation, it has effectively controlled the spot commodity to the extent necessary to enable it to convert its dominant long futures position into an illegal corner or squeeze.[75]

In Cargill, the court reasoned that:

> A corner amounts to nearly a *monopoly of the cash commodity*, combined with ownership of long futures contracts in excess of the amount of that commodity. [emphasis added].[76]

Similarly, in Abrams the ALJ stated that

> It is when [the manipulator] *knows* by virtue of his ownership of deliverable supply, that supplies will be short that his actions may be considered manipulative. . . . Unless the respondent either physically controls most of the deliverable supply, or is otherwise privy to some 'inside information'. . . it is not clear how [he] could possibly know what deliverable supply will be[77] [emphasis in original].

Although none of these statements goes as far as to assert that ownership of the deliverable is necessary for manipulation, all strongly suggest that it may be very difficult to prove manipulation if the accused does not possess some of the physical commodity. It is clear, however, that a long futures position and a unit of the deliverable commodity are equivalent in their contribution to manipulative profit. This is true because a futures contract and a unit of the commodity both represent a claim on the same commodity in the same market at the same time. Thus, as a logical matter such a plausible reading of the cases is inconsistent with an understanding of the economics of manipulation.

The reasoning in Abrams is particularly troubling. Put in their best light, one can interpret the statements made in this case to mean that a long in possession of the deliverable supply can readily purchase futures contracts at the competitive price from shorts ignorant of this fact; other traders sell freely because they perceive the open interest small to the deliverable supply, which they presume to be held by competitive traders. Such an situation would certainly benefit the long (as it did in Cargill, for instance), but there are cases (the Hunt soybean and Ferruzzi soybean episodes, for example) in which the long either owned no physical supplies, or knowledge of the long's physical position was widespread when he entered the futures market. Thus, secret ownership of the deliverable is not even necessary for a long to acquire a dominant futures position. Moreover, if the trader can acquire the physical commodity at the competitive price from those oblivious to his intent, he should be able to acquire futures contracts at the competitive price as well. As a result, the asymmetric treatment of the physical commodity and futures contracts implicit in the ALJ's argument is highly suspect.

Read more critically, the ALJ's assertion is nonsense. If the term *deliverable supplies* is interpreted narrowly to mean the stocks certified regular for delivery, the claim is patently incorrect, since exchanges regularly publish deliverable supply figures. If the term is interpreted broadly to mean those stocks that could be made deliverable (at unspecified cost), it is clear that the large long could never know for certain "what the deliverable supply will be" no matter how much he owns; he just knows how much shorts *cannot* deliver to him. This may be important information, but it does not provide the certainty that the ALJ (erroneously) asserts is crucial to a successful squeeze.[78]

In conclusion, major precedents concerning the evidence necessary to determine causation in a manipulation case may provide substantial legal shelter to a cornerer. Most important, the potential for the accused to refute causation by convincing a court or commissioners that the deliverable supply is large may allow him to escape unscathed. Indeed, since several cases suggest that any supplies that shorts can physically make deliverable should be included in the deliverable supply regardless of the cost of doing so, the concept of deliverable supply is so elastic as to provide no meaningful check on manipulative conduct. Moreover, since these cases can be interpreted to mean that a short that pays a high price to escape his obligation to deliver (regardless of the level of the marginal cost of delivery) is in fact the "cause" of the artificial price, as a practical matter it may be impossible to find any large long trader guilty of manipulation.

Like the current interpretations of price artificiality, therefore, one can make a very strong case that several (although not all) causation precedents legalize manipulation de facto. Moreover, the following section demonstrates that the third leg of the prevailing doctrinal triad--intent--also places an extreme burden on anyone attempting to prove manipulation.

5.3.2.3. Intent

"Intent," stated the commissioners in Indiana Farm Bureau, "is the essence of manipulation."[79] Although requiring a finding of an intention to create an artificial price to prove guilt is justifiable, the definition of intent that has evolved over time is not. As is the case for price artificiality and causation standards, the prevailing intent doctrine seems calculated to permit manipulation in many circumstances. The prime culprits are again Indiana Farm Bureau, Cox, Abrams, and Volkart, but the better-reasoned opinions in Cargill and Great Western muddy the waters somewhat as well; indeed, errors in the later decisions stem largely from statements in the earlier ones.

The major problem with the existing case law on intent concerns the notion of a "natural" corner or squeeze. In Cargill, the court argued that "many squeezes do not represent intentional manipulation."[80] They instead arise when an unexpected shortage occurs due to drought, unusually high demand, or transportation problems. Similarly, in Volkart the case cited the Federal Trade Commission's landmark grain study from the 1920s as authority for its claim that many squeezes are unintentional, again because events unforeseen at the time a trader creates a position may confer market power on him subsequently.[81] Moreover, the court in Great Western also cited the authority of the F.T.C. report when it asserted the existence of an "unpunishable. . . *unintentional* corner" (emphasis added).[82]

It is a short (but wrong) step from the assertion that exogenous events may facilitate manipulation to the conclusion that if such an event occurs, a trader who exerts market power cannot have intended the result. In Cargill the court did not take this step. In fact, it deliberately rejected it.[83] Thus, although the court in Cargill recognized that natural conditions facilitate some squeezes, a long trader cannot exploit these conditions. In Indiana Farm Bureau, however, the majority of the commission drew the opposite conclusion. According to this opinion, the Indiana Farm Bureau did not initiate its position with the intent of manipulating; it was legitimately hedging instead.[84] Between the time the hedge was placed and contract expiration, however, conditions evolved that placed the Bureau in a position to squeeze the market.[85] The commission found the Bureau blameless for "seeking the best price from the existing situation"[86] and asserted that a long has "a contractual right to stand for delivery or exact whatever price for its long position which a short is willing to pay to avoid having to make delivery."[87] The court in Volkart reasoned similarly.[88]

According to the CFTC's decision in Indiana Farm Bureau, only if a trader deliberately "exacerbates the congestion" at contract expiration can intent be inferred.[89] Exacerbating acts include buying additional futures positions in the delivery period and intentionally decreasing the cash supply.[90] Since a trader can amass a position that confers market power without engaging in such acts, it is clear that this opinion--which has been cited as authoritative the two subsequent manipulation cases of Cox and Abrams--permits manipulation in many circumstances. Only in a case like Cargill, where the firm engaged in just this sort of conduct, can one infer intent under the guidelines established in the Farm Bureau case.[91]

Together these decisions imply that a trader's intent at the time he *initiates* a futures position is relevant to determining whether his actions during the delivery period are manipulative. It is readily apparent, however, that a trader's state of mind when he creates a futures position has no bearing on whether he exercises market power in the delivery month or on his state of mind during the delivery period. The doctrine of a "natural" squeeze therefore provides a large trader with a manipulation option; if he creates a long large position for a legitimate hedging or speculative purpose, he can exercise his option to squeeze the market if conditions subsequently change so as to make manipulation profitable. One can imagine the havoc that would result if judges were to find only those who meticulously planned a murder guilty of the crime and freed all those that merely killed impulsively when the opportunity presented itself. The precedents in manipulation law create the conditions for such chaos in futures markets.

The reasoning in the Abrams decision presents still further difficulties to any attempt to prove manipulative intent. In Abrams the ALJ argued,

> Abram's actions were taken with the purpose of exacting the best possible price for his long positions, which he established after correctly divining the market's future direction. Under the Commission's precedents, Abrams did nothing beyond what speculators normally do, and indeed must do to make markets function.[92]

If widely adopted, this reasoning has very mischievous implications. If a rise in price during the delivery period is interpreted merely as evidence of his prescience in "divining the market's future direction," a large long can effectively escape conviction even if he does manipulate the market.[93] A successful manipulation *causes* the price to rise. The Abrams decision implies that a rise in price is sufficient to deny any intent to manipulate the market because the long can cite this price increase as evidence of his legitimate speculative motives for buying futures. If a price rise is considered dispositive evidence of legitimate speculative intent and if a finding of manipulative intent is necessary to convict a cornerer, application of the reasoning in Abrams makes it impossible to convict a successful manipulator.

Another difficulty with the prevailing view of intent is the emphasis placed on ownership of the deliverable commodity before the completion of a squeeze. Cargill,[94] Great Western,[95] Volkart,[96] Indiana Farm Bureau,[97] and Abrams[98] all mention the importance of the ownership of deliverable stocks in determining intent. Again, since such ownership is neither necessary nor sufficient for a successful manipulation, this emphasis is misplaced and highly misleading. Since a manipulator must take deliveries of virtually the entire deliverable stock, however, ownership of this stock *after* the expiration of a futures contract is strong evidence that a particular trader intended to corner the market. Thus, courts and the CFTC have focused on the deliverable stock at an inappropriate time.

In conclusion, the precedents concerning intent provide a would-be manipulator with considerable latitude. As long as he can demonstrate a legitimate intent for initiating a futures position (such as, hedging or informed speculation) and does not purchase the deliverable commodity, he can utilize these precedents in his defense.

5.3.2.4. Summary

The existing court and regulatory decisions on manipulation resemble a rickety three-legged stool, ready to collapse under the slightest weight. Each leg--artificial price, causation, and intent--is rotted through. Taken collectively, the relevant decisions (especially the most recent ones--Indiana Farm Bureau, Cox, and Abrams) (1) make it difficult to employ the most valuable evidence concerning price distortions, (2) obscure the determinants of market power, and (3) make it possible for those who intend to exercise market power in the delivery period to deny effectively this intent. With such a collection of precedents, it is no wonder that some believe that the prosecution of manipulation is futile.

It is also important to note that the prevailing confusion does not simply jeopardize *ex post* prosecutions of accused manipulators. It also undermines the foundations for interventions by regulators and exchanges, such as emergency actions and forced liquidation (as occurred in the 1989 Ferruzzi episode).[99] Any exchange or regulatory body that attempts to force a particular trader to liquidate a position because of a fear of an impending manipulation runs the risk that the accused will challenge the action on the grounds that existing precedents imply that his actions do not satisfy the established criteria of price artificiality, causation, or intent. It is certainly possible that a court will accept the challenge and overturn the emergency action. Moreover, although subsequent appeals may reinstate the emergency order, given the time required to complete appeals it is almost certain that the futures contract will expire (and the manipulation succeed) before the process ends. If the trader stalls emergency intervention successfully through the courts, he need only worry about *ex post* adjudication. Given the highly favorable odds the existing precedents provide, this prospect may be less than daunting.

5.3.3. Legal Commentary on Manipulation Law

Given the foregoing analysis, it is unsurprising that the literature on manipulation case law (some of which has been cited heretofore) is almost uniformly critical. Some of these criticisms overlap those that I have just made, while others are quite different. The most important difference between these criticisms and mine is that, as noted earlier, several commentators strongly criticize the law's reliance on evidence of price artificiality to decide manipulation cases. In contrast, I consider this evidence crucial.

The legal commentators focus on intent or conduct and either denigrate the importance of establishing price artificiality in manipulation litigation or fail to provide any tests to establish the existence of price abnormalities that address the problems raised by Cox and Indiana Farm Bureau. As a result, the they proposed alternatives do not provide a complete methodology that a court can apply to determine whether a particular set of facts supports or does not support a conclusion that a trader manipulated the market.

For example, Perdue proposes the following "price impact" test: Did the trader act as he did in the expectation that his action would affect the market price? That is, but for the anticipated price increase would he have engaged in this conduct?[100] Friedman modifies Perdue's formulation by adding the following question: "If the only sanction for a short's default [on a futures contract] were the ordinary measure of contract damages, would the long trader have withheld supply to a lesser extent than he did?"[101] McDermott proposes a conduct-based test. Calling for a test analogous to the common law standard of hindrance, he argues that a long manipulates only if the long "engages in unjustifiable economic transactions as cash and futures markets are merging [that is, during the delivery period]. In effect, the long buys or threatens to take delivery of the same product twice."[102] In reasoning that parallels that in Indiana Farm Bureau, McDermott considers purchases of additional cash or futures contracts during the delivery period as a hindering action that provides evidence of manipulative intent.[103] This author also argues that holding a futures position that is larger than the deliverable stock is also evidence of manipulative intent.[104]

These tests do not overcome the obstacles to a successful prosecution of a cornerer laid by the decisions in Indiana Farm Bureau and Cox. Most important, although the Perdue alternative is eminently defensible as a test for intent, it is incomplete because it does not allow a fact finder to determine whether the alleged conduct actually had any impact on price. Moreover, since (as noted earlier) Perdue attempts to discredit the main means of establishing whether anyone's conduct had an impact on price, it seems that she creates a standard that relies on proving intent to raise prices without proving that such an increase in price actually occurred.

Furthermore, as I argue below, it is extraordinarily difficult to prove intent (and thus, to implement Perdue's test) without relying on price data to demonstrate the existence of artificiality. The defendant can claim other motives for his conduct and it is therefore necessary to compare the observable implications of his explanation for his conduct to the implications of the alternative explanation that he acted in order to squeeze the market. Since (as I will show below) price effects are among the most important of these implications, Perdue's discrediting of the utility of price data undermines the most effective means of carrying out her test.

In contrast, Friedman does not discount the use of price data to determine whether a manipulation occurred. To the contrary, he notes that manipulation necessarily distorts prices and therefore argues that price data can be very helpful in establishing whether an offense occurred.[105] His proposed test is therefore a very useful means of refining the inquiry into intent, with the added advantage that he does not (unlike Perdue) rule out the examination of the most powerful evidence available to implement his test. However, given the current state of manipulation case law and legal commentary and the resulting confusion and suspicion surrounding what constitutes an artificial price, Friedman's test alone is an insufficient foundation on which to erect a complete legal analysis of manipulation. Moreover, the measure of damages that Friedman uses to motivate his analysis equals the difference between the market price and the but-for manipulation competitive price.[106] That is, his test requires the fact finder to quantify the price distortion. Determining this distortion without relying on historical data analysis discredited in Indiana Farm Bureau and Cox is problematic, to say the least. Thus, implementation of Friedman's test of intent requires a rehabilitation of the price artificiality doctrine.

McDermott's conduct test also fails to address the fundamental problems with manipulation law. Inasmuch as it relies on deliberate, exacerbating conduct during the delivery period, it is subject to the same criticism as the decision in Indiana Farm Bureau. Namely, a squeeze can succeed even if the manipulator does not engage in this aggravating conduct. Moreover, the other form of conduct that McDermott deems manipulative--holding a position in the delivery month that exceeds the deliverable stock--requires measurement of this quantity and the definition of the relevant market. As the preceding analysis makes clear, this raises intractable difficulties.

Still other commentators despair altogether of establishing any test or standard that judges can employ to determine whether a defendant has manipulated the market.[107] These scholars therefore conclude that it is necessary to replace the common law-like adjudication after the fact with expansive *ex ante* restrictions on trader conduct. This alternative regulatory structure resembles a civil code system of justice, in that it attempts to foresee every eventuality, to define clearly the line between allowed and disallowed behavior before any case has arisen and to intervene while a transgression is in progress.

This view is subject to severe criticism on the grounds that it discards valuable information about the economic effects of any trader's actions that is available only after the fact. Both an *ex post* fact finder and an *ex ante* fact finder can determine whether a particular trader engaged in a particular form of conduct. Only the *ex post* fact finder, however, can determine whether that conduct had detrimental economic effects. Moreover, only an *ex post* fact finder can observe (1) whether the price in the delivery market plunged after the end of an alleged manipulation, (2) whether the accused manipulator sold the commodity immediately after the delivery period and (3) whether the accused both took deliveries and sold futures contracts. Observation (1) is a crucial test of whether a manipulation occurred, while observations (2) and (3) are necessary to determine whether the accused acted with manipulative intent. Thus, if closely related forms of conduct can have widely divergent economic effects, *ex post* adjudication dominates because it can exploit more information. Therefore, it is more discriminating and less likely to demoralize legitimate actions that are difficult to differentiate from illegitimate ones on the basis of information available before the end of the delivery period.[108]

If some forms of conduct are uniformly harmful, there is little difference between *ex post* and *ex ante* measures. The case law and legal scholarship demonstrate clearly, however, that no one has yet established such a "smoking gun," conduct-based test. Nor is this surprising. An action (such as, buying a large number of futures contracts or taking deliveries of large quantities) that is manipulative in one set of circumstances is innocuous in others because changeable underlying fundamental conditions (such as, supply in the delivery market, transport costs) affect a market's response to a trader's actions. Given these difficulties, there is no reason to believe that broad proscriptions of various forms of conduct will provide benefits (in the form of manipulation deterrence) that more than offset the costs resulting from demoralization of legitimate trading activity. To put the issue in the form of a question, if conduct alone is sufficient to infer intent and effect and the undesirable forms of conduct are known and identifiable, why haven't the courts simply proscribed these actions? Moreover, why should regulators be able to detect and deter these actions with less information *ex ante* than the courts have available *ex post*?

In sum, legal scholars have identified many failings with the existing law of commodity market manipulation. They have not, however, provided a viable alternative set of standards and tests that would improve the performance of courts and regulators. Most important, despite numerous assertions to the contrary, the suggested alternatives to the existing rules fail to provide a reliable methodology to determine whether a manipulation actually occurred. Conduct-based standards require no analysis of price effects, but are overinclusive. The denials of some authors notwithstanding, moreover, intent-based standards are dependent on a price analysis. Those advancing such standards fail to show, however, how such an analysis should be carried out (if they do not denigrate price analysis altogether).

Although far from encouraging, the analysis of court cases and legal commentary should not be considered as grounds for complete despair. It is not *inherently* impossible to determine whether a particular trader has exercise market power; rather, certain decision makers have simply failed to understand the workings of manipulation and have strayed into logical dead ends as a result. That is, I concur with Richard Friedman's assessment that:

> I prefer to hope, until hope appears vain, that the apparent intractability in manipulation litigation does not inhere in the subject, but results from a failure to understand it. Asking the right questions, ones that accurately describe the phenomenon at issue, will make the fact finder's task easier, and in any event more rational.[109]

The following section presents an economically defensible antimanipulation doctrine by relying on the analysis of manipulation contained in my earlier work and outlined in Section 5.2; in this section, I attempt, as Friedman suggests, "to ask the right questions." Most important, I wed the predictions of the manipulation model to classical statistical hypothesis testing techniques to create a reliable methodology to determine whether a trader exercised market power. This methodology also allows a fact finder to implement the tests of intent derived by Friedman and Perdue. Thus, it both expands on and complements existing analyses of manipulation law.

5.4. An Alternative Manipulation Deterrence Doctrine

5.4.1. Introduction

The proper objective of an antimanipulation strategy is to deter the exercise of market power in derivative product markets. To do so, an *ex post* deterrence mechanism must be able to determine reliably whether a manipulation has occurred and assign liability for this conduct. In this section I propose a methodology that allows a decision maker to perform these tasks with considerable precision.

5.4.2. An Alternative Test for Market Manipulation

The detection of manipulation and assignment of liability to a particular trader require the answers to three questions:

1. What is the probability that competitive interactions between traders produced the observed market outcomes?

2. If competitive interactions were unlikely, is the accused trader's conduct consistent with the exercise of market power?

3. Are there any non-manipulative explanations for this conduct?

If the answer to question 1 is a small number, an investigator may infer with confidence that some trader or traders exercised market power. Question 2 aims to identify a particular trader acting in a noncompetitive fashion. Question 3 examines whether there is some alternative explanation for his conduct.

In many respects, the structure of these questions parallels the structure of the existing law discussed earlier. Question 1 corresponds to price artificiality; question 2 corresponds to causation; question 3 corresponds to intent. Thus, one can view the analysis that follows as a rehabilitation of the existing doctrine. Given the disreputable state of that doctrine, however, it is desirable to wipe the slate clean and discard the old terms to prevent them from contaminating the new analysis. Moreover, the questions focus the issues more clearly on the relevant issue of market power at contract expiration than the original three terms. This should reduce the probability that inquiries based on these questions will go astray, as have those based on the original classification.

5.4.2.1. Answering Question 1

The analysis of Section 5.2 presents five economic effects of manipulation. By undertaking a systematic empirical examination (using established statistical methodology) of these symptoms or implications, it is possible to quantify the likelihood that some trader has exercised market power.

This is accomplished by testing *the null hypothesis that all traders acted competitively at expiration of a particular contract where manipulation is suspected.*[110] Under the null, the price, shipment and receipt and delivery patterns during the expiration period should be statistically indistinguishable from the past patterns exhibited in that market. Under the *alternative hypothesis that manipulation occurred*, the five effects are pronounced. Given the historical variability in the relevant variables, one can calculate the probability of falsely rejecting the null hypothesis. That is, one can calculate the likelihood of incorrectly finding a competitive trader guilty of exercising market power. Since (1) the specific hypotheses tested are derived from a rigorous model of the effects of manipulation and competition on prices and (2) the testing methods are the standard ones employed in both the social and physical sciences, this proposed standard addresses the criticisms raised in Cox and Indiana Farm Bureau and the legal literature and avoids the ad hocery implicit in the alternatives proposed in these decisions.[111]

An examination of the relevant implications shows that they represent an enhanced price artificiality standard. It is an enhanced standard because it relies on quantity data (delivery point receipts and shipments and the number of deliveries) as well as price data. By utilizing historical data and universally accepted statistical hypothesis testing techniques, an investigator can determine the probability the prices and quantities observed during an alleged manipulation were the result of competitive behavior by all traders. If the estimated probability is very small, it may be reliably inferred that a manipulation occurred. Since these tests are likely to be statistically powerful, especially in combination, this methodology can separate competitive and manipulative episodes with a high degree of precision.

An example demonstrates how these tests can be employed and how very powerful they can be. In April 1991, there was an allegation of a corner in zinc, which is traded on the London Metal Exchange. I focus on this episode because in work with my colleague Victor Ng, I have studied closely the dynamics of industrial metals prices.[112] Therefore, I can speak with some authority about this market because I have considerable familiarity with the behavior of zinc prices.

In particular, consider a test of implications 1 and 4. Recall that these implications state that during a manipulation, the spot price should first rise precipitously relative to the deferred futures price and then fall even more precipitously at the end of corner.

From April 10, 1991 to April 15, 1991, the spot price of zinc rose 11.6 percent.[113] During this same period, the price of zinc for delivery in three months (that is, the deferred futures price) *fell* 1.7 percent. Thus, as one would expect to occur during a manipulation, the spot price rose appreciably (more than 13 percent) *relative* to the futures price.

The corner ended on April 15, 1991. The next day the spot price of zinc fell 10 percent while the futures price fell by .1 percent. On April 17, the spot price fell by another 1.97 percent, while the futures price declined again by only .1 percent. Again, this price pattern is strongly consistent with the burying-the-body effect, which is symptomatic of manipulation.

Figure 5.1 illustrates the price pattern over the relevant period. Note the dramatic spike in the spot price and the lack of movement in the forward price. Also note that the spot price after the end of the corner was lower than it was prior to the alleged corner. Figure 5.2 plots the difference between the logarithms of spot and forward prices (the difference in the log transformed prices essentially measures the spread as a percentage of the spot price).[114] This price difference called the *spread* in the argot of commodities markets. This figure shows clearly the large increase in the spot price relative to the forward price. It also shows that the ratio between the spot and forward prices was lower after the alleged corner than before (that is, the spot price fell relative to the forward price). The pattern illustrated in the figures is therefore consistent with the existence of a corner in zinc.

In order to fully implement the proposed methodology, it is necessary to compare these relative price changes, which are superficially consistent with a corner, to some measure of the "natural" variability of prices. If the spot price of zinc was extremely variable relative to its futures price (for example, on the order of 5 percent per day) even if all traders had acted competitively, the price changes observed in the April 10 through April 17 period may have occurred with a high probability even if no one had manipulated the market. Thus, one can confidently reject the null hypothesis of no-manipulation only if the observed price changes were large relative to their normal variation.

FIGURE 5.1

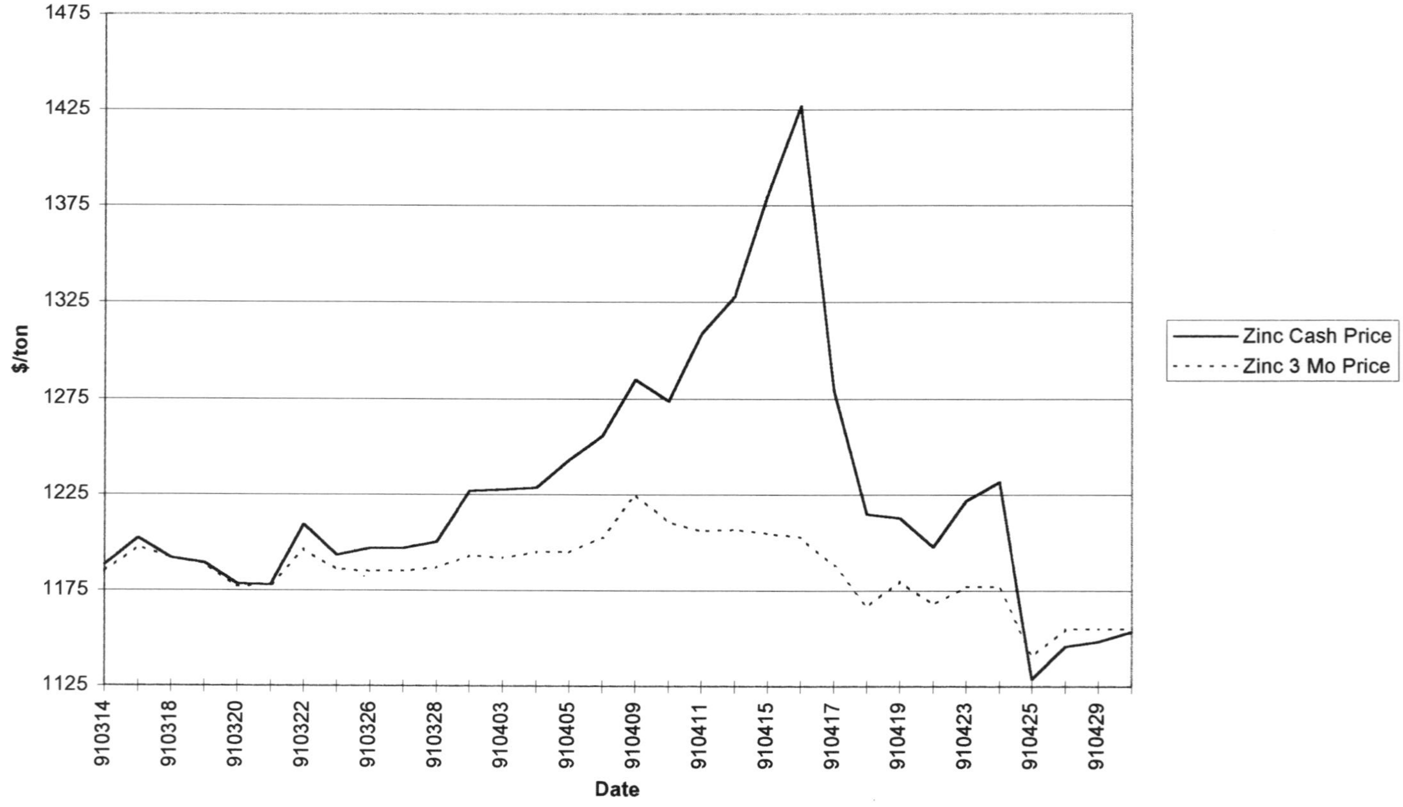

1475
1425
1375
1325
1275
1225
1175
1125
$/ton
910314
910318
910320
910322
910326
910328
910403
910405
910409
910411
910415
910417
910419
910423
910425
910429
Date
Zinc Cash Price
Zinc 3 Mo Price

FIGURE 5.2

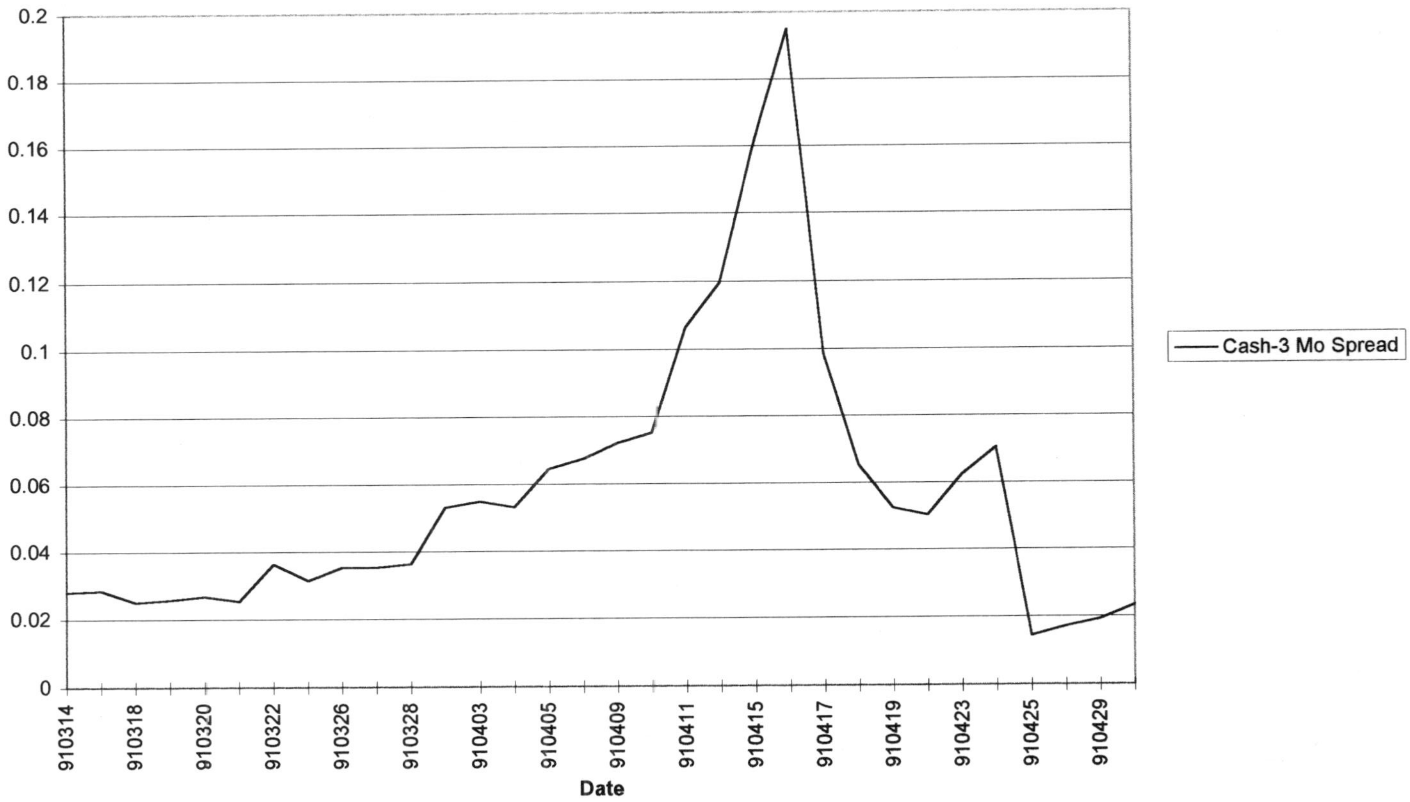

0.2
0.18
0.16
0.14
0.12
0.1
0.08
0.06
0.04
0.02
0
910314
910318
910320
910322
910326
910328
910403
910405
910409
910411
910415
910417
910419
910423
910425
910429
Date
Cash-3 Mo Spread

The traditional measure of variability is the standard deviation. In this context, the standard deviation measures the average deviation of actual price changes from their expected value of zero. Therefore, the larger is the observed price change relative to the standard deviation, the smaller the probability that the price change resulted from chance, rather than from a manipulation.

Based on a model of spot and futures price dynamics that allows the standard deviations of sport and forward prices and the correlation between these prices, to vary with fundamental supply and demand conditions,[115] the increase in the ratio of the spot price to the forward price over the period April 10 through April 15 was 6 standard deviations away from the change that would be expected under competition. Under the null of competition, such a large gap between observed prices and their expected value would occur by chance with probability .0011, about one time in a thousand. Similarly, the relative price decrease during the period April 16 through April 17 was 4.44 standard deviations below the expected value (under the competitive null) of 0. If all agents in the zinc market acted competitively, this would occur by chance with a probability of .0039. Thus, if all traders were acting competitively in the period April 10 through April 17, the large increase in relative price and the subsequent large decrease in relative price were both extremely unusual events. Together, they were truly extraordinary. The probability that they *both* would have occurred if all traders had acted competitively equals .0000044. Thus, these data overwhelmingly reject the null hypothesis that no manipulation occurred in the zinc market in April 1991, in favor of the alternative that the market was squeezed.

Put another way, the data reject the null hypothesis at a confidence level of .00044 per cent. This is far higher than the 1 per cent and 5 per cent levels of confidence commonly employed in scientific work. This implies that if a trader were found guilty of manipulation of the zinc market on the basis of this evidence, the odds of a wrongful conviction would be on the order of four chances in 1,000,000.[116]

Some other available data bolster the conclusion that the zinc market was cornered. In particular, consistent with implication 2, the deliverable stocks of zinc rose dramatically between April 10, 1991 and April 18, 1991. This implies that receipts of zinc to exchange warehouses rose and/or shipments of zinc from these warehouses fell during this week. Correcting for how changes in stocks in one week are related to changes in previous weeks and for the effect of the difference between spot and futures prices, these stocks rose by 40 percent during the week of the alleged corner. This is more than 40 standard deviations away from the expected value of zero. Given the variability of changes in deliverable supplies observed in the data, the probability that such a large increase in stocks would occur by chance is on the order of magnitude of the probability that an individual will be struck by lightning. Thus, the deliverable stock data are also inconsistent with the hypothesis that nothing unusual happened in the zinc market in mid-April 1991. Like the price evidence just discussed, the increase in deliverable stocks is therefore strongly consistent with the view that the zinc market was manipulated during that period.

Viewed together, the observed behavior of prices and deliverable stocks provides even stronger evidence of a squeeze. Recall from Section 5.2 that the theory of storage implies that in competitive markets the spot price should *fall* relative to the forward price when stocks increase dramatically. The spread between forward and spot prices measures the return to storing the commodity. This is true because the forward price must rise relative to the spot price in order to make storage of additional quantities of a commodity profitable. In the present case, however, we observe the exact opposite. Although contrary to what one would expect to observe in a competitive market, the comovements of prices and stocks in zinc in April 1991 are exactly what one would expect to observe during a market-power manipulation. Thus, when considered jointly, the price and deliverable stock evidence provides even stronger support for the alternative hypothesis of market-power manipulation in this episode.

This brief overview of an analysis of the events in the zinc market demonstrates clearly how price and quantity data can be used to determine the probability that a market was cornered. I have already addressed some common objections to this methodology. The example shows that these criticisms are irrelevant to the analysis of a large manipulation. These are just the corners that it is most beneficial to deter. It should also be noted that the elimination of large manipulations also improves the ability to detect smaller ones. Recall that this methodology implicitly assumes that a competitive process generates the observed historical data. If some past episodes of manipulation contaminate the data, they are noisier and therefore less powerful as a means to detect the existence of a corner or a squeeze; this is especially true in the case of smaller manipulations. The employment of a reliable set of tests for market power, however, will deter the more dramatic squeezes. This, in turn, reduces the "noisiness" of the data, and they can be used to detect less pronounced manipulations that were difficult to distinguish statistically before the larger manipulations were deterred. These smaller corners are now detectable and deterrable, which reduces the noisiness of the data still further. Thus, the adoption of a reliable set of manipulation tests commences a bootstrapping process that largely renders null and void the criticism that historical data contaminated by past episodes of market power are an unreliable means of establishing price abnormalities allegedly resulting from manipulation.

In carrying out such an investigation, it is necessary to distinguish between "surprise" manipulations (such as those alleged in Cargill, Indiana Farm Bureau, and Cox) that occur during the last moments of futures trading for a particular contract and those that become manifest prior to this time. This is true because the implications of the two types of manipulation are somewhat different. The possibility that traders become aware of a manipulation only gradually dictates how an investigator must implement the tests of these implications. Most important, tests of implications 1 and 3 require comparisons of relative price *levels* during the delivery period rather than relative price *changes* prior to that time because the normal noise in prices is likely to obscure the gradual trend in relative prices. This does not imply that relative price *changes* are irrelevant altogether, however. Tests of implication 4 can utilize price change data because spot price declines (absolute and relative) in the delivery market are likely to occur very rapidly after the end of a manipulation.

Moreover, it is necessary to replace implication 4 with the following:

S4. The futures price rises relative to delivery market spot bids at the time that the manipulator liquidates his position.

This implication requires some comment. The use of cash-futures comparisons has been criticized[117] because cash and futures prices are supposed to converge (that is, become equal) during the delivery period. To the extent that a manipulation is anticipated, this is correct, and this is why that the original implications discussed above exclude any comparison of the expiring futures price and delivery market spot prices; during an anticipated manipulation shorts bid up the spot price to equal the futures price as they can extinguish their position either by purchasing the deliverable and tendering it, or by buying a futures contract. In equilibrium, the costs of these actions must be equal. Given the nature of most spot-price data, however, it is quite possible that convergence does not occur in a surprise squeeze. Spot-price data for most physical commodities including grains, petroleum products, and metals, consist of bids to purchase the commodity rather than transactions prices determined in transparent competitive auctions. As a result, these prices tend to be somewhat sticky. Although this feature is frequently a source of criticism of these data, in this context it is quite important. Bidders do not react immediately to surprise events such as a last minute squeeze, so the occurrence of such an event causes an unusual divergence between spot and futures prices. If other factors (such as, weather news or information about demand) can be excluded as a cause of the futures price shock, an unusually large spot-futures divergence is inconsistent with competitive behavior by all market participants. Moreover, the failure of spot bids to rise dramatically *subsequent* to the increase in the futures price at contract expiration and/or the failure of the deferred futures price to rise at this time make it highly unlikely that exogenous factors caused the rise in the expiring futures price. One can again analyze historical data using classical methods to estimate the probability that a rise of a given size in the expiring futures prices is not followed by a similar rise in the spot price, or accompanied by a similar rise in the deferred future.

One potential difficulty in diagnosing a surprise squeeze is that if one occurs, shorts may not have time to acquire supplies elsewhere to make deliveries. Implications 2 and 5 do not hold, therefore, for this type of squeeze.

Finally, use of the quantity data requires some care. In particular, since many commodities against which futures are traded (such as, grains) exhibit pronounced seasonal variations in shipments, receipts, and stocks, it is necessary to correct for this seasonality. Moreover, since delivery point receipts and shipments frequently show considerable positive autocorrelation (rises (declines) tend to be followed by rises (declines)), tests of implications 2 and 5 are likely to be very powerful, as they imply a negative autocorrelation around the end of the delivery period. That is, in contrast to their normal pattern, during a corner increases (declines) tend to be followed by decline (increases).

In conclusion, market power leaves telltale footprints in the form of distorted prices, shipments, receipts, and deliveries. The price and quantity indicia of manipulation differ markedly from the effects of other unusual events in futures markets. Under the assumption that historical price and quantity data represent a sample of competitive outcomes drawn from the same universe of underlying conditions as those prevailing during an alleged manipulative episode, an investigator can employ classical statistical techniques to determine the likelihood that the prices and quantities observed during this episode were in fact consistent with competition. If the estimated probability is small, there is strong evidence that some trader(s) has (have) exercised market power. This permits the investigator to proceed to question 2 and determine who exercised this power.

5.4.2.2. Answering Question 2

The analysis of causation in Section 5.4 notes that courts and commissions have attempted to determine whether a particular trader had the ability to influence market price and that this has led to considerable confusion and misunderstanding. In particular, this standard requires a detailed understanding of costs that are difficult, if not impossible, for *ex post* adjudicators to calculate. Fortunately, the analysis of Section 5.2 identifies several actions that a large trader must undertake in order to exercise market power. It is possible, therefore, to replace a standard that requires the determination of *ability* to exercise market power (a difficult task that requires knowledge that is extremely costly to collect) with a standard that relies on the identification of readily observable conduct by the accused.

Specifically, recall that a long manipulator

1. Stops an abnormally large number of deliveries, but liquidates a substantial proportion of his position,

2. Stops a large fraction of deliveries relative to the total number of deliveries made, and

3. Liquidates his futures position at a price that exceeds the value of the units delivered to him.

Each of these implications is testable, although an investigator must exercise care in doing so. First consider implication 1. It is necessary to establish a standard in order to test whether the number of deliveries a long takes is large or small. This standard should correct for the identity of the trader and his past behavior, whether or not he owns a substantial portion of the deliverable unbeknownst to shorts, and certain conditions that may affect the marginal cost of delivery.

A trader's type and past behavior are relevant because some traders (especially commercial traders and some arbitrageurs) take delivery as a part of their normal commercial operations. An investigator should therefore compare the number of deliveries stopped by the accused trader with the number of deliveries taken concurrently (that is, at the time of the alleged manipulation) by other traders of a similar type (such as, compare an alleged commercial manipulator with other commercials, or an alleged arbitrageur manipulator with other arbitrageurs); and the number of deliveries taken by traders of a similar type during previous delivery periods.

In making the latter comparison in particular, it is necessary to correct for certain factors that influence the economics of taking delivery. These include contract month (there are more corn deliveries in December than July), stocks on hand in the delivery market, and (especially) futures spreads--the annualized percentage difference between the price of the deferred future and the expiring futures price net of the cost of storage and the time value of money. This last correction is motivated by the fact that it is much costlier to take delivery and hold inventories when a market is *inverted* (that is, the difference is a large negative number) rather than when it is at *full carry*. In a full-carry market, the futures price exceeds the spot price by the costs of storing inventory until the expiration of the future. In such a market, the trader taking delivery can short the deferred future and receive a payment sufficient to cover the costs storage and forgone interest that he incurs before he can deliver against the deferred contract. If the market is not at full carry, however, the trader suffers a loss from holding inventory until the expiration of the deferred contract.

This discussion suggests testing a regression model of delivery behavior. Specifically, the number of deliveries taken by a commercial trader (D), is a function of the contract month C_i, a dummy variable equal to 1 in month i and 0 in other months, where $i=1, \ldots n$, and n is the number of delivery months in a year; stocks on hand in the delivery market, S; and the return to holding inventory, R, where $R=F_D-F_E-c-rF_E$, and F_D is the deferred futures price, F_E is the expiring future, c is the dollar cost of storing inventory until the expiration of the deferred contract, and rF_E is the dollar value of interest forgone on the value of the commodity from the expiration of the nearby contract to the expiration of the deferred contract. Formally, one estimates the model:

$$D=a+b_1C_1+\ldots+b_{n-1}C_{n-1}+b_sS+b_RR+e,$$

where e is a random error term, and the b_i are parameters.

Given historical data on deliveries taken by traders of the same type as the manipulator and assuming competitive behavior during the sample period, one can estimate the parameters of this model (including the variance of the error) over the sample period, calculate the fitted value of D for the period of the alleged manipulation and determine whether the fitted value is statistically significantly different from the value observed during the delivery period in question. If the probability that the difference between the fitted and observed values (estimated by using the relevant values for the C's, R, and S) is consistent with competition is sufficiently small, an investigator can infer manipulative conduct.

The primary potential obstacle in implementing this test is data availability. This test requires historical data on the number of deliveries taken by this trader or other similar traders in the past. This is not publicly available and an investigator would probably have to secure it by competitive means it; it may be especially difficult to acquire from those other than the accused.

This problem does not affect tests of the other implications as seriously. In particular, an investigator can rely on publicly available price data and information on the alleged manipulator's postexpiration actions.

Indeed, the information used to verify the burying-the-body effect and the spread between spot and deferred futures prices relate directly to this issue. The finding of a substantial spot-price decline in the delivery market (especially relative to other prices) at the end of an alleged anticipated squeeze implies a significant difference between liquidation prices and the value of the commodity received via delivery. An anomalous futures spread has a similar implication. In fact, although an accused manipulator may try to argue that the decline in the spot price was unexpected (the expected the price of the deliverable after contract expiration to approximately equal the price at which he liquidated futures contracts), this claim is unpersuasive if the deferred futures price (which is a publicly available measure of the expected spot price) is depressed.

Similarly, in a surprise squeeze, a disparity between the price at which an accused manipulator sells futures contracts and contemporaneous spot bids is strongly consistent with the existence of a manipulation; the spot bids represent an independent measure of the true value of the commodity. What if the accused alleges that the price pattern resulted from other traders' incorrect perceptions of his intentions? Assuming this is true, the alleged manipulator would consider the post-delivery spot price too low and should purchase deferred futures and/or spot supplies at that time. Thus, this potential defense is contradicted if he sells (rather than buys) the commodity after the manipulation.

In conclusion, it is possible to determine whether a particular trader has behaved in a manipulative fashion by comparing the number of deliveries he takes to his past performance and the performance of other traders, correcting for various factors that affect the delivery calculus. It is also very informative to compare the value of the deliveries he takes relative to the price at which he liquidates futures contracts.[118] This analysis does not require an estimation of potentially amorphous quantities like the deliverable supply. Instead of estimating the *ability* of a trader to manipulate, the proposed method examines whether his conduct mimics that predicted by the model of manipulation. If it does, and one can rule out alternative explanations of the accused trader's conduct, the probability of mistakenly assigning liability to the trader is very small. I next examine criteria for evaluating the accused's possible excuses for his conduct.

5.4.2.3. Answering Question 3

The objective of this final question is to address an alleged manipulator's potential defenses.[119] In particular, he may argue that his actions were not motivated by a desire to manipulate the market, but instead were the product of some legitimate strategy. The alternative rationales include (1) a desire to obtain the physical commodity for commercial purposes, (2) legitimate speculation, (3) hedging, (4) tax considerations, and (5) stupidity or ignorance.

Each alternative rationale has observable implications that differ from the implications of manipulative conduct. Thus, one can reliably test the validity of the claims of a suspected manipulator by comparing her actual conduct to that implied by the manipulation theory and that implied by the theory advanced as a defense. I consider each rationale in turn.

Since manipulators stand for excessively large numbers of deliveries, some claim that their actions were motivated by a need to obtain the cash commodity for commercial reasons. As noted in Section 5.2, however, successful frictional manipulators also liquidate large numbers of contracts. An accused manipulator must therefore explain why he did both. In order for such behavior to be consistent with competitive (price taking) behavior, the marginal value of a delivery taken (its price) necessarily equals the liquidation price on the marginal contract.[120]

If an investigator documents a burying-the-body effect, however, the accused cannot claim that he chose the number of deliveries in order to minimize the cost of acquiring the physical commodity. This is true because the burying-the-body effect implies that the value of the marginal contract liquidation exceeded the value of the marginal delivery at contract expiration. This is inconsistent with competitive price-taking behavior.

Moreover, if the long takes deliveries to satisfy an existing sales commitment (that is, a short position in the cash or futures markets), this "defense" actually undermines the accused's case if he liquidates some contracts as well. The primary cost of executing a manipulation is the loss incurred on deliveries taken due to the burying-the-body effect. That is, a manipulator takes delivery of a large amount of the commodity that must be disposed of. A trader who has no short position in the same commodity must sell these deliveries at a low price. In contrast, a trader with an outstanding short position is hedged against the price decline that results at the end of a manipulation. Thus, *ceteris paribus*, traders with existing sales commitments actually find manipulation more profitable than those without such commitments. As a result, the existence of such commitments is less a defense against a charge of manipulation than an inducement to execute one.

Other information may also disprove an accused squeezer's claim that the futures market was the cheap source of the cash commodity. In particular, bids on the cash market that are lower than the futures price is strong evidence that there are cheaper sources of the deliverable. This is particularly true if the accused is one of the bidders (as was the case in Indiana Farm Bureau).[121] Moreover, if the fraction of the open futures position the trader owns grows as expiration approaches, his claim is open to serious question. The change in market share indicates that his behavior is opposite that of other longs: he is buying (or holding a long position) while they are actively selling. To explain this behavior, the accused must demonstrate why the futures market is a cheaper source of cash supplies for him but not for those longs who liquidate.

Rational competitive speculation also requires an equation of the price at which the trader liquidates the marginal contract and the value of the marginal delivery. To explain his behavior as the product of a speculative strategy, therefore, an accused manipulator must argue that he valued the physical commodity at the high liquidation price he accepted. That is, he must argue that the expiring futures price is cheap relative to prices at other locations and deferred futures prices. Again, if there is a large and rapid spot price decline in the delivery market (that is, there is a burying-the-body effect), the failure of the trader *to purchase* more of the spot commodity contradicts his assertion that the expiring futures price was cheap.[122] Similarly, sale of the cash commodity or sale of deferred futures contracts is inconsistent with the speculative rationale. Again, there are several behavioral implications of the assertion of a speculative motive and an investigator can compare these implications with the trader's observed conduct.

Moreover, if an investigator establishes relative price distortions, an accused manipulator bought the commodity that was atypically dear (that is, he purchased the deliverable commodity when it was unusually expensive relative to the same commodity at other times and other locations, and to other commodities). Since the old speculative adage is "buy cheap and sell dear," any accused manipulator will find it extraordinary difficult to provide an explanation for such behavior. This is especially true if his market share grows as the contract nears expiration, as this suggests that other traders disagree with his claimed rationale.

Some traders may also claim that their large positions are hedges; others (speculators who do not trade on the cash market) cannot employ this rationale. Hedging is a potentially plausible explanation well prior to contract expiration but is far less credible immediately before the end of trading. The expiring future can hedge only those cash-market transactions that take place in the time remaining before the end of trading. Thus, as trading in a particular contract nears its end, a trader with a large long futures position must be able to show that he has a fixed-price sales commitment of approximately the same size as the futures position and that the long plans to acquire the commodity to meet that commitment prior to the end of the futures trading. This rationale is patently ridiculous if the long holds a substantial position to the very end of trading. Moreover, if the long liquidates earlier, his behavior provides an acid test of his motives. Specifically, in order for the hedging rationale to withstand scrutiny, it must be the case that prior to or immediately following the liquidation the trader acquires the cash commodity in an amount approximately equal to the size of his futures position. A failure to do so, or sales the cash commodity on the spot market, contradicts the hedging rationale.

Furthermore, as in the speculative explanation, the accused manipulator can be questioned closely about the reasonableness of his actions. Again, given a wide spread between the expiring and deferred futures, a legitimate long hedger could reduce his hedge costs by selling the expiring contract at a high price and buying the deferred future at a low price. A trader's failure to do so is strongly consistent with manipulative intent.

The defendants in one manipulation case, N. B. Hunt, W. H. Hunt, and Lamar Hunt claim that they stood for large numbers of deliveries against silver futures contracts for tax purposes and had no intent to manipulate the market.[123] Their reasoning was this. Any profits earned on a liquidated contract are taxed at the time the position is closed. Profits earned on the sale of a commodity acquired by taking delivery on a futures contract are not taxable until the commodity is sold; a trader can defer taxes for as long as he desires. Deferring taxes is valuable if interest rates are positive. Deferral is especially beneficial to a trader if short-term gains are taxed at a higher rate than long-term gains, as was the case in the late 1970s and early 1980s.

The tax advantages of taking delivery do not necessarily imply that a trader has *not* manipulated a market if he takes a large number of deliveries. If a trader does not exert market power, he should either liquidate his entire position, or take delivery on his entire position. This is true because if a trader does not exert market power, the spot and futures prices do not depend on the number of contracts he liquidates. Thus, if prices are such that tax considerations imply that the trader is better off taking delivery on one contract, he should take delivery on all of them. Tax considerations therefore do not explain why a competitive trader would liquidate some contracts and take delivery on others. As a result, even if these tax considerations are relevant, a trader that both liquidates contracts and accepts deliveries acts like a trader that exerts market power.

Moreover, if a trader exercises market power, the advantages of deferring taxation may indeed induce him to take more deliveries than an untaxed trader would. However, this should not excuse his actions because the additional deliveries merely exacerbate the distortions resulting from the exercise of market power. That is, *ceteris paribus*, a taxable trader who manipulates does more damage than a nontaxable one. Since the objective of manipulation law is to reduce the frequency and intensity of price and quantity distortions, it would be perverse indeed to allow a manipulator to use the tax advantages of taking delivery to escape penalty. Put another way, the Commodity Exchange Act states that it is unlawful to corner the market; it does not say that it is unlawful for a trader to run a corner *unless* she can reduce her taxes by doing so.

When all else fails, a manipulator may claim stupidity or ignorance. It is impossible to refute definitively either explanation using reasoning similar to that used heretofore. If the accused is an experienced or sophisticated trader, however, such a defense is easily dismissed.

5.4.3. Summary and Conclusions

A trader that exercises market power undertakes certain actions that are readily observed. These actions, in turn, have pronounced and well-defined effects on prices and quantities. By testing these implications of manipulative conduct, therefore, it is possible to determine whether an observed set of prices and the actions of a particular trader are consistent with competitive behavior. Thus, when properly understood, manipulation is not "unprosecutable." Rejection of this hypothesis with a high degree of confidence implies that it is very likely that a trader exerted market power. Moreover, examination of an accused trader's actions allows a fact finder to determine whether she exercised this power. The existence of an offense is readily identified and manipulative conduct is readily distinguished from competitive conduct.

5.5. Conclusion

This chapter has (1) examined the state of commodity market manipulation law and (2) proposed a new set of tests that promises to address many of the defects in the existing decisions in manipulation cases. Two findings deserve emphasis.

First, the existing case law on manipulation is extraordinarily misguided. In particular, many of its precepts are based on a complete misunderstanding of the economics of manipulation. In its current state, the law is less a deterrent to manipulators than an invitation to them.

Second, this state of affairs is not irredeemable. It is possible to assign the liability for manipulative conduct with a considerable degree of precision by employing a set of criteria firmly grounded in an understanding of the economics of manipulation. A corner leaves a trail that is readily followed to its source if one recognizes the telltale markers--price effects, quantity effects, and trader conduct. Straightforward application of statistical inference techniques allows an adjudicator to determine *ex post* whether a market was manipulated and who manipulated it with a high degree of precision. Thus, I strongly concur with Friedman's statement that by asking and answering the right questions--questions motivated by a clear understanding of the predictable effects of the offense--courts can effectively detect and deter manipulation. *Ex post* deterrence is not predestined to failure but is capable of reform and redemption.

I readily admit that this conclusion is controversial. Some noted scholars have argued that it is virtually impossible to detect manipulation using price and quantity data. They conclude from this that *ex post* deterrence is either fruitless or that it must proceed on very different lines than proposed here. I find these objections completely unpersuasive, however. Most important, they often ultimately rest on the syllogism that since econometric and statistical techniques are fallible, they are unsuitable for use in legal proceedings. It is no doubt true that the methodology that I have promoted here is vulnerable to error. Indeed, the hypothesis testing technique essentially quantifies the probability of making a mistake, and this probability is never exactly zero. The problem with the syllogism, however, is that *all* deterrence methods are fallible; for example, *ex ante* preventative measures are also subject to error. In fact, any potential alternative is subject to the same species of difficulties as *ex post* deterrence. It is quite plausible, moreover, that they are more vulnerable to mistakes than the methodology that I have proposed here.

This implies that the relevant questions that need to be answered in order to determine whether *ex post* deterrence is fundamentally flawed by the potential for error are, Which deterrence method is least subject to errors, and for which deterrence mechanism are these errors least costly? That is, of the various fallible methods available to us, which is the most efficient? Answering these questions requires a full comparative analysis of the costs and benefits of the alternative mechanisms. Heretofore, this comparison of alternative mechanisms has not been undertaken in a thorough and unified way. The next chapter presents my attempt at such an analysis.

Endnotes

[1] Section 13(b) of the Commodity Exchange Act (CEA) makes manipulation or attempted manipulation a felony. 7 U.S.C. § 13. Section 7(d) of the CEA requires Boards of Trade (that is, commodity exchanges) to prevent "the manipulation of prices and the cornering of any commodity." 7 U.S.C. § 7. The Commodity Exchange Act was originally titled the Grain Futures Act, which was passed in 1922.

[2] The ALJ in In re Henner, 30 Agric. Dec. 1151 (1971) included a twenty-eight page appendix excoriating the reasoning in Volkart Bros., Inc. v. Freeman, 311 F.2d 35 (5th Cir. 1962) (Volkart), even though the Henner case was not a market-power manipulation case. The 8th Circuit Court's decision in Cargill v. Hardin, 452 F.2d 1154 (8th Cir. 1971) (Cargill) also pointedly criticized Volkart.

[3] For example, the decision of the Commodity Exchange Authority in In re Vincent W. Kosuga, 19 Agric. Dec. 603,615 (1960) states that "Drawing a line between legitimate trading and trading with manipulative intent is sometimes a very difficult task." Similarly, the Commodity Futures Trading Commission opined that the "lack of objective standards for identifying and preventing disruptive situations in futures markets." Proposed Limits on Futures Positions Exceeding 25 percent of Open Interest in the Delivery Month of a Commodity Futures Contract, 43 Fed. Reg. 15,438, 15439.

[4] Jerry Markham, The Manipulation of Commodity Futures Prices--The Unprosecutable Crime, 7 Yale J. on Reg. (1991); Davidson, Squeezes and Corners: A Structural Approach, 40 Bus. Law 1283 (1985).

[5] The supply of storage curve has been analyzed by Holbrook Working, The Theory of the Inverse Carrying Charge in Futures Markets, 39 J. Farm Econ. 1 (1948), Lester Telser, Futures Trading and the Storage of Cotton and Wheat, 66 J. Pol. Econ. 233 (1958), Jeffrey Williams, The Economic Function of Futures Markets (1986), and Jeffrey Williams and Brian Wright, Storage and Commodity Markets (1991). The curve plots the spot-futures basis adjusted for carrying costs against the amount of the deliverable commodity in store.

[6] Marginal costs of delivery are typically increasing for "spatial commodities"; that is, commodities which are (1) produced and consumed over a wide geographical area and (2) costly to transport. Examples that such goods include grains and industrial metals. The marginal cost of delivery is increasing for such commodities because it is necessary to acquire additional supplies from progressively less economical locations. Manipulation is not limited to spatial commodities, however. Any transaction cost that makes it costly to increase deliverable supply can facilitate manipulation. Thus, a corner may occur in a financial market, although the

conditions in such markets are typically less conducive to manipulation than is the case in physical commodity markets.

[7] The postmanipulation spot price is below the no-manipulation spot price because the corner increases supplies in the delivery market.

[8] This phrase is attributed to the noted grain trader and meat magnate P. D. Armour. He was once asked whether it was easy to manipulate the market. Armour replied that the manipulator faced the same problem as a murderer: "It is easy to commit the murder, but difficult indeed to dispose of the corpse." That is, it is easy to drive the price up by buying huge quantities but hard to sell what you buy at a profit.

[9] Frank Easterbrook, Monopoly, Manipulation, and Fraud, 59 J. of Bus. S107 (1986) also argues that the price and quantity effects of manipulation are distinctive.

[10] A systemic shock is one that affects all markets in common in a similar fashion. That is, a systemic shock is not concentrated in the delivery market alone.

[11] Unless, of course, one was willing to believe that the export boom collapsed on a single day that just happened to correspond with the expiration of a futures contract.

[12] Some analysts have asserted the existence of a so-called "natural corner." Most important, 7 Report of the Federal Trade Commission on the Grain Trade 243-244 (1926), asserts the existence of natural corners. This is said to occur when some exogenous development reduces supplies of a commodity and allows a trader with a relatively small position to exercise market power. It is sometimes claimed that the trader that does so is blameless because he simply took advantage of the prevailing conditions; several judicial and regulatory decisions discussed below adopt this view. I argue below that this is a very dangerous proposition that gives large traders a "manipulation option."

[13] One subtle point deserves mention in this context. Many commercial futures traders engage in socalled exchange for physical (EFP) transactions. In an EFP, a trader short futures makes the following arrangement with a trader long futures: the short delivers the commodity to the long and buys a futures contract from the long. This transaction is essentially equivalent to the short simply delivering the commodity to the long, because the two traders' futures positions cancel and the short tenders the good to the long. The only important difference between a delivery and an EFP is that, in the latter, the parties can choose to make or take delivery outside the delivery market and/or before the delivery period. In the context of a manipulation, an EFP is not a substitute for a delivery, as the long must agree to the transaction. Thus, shorts cannot unilaterally use EFPs to escape a corner.

[14] McDermott, Defining Manipulation in Commodity Futures Trading: The Futures "Squeeze", 74 NW. U.L. Rev 202-205 (1979).

[15] Great Western Food Distributors v. Brannan, 201 F.2d 476 (7th Cir. 19).

[16] Cargill v. Hardin, 452 F.2d 1154 (8th Cir. 1971).

[17] Volkart Bros., Inc. v. Freeman, 311 F.2d 53 (5th Cir. 1962).

[18] In re Hohenberg Bros., [1975-1977 Transfer Binder] Commodity Futures Law Reporter (CCH) ¶20,271 (CFTC 1977).

[19] In re Indiana Farm Bureau Cooperative Association, [1982-1984 Transfer Binder] Commodity Futures Law Reporter (CCH) ¶21,796 (CFTC 1982).

[20] In re Cox, [1986-1987 Transfer Binder] Commodity Futures Law Reporter (CCH) ¶23,786 (CFTC 1987).

[21] In re Abrams, [1988-1989 Transfer Binder] 2 Commodity Futures Law Reporter (CCH) ¶24,408 (CFTC 1989).

[22] Philip McBride Johnson and Thomas Hazen, 3 Commodities Regulation 32-54 (1988).

[23] Cargill, Inc. v. Hardin, 452 F.2d at 1164.

[24] Id. at 1167-1170.

[25]Great Western Food Distributors v. Brannan, 210 F.2d at 483.

[26] Id. at 483.

[27] In re Cox [1982-1984 Transfer Binder] Commodity Futures Law Reporters (CCH) ¶21,267 (CFTC 1982) at 27,092-27,101; In re Indiana Farm Bureau at 27,280-27,281.

[28] In re Indiana Farm Bureau at 27,280-27,281.

[29] In re Cox at 27,072, 27093.

[30] In re Indiana Farm Bureau at 27,281.

[31] In re Indiana Farm Bureau Cooperative Association at 27,287.

[32] Id.

[33] In re Cox at 34,064.

[34] Wendy Perdue, Manipulation of Futures Markets, 56 Fordham L. Rev. 345 (1987); McDermott, supra note 14. Van Smith, Preventing the Manipulation of Commodity Futures Markets: To Deliver or Not to Deliver? 32 Hastings L.J. 1569 (1981); Lower, Disruptions of the Futures Market: A Comment on Dealing with Market Manipulation, 8 Yale J. on Reg. 391 (1991); Johnson and Hazen, supra note 22.

[35] Perdue supra note 34, at 365-367.

[36] McDermott supra note 14, 211-212.

[37] Lower, supra note 34, at 393.

[38] Dan Fischel and David Ross, Should the Law Prohibit "Manipulation" in Financial Markets?, 105 Harvard L. Rev. 503 (1991).

[39] The author of Note, The Delivery Requirement: An Illusory Bar to Regulation of Manipulation on Commodity Exchanges, 73 Yale L. J. 171 (1963), makes a similar argument: "While some miscreants may inevitably escape under the cover of ambiguity, this is not a sound reason for refusing to punish those who can not."

[40] Stephen Craig Pirrong, Roger C. Kormendi, and David Haddock, Grain Futures Contracts: An Economic Appraisal, chs. 2 and 5 (1993).

[41] See Charles Taylor, History of the Chicago Board of Trade (1917) and William Ferris, The Grain Traders (1988). As an example, the collapse of the Leiter corner in 1898 resulted in a nearly 39 per cent price decline in the period of minutes. The collapse of the gold corner during "Black Friday" in 1869 resulted in an equally calamitous price shock.

[42] The 1988 drought provides a clear example of this phenomenon. Prices skyrocketed during the summer of that year, but spreads between spot and futures prices and between futures prices for different maturities, did not exhibit the tell-tale backwardation symptomatic of manipulation. Indeed, prices were nearly at full carry. That is, the futures prices for new crop months (November for soybeans and December for corn) exceeded the relevant spot prices by the interest and storage costs of carrying inventory from the summer until the new crop months. Thus, it is easy to dismiss the hypothesis that market-power manipulation caused the large price rises that occurred during the summer of 1988. This ability to distinguish manipulative price shocks from shocks caused by changes in supply conditions is likely to be quite common in markets for seasonally produced agricultural products. The primary sources of price and spread changes for these products are changes in expected supplies at harvest. Kenneth French, Detecting Spot Price Forecasts in Futures Prices, 59 J. of Bus S39 (1986), shows that when a harvest is expected to be small, prices rise but spreads should fall. The intuition behind this result is straightforward. Agents should store more when future supplies are expected to be

small. In competitive markets, the theory of storage implies that an increase in storage drives the spot price down relative to the futures. This pattern of storage and relative price changes is exactly opposite what occurs during a manipulation.

Matters are somewhat different in markets for products that are produced continuously, rather than seasonally. These include industrial metals and energy products. In these markets it is unlikely that prices rise explosively while spreads move to full carry. Nonetheless, manipulation-caused backwardations can be distinguished from backwardations that result in competitive markets. Increases in deliverable stocks accompany manipulative backwardations, whereas declines in stocks accompany competitive backwardations.

[43] Working, supra note 5.

[44] Friedrich Hayek, The Use of Knowledge in Society, 35 Am. Econ. Rev. 519 (1945). Thomas Sowell, Knowledge and Decisions (1981).

[45] In re Cox at 34,076.

[46] Richard Friedman, Stalking the Squeeze: Understanding Commodities Market Manipulation, Michigan L. Rev. 30 (1991), makes this point as well.

[47] In re Indiana Farm Bureau at 27,287, 27,307.

[48] Id.

[49] Id.

[50] Id.

[51] In re Cox at 34,062.

[52] Id. at 34,063.

[53] Id.

[54] See Section 2.3.2 of Chapter 2 for details. The decision in Cox is also contrary to a stated objective of the CEA. As a part of the CEA's clear antimanipulation intent, Section 7a(10) requires exchanges to choose delivery points and delivery differentials in order to prevent the disruption of commodity flows. The Cox decision, in contrast, encourages such distortions.

[55] This latter fact raises questions concerning the culpability of shorts in failing to prepare to make deliveries, which I discuss later.

[56] In re Indiana Farm Bureau at 27,290.

[63] Cargill, Inc. v. Hardin, 452 F.2d at 1165-1166.

[58] Great Western Food Distributors v. Brannan, 201 F.2d at 480-481.

[59] Evidence from Indiana Farm Bureau provides further illustration of this fact. Specifically, the delivery stock estimates provided by the CFTC's Division of Enforcement also conflict with the facts of the case. The Commission's staff estimated that deliverable stocks were only about 500,000 bushels, but the Farm Bureau took delivery of over 2 million bushels. In re Indiana Farm Bureau at 27,280. This again illustrates that delivery stock estimates may be very arbitrary when issues like commitment and the ability to bring new supplies to the market are relevant. Under these circumstances, the amount that will be delivered is an increasing function of price. That is, there is no single number that gives "the" deliverable stock. Price changes around contract expiration are the most reliable estimates of the marginal cost of delivering the commodity. Thus, a priori estimates of deliverable stock provide little information not already communicated by prices. In his concurring decision, Commissioner Stone criticized the "binary" treatment of stocks as deliverable or unalterably committed regardless of price. Id. at 27,302.

[60] Robert Bork, The Antitrust Paradox (1978).

[61] Volkart Bros., Inc. v. Freeman, 311 F.2d at 60.

[62] In re Indiana Farm Bureau at 27,289.

[63] In re Cox at 34,062.

[64] Cargill, Inc. v. Harding, 452 F.2d at 1165-1166. Great Western Food Distributors v. Brannan, 201 F.2d at 481.

[65] Cargill, Inc., v. Hardin, 452 F.2d at 1173.

[66] Id.

[67] In re Cox at 34,062, 34,067.

[68] Fischel and Ross, supra note 38, at note 182, argue that manipulation is "self-deterring" because the possibility of manipulation gives shorts a strong incentive to obtain additional deliverable supplies. This is true, but it is not sufficient to justify a reliance on short self-protection to deter market-power manipulation. These actions by shorts distort consumption and production decisions. Therefore, even if they markedly reduce the frequency and severity of corners, it is more efficient to deter manipulation through legal sanctions if the costs of deterring manipulation in this manner are smaller than the deadweight costs attributable to the distortions inherent in short self-protection. Put differently, the fact that shorts take precautions against corners does not imply that legal prohibitions against manipulation are superfluous, as Fischel and Ross suggest. An analogy makes this

point clearly. Burglary is similarly "self-deterring" because homeowners and businesses routinely purchase locks, security systems, and dogs to protect their property against thieves. It is a non sequitur to conclude, however, that these expenditures of real resources to deter crime vitiate the need for laws against burglary. Indeed, the resource costs of self-protection (which may be quite high due to free-rider and public-good problems) can make punishment of theft by the state efficient. This argument applies exactly to the case of market manipulation.

[69] Shorts may take few precautions for another reason as well. Specifically, if there are many shorts, a free-rider (that is, externality) problem may exist. The preparations taken by individual short A benefits other shorts B, C, etc. because all shorts benefit from any action that reduces the probability and severity of corners. However, short A will not take the benefits accruing to other shorts into account when deciding on the level of precautions to take. As a result, the other shorts free-ride off of A's efforts. Similarly, A free-rides off of the efforts of other shorts. It is well known that the existence of such a positive externality induces the shorts to take too few precautions.

The existence of this type of free-rider problem does create an incentive for a single trader to consolidate all of the short positions and thereby internalize the externality. This may not be a practical response in futures markets. Wealth constraints may preclude one trader from assuming the entire open interest. Moreover, in the present regulatory environment, position limits would make it very difficult for a single individual or firm to acquire all open short positions.

[70] In essence, under Indiana Farm Bureau and Volkart it is axiomatic that if a corner occurs, the shorts failed to take sufficient precautions. Moreover, under these two decisions such a failure on the part of shorts is sufficient to absolve the cornerer from any legal responsibility. Thus, taken to their logical conclusion, these decisions return us to the laissez faire regime that prevailed prior to the passage of the GFA and CEA.

[71] Recall that Result 21 from Chapter 2 implies that manipulation by short traders is extremely unlikely if conditions favor the execution of a long manipulation. Therefore, deterring long manipulation (which has historically been far more prevalent than short manipulation) essentially makes the market competitive during the delivery period. Put another way, if a corner is analogous to pulling on a rope, shorts who attempt to exercise market power at the end of the delivery period will have as much success as someone who tries to push a rope.

[72] The Indiana Farm Bureau rule may actually inflate the costs of enforcing antimanipulation laws as well. In order to reach a verdict in a case under this rule, it is necessary for the fact-finder to determine whether the short took the proper precautions. Such an investigation is costly, but would be unnecessary under the alternative rule that simply proscribes the exercise of market power by longs regardless of the precautions taken by shorts. Moreover, it is uncertain how much preparation by shorts is enough. This inherent ambiguity is costly to resolve. Such resolution would be unnecessary under the alternative rule. Finally, the Indiana

Farm Bureau rule increases the returns to manipulation because a cornerer can escape punishment if shorts are found culpable. This increase in the returns to manipulation should increase its frequency, thereby increasing the number of cases that arise under the anticorner provisions of the CEA. All of these factors tend to make the Indiana Farm Bureau rule more costly to implement than the alternative rule. As a result, the Indiana Farm Bureau rule is likely to entail both higher deadweight costs due to excessive precautions by shorts and higher litigation expenses.

[73] The reason underlying placing the onus for deterring manipulation on shorts in Volkart, Indiana Farm Bureau, and Cox seems to be a fear that prosecuting manipulators would give shorts an incentive to evade their contractual obligations and thereby compromise the surety of performance on futures contracts. In Volkart, the New York Cotton Exchange submitted an amicus curiae brief which stated that a finding of manipulation in that case would allow shorts to escape their delivery obligation and therefore undermine the markets. Volkart Bros., Inc. v. Freeman, 311 F.2d at 57. The court relied on similar reasoning in its decision. "The petitioners can be held to a purpose to create prices not responsive to the forces of supply and demand only on the assumption that shorts should not be held to their contract obligation to deliver the cotton. . . . For the respondents to proceed on the assumption that the shorts should not be required to deliver at maturity would to be to put them in the position of regulating a gambling institution rather than a legitimate futures exchange. That, of course, was not the intention of the statutes prohibiting manipulation." Id. at 60 (emphasis added).

This reasoning is specious. Sanctioning large long traders who corner or squeeze a market does not free shorts from their obligation to perform on their contracts. Under the operation of a legal regime that imposes penalties on traders that exercise market power, exchanges can (and should) continue to take strong measures to give shorts and longs an incentive to perform. Although enforcing strict performance on contracts may allow a large long to manipulate the market (as emphasized by Friedman, supra note 46), such bad behavior can be deterred by imposing sufficiently punitive sanctions on those who do so. Put another way, although the large penalties for defaulting on contracts facilitate manipulation, it is a non sequitur to assert that sanctioning traders who exercise market power makes default by shorts attractive. Sanctioning shorts for failure to perform and sanctioning longs for cornering are two separate, independent, and mutually compatible actions.

The hostile attitude towards shorts expressed in these decisions echoes the sentiments of exchanges during the preregulation era of futures trading. During this era, exchange members frequently blamed shorts for corners and argued that shorts deserved no protection against the demands of large longs. For example, a Chicago Board of Trade committee investigating an alleged barley corner in 1868 asserted that "the market is virtually cornered by reason of parties selling what they did not possess at the time of making their contracts, and which they could not procure at the time of the maturity of such contracts. " 7 Report of the Federal Trade Commission on the Grain Trade 252 (1925). Similarly, the secretary of the Minneapolis Chamber of Commerce (a grain exchange) stated that "speaking frankly, I would say that some of those who have cried out against alleged manipulations in the markets . . . have been conducting their own business in a rather unintelligent fashion in permitting their hedges to remain until the last hour, hedging grain that was not geographically so located to be deliverable there, possibly grain that is not deliverable there." 2 Report of the Federal Trade Commission on the Grain Trade 17 (1921).

This reasoning contradicts the correct economic justification for futures markets. Futures markets serve an important economic purpose in because (1) they allow traders in all markets (not just the delivery markets) to hedge their transactions by selling futures in a central location and (2) traders with information about fundamentals can trade in order to improve price informativeness without handling the actual commodity. Both of these essential functions require some traders to "sell what they do not possess." Therefore, the blaming of shorts for squeezes imposes costs on those who are using the markets in a perfectly legitimate and socially useful fashion. Moreover, the use of this logic to absolve cornerers from any responsibility for the exercise of market power rewards those that impose these costs on the legitimate users.

[74] Steven Shavell, The Optimal Structure of Law Enforcement 36 J. of Law and Econ. 255 (1993) argues that ex post deterrence (that is, sanctioning manipulators after they have exercised market power) dominates ex ante deterrence (that is, imposing restrictions such as position limits, or intervening in the market before the end of the delivery period in order to prevent the exercise of market power) for offenses that (1) are detected with high probability, (2) cannot occur without the knowledge of the malfeasor, and (3) are executed by individuals or firms with substantial wealth. All three conditions obtain in a market-power manipulation. Section 5.5 below demonstrates that corners have marked effects on prices and quantities that are easily observed. Moreover, corners require substantial planning. Finally, only individuals or firms with large financial resources can corner a market. Since they are almost certain to be detected, wealthy manipulators can be deterred by levying substantial fines on them. Chapter 6 shows how these factors tend to make ex post deterrence more efficient than alternative means of reducing the frequency of manipulation.

[75] Volkart Bros., Inc. v. Freeman, 311 F.2d at 59.

[76] Cargill, Inc. v. Hardin, 452 F.2d at 1162.

[77] In re Abrams at 35,785.

[78] The ALJ in Abrams also stated that since warehouse receipts can be retendered, shorts can deliver an amount greater than the deliverable stocks on hand. The ALJ argued that this would constrain the long's ability to influence price. Id. at 35,782. This reasoning is incorrect. Warehouse receipts can be retendered only if the long who initially receives delivery sells them. A profit-maximizing manipulator who receives delivery of warehouse receipts would sell them only at a price equal to the

price at which he is willing to sell futures contracts. Thus, retendered warehouse receipts do not represent an additional source of the deliverable commodity.

[79] In re Indiana Farm Bureau at 27,282.

[80] Cargill, Inc. v. Hardin, 452 F.2d at 1162.

[81] Volkart Bros., Inc. v. Freeman, 311 F.2d at 59.

[82] Great Western Food Distributors v. Brannan, 201 F.2d at 479.

[83] Cargill, Inc. v. Hardin, 452 F.2d at 1173.

[84] In re Indiana Farm Bureau at 27,286. Fischel and Ross, supra note 38, at 545, also argue that market power can result from legitimate trades. They therefore conclude that the exercise of market power is not manipulative per se. This is clearly at variance with United States law, which explicitly proscribes corners. Moreover, this view is rather eccentric, inasmuch as most of the academic literature recognizes that a the exercise of market power is the most important form of manipulation. See, for instance, Markham, supra note 4; Easterbrook, supra note 9; Johnson and Hazen, supra note 22; and Ronald Anderson, The Industrial Organization of Futures Markets: A Survey, in The Industrial Organization of Futures Markets (R. Anderson ed. 1984). Moreover, semantics aside, it is clear that the exercise of market power can impose substantial deadweight losses, and allowing cornerers to use the reasoning advanced in Indiana Farm Bureau or by Fischel and Ross to escape punishment for such exercise could dramatically impair the efficiency of derivatives markets. Put differently, many guns are obtained through legitimate transactions, but this is no reason to allow people to use firearms so obtained to rob or murder; similarly, there is no reason to allow traders who acquire market power through legitimate means to exercise that power to the detriment of market efficiency.

[85] Id. at 27,285.

[86] Id.

[87] Id. at 27,286.

[88] Volkart Bros., Inc. v. Freeman, 311 F.2d at 59.

[89] In re Indiana Farm Bureau at 26,285.

[90] Id.

[91] This case contains other examples of peculiar reasoning as well. The majority decision noted that the Farm Bureau utilized the corn delivered to it to satisfy outstanding sales commitments and claimed that this demonstrated that the

Bureau's actions were commercially legitimate. In re Indiana Farm Bureau at 27,286. This is balderdash. Result 3.6 from Chapter 2 implies that a trader with an outstanding short position (like the Farm Bureau) is an especially dangerous manipulator because it has already acquired a plot in which to bury the corpse. In Volkart, the defendants had shorted deferred futures, similarly "insuring" the firm against a drop in price after the termination of the squeeze. Volkart Bros., Inc. v. Freeman at 63. The Commissioners' assertion also overlooks the fact that the Bureau liquidated a large number of contracts, even though it still had some sales commitments that remained open. If the futures market was truly the cheap source of corn (as the Commission's logic requires), and if the Farm Bureau needed more corn to satisfy its sales requirements, it should have taken more deliveries. This reasoning suggests that the commissioners possessed only a dim understanding of how manipulation works.

[92] In re Abrams at 35,786.

[93] Id.

[94] Cargill, Inc., v. Hardin, 452 F.2d at 1159.

[95] Great Western Food Distributors v. Brannan, 201 F.2d at 480.

[96] Volkart Bros., Inc. v. Freeman, 311 F.2d at 59.

[97] In re Indiana Farm Bureau at 27,285.

[98] In re Abrams at 35,782-35,785.

[99] The CFTC did not order an emergency action in this episode; the Chicago Board of Trade did. According to Commissioner Fowler West, the CFTC did not act because it had adopted such a cramped definition of manipulation that it was "virtually impossible" to prove the existence of a squeeze. Ingersoll, As Congress Returns, Will the CFTC Feel the Squeeze on Soybean Flap? Wall St. J., Aug. 22, 1989, at C1.

[100] Perdue, supra note 34, at 393.

[101] Friedman, supra note 46, at 50.

[102] McDermott, supra note 14, at 214.

[103] Id. at 204-205, 214-219.

[104] Id.

[105] Friedman, supra note 46, at 54-55.

[106] Id. at 48.

[107] Davidson, supra note 4; Markham, supra note 4.

[108] The criteria discussed by Shavell, supra note 74, at 255, imply that ex post deterrence of manipulation is preferable to ex ante deterrence.

[109] Friedman, supra note 46, at 60.

[110] It is of course possible to reverse the null and alternative hypotheses. That is, one could treat the hypothesis that a particular contract was manipulated as the null. This reversal essentially shifts the burden of proof to the defendant. If under this hypothesis the statistical tests are met, manipulation would be considered proved, unless the defendant could provide evidence to support an alternative explanation. It is clear that who bears the burden of proof is an important question. However, it is not the objective of this paper to answer it. Instead, my objective is to create a methodology that can be employed to determine reliably whether a manipulation occurred. The validity and power of this methodology is independent of who bears the burden of proof.

[111] Indeed, the observable implications of the manipulation model and the data available to test them are far more exact than those employed in other types of cases where similar issues arise. In particular, the contrast between the clearness of these implications and tests and those employed in antitrust cases is strikingly evident.

[112] Victor Ng and Stephen Craig Pirrong, Fundamentals and Volatility: Storage, Spreads, and the Dynamics of Metals Prices, 67 J. of Bus. 207 (1994).

[113] All reported percentage price changes (*returns*) have been stripped of their predictable components. That is, the reported returns are equal to actual returns net of the expected return. Such returns are sometimes called *residual returns*. The use of residual returns is motivated by the fact that some fraction of price movements on a given date t can be predicted using information available on date t-1. Such information includes past price changes and past price levels. In the zinc data, Ng and Pirrong estimate this predictable component using an ordinary least squares regression model. As is the case for most financial data, a very small fraction of the movements in zinc returns are predictable; past price changes and price levels explain less than 2 percent of the variation in zinc spot and forward prices. Thus, observed price changes are almost identical to price changes net of the predicted price changes. Moreover, since residual returns have been stripped of their predictable components, the expected residual return equals zero. The data on changes in deliverable stocks have also been stripped of their predictable components through the use of a regression model. As a result, the expected change in stocks under the null hypothesis is zero.

[114] The spread also corrects for the effects of interest rates and the costs of warehousing zinc. See Ng and Pirrong, supra note 112, at 207, 217-218, for details.

[115] Id. Specifically, the model adjusts standard deviations to reflect the fact that even in competitive markets, spot and futures prices become more variable and vary more independently, when the spot price is high relative to the futures price. This is true because the spot price increases relative to the futures price when supply conditions tighten (holding demand constant) or demand increases (holding supply constant). Thus, although a rise in the spot price relative to the futures price could signal an impending corner, it could also reflect a natural tightening of supply conditions which would tend to make prices more volatile. Given that a corner causes the spot price to rise relative to the futures price, use of this model tends to favor an accused manipulator. In particular, under the null hypothesis the model attributes the initial rise in the spot price-forward price ratio to a fundamental shock to supply or demand conditions and increases the estimated standard deviation of spot and forward prices. This increase in these statistics makes the price plunge that is attributable to the burying-the-corpse effect seem less unusual. The example in the text shows that even given this advantage to the accused, the statistical test for the existence of a corner can be extremely powerful.

[116] The null can be rejected at any level of confidence. This is a choice variable for the court. This choice corresponds to the selection of a burden of persuasion. A "to the preponderance of the evidence" standard corresponds to a wide confidence interval (such as, 50 percent). A "beyond a reasonable doubt" standard corresponds to a narrow confidence interval (such as, 5 percent or 1 percent). It is not my aim to establish the appropriate burden of proof. Again, my objective is to create a set of tests that can be employed under any proof-burden standard. However, the example just discussed shows that the effects of manipulation can be so pronounced that even a very strict burden is not insurmountable. Since it is most beneficial to deter the most egregious episodes of manipulation, and since the costs of demoralizing legitimate trading activity through the use of a low threshold may be large, a narrow confidence interval is likely to be optimal. The decision in Great Western states that a showing that the preponderance of the evidence implies manipulation is necessary in order to obtain a conviction. Great Western Distributors Food v. Brannan, 201 F.2d. at 474.

[117] Perdue supra note 34; McDermott supra note 14; Bianco, The Mechanics of Futures Trading: Speculation and Manipulation, 6 Hofstra L. Rev. 27 (1977); Philip McBride Johnson, Commodity Market Manipulation, 38 Washington & Lee L. Rev. 725 (1985); Lower, supra note 34.

[118] It is possible to use other information to improve this analysis. Specifically, an accused manipulator may claim that the actions of other long traders, rather than his own actions, caused the price and quantity anomalies. Data on market share is directly relevant in this case.

[119] The analysis in this section bears some similarities to that of Perdue, supra note 34, and Friedman, supra note 46. Each proposes that the test of manipulative intent should be; would the accused trader behave as observed but for the desire to influence price? Friedman's proposed methodology for answering this question implicitly requires a knowledge of the competitive price. He asks whether the shorts submit to the demands of a large trader only because there are stiffer penalties for default on futures contracts than there are for failure to perform under contracts governed by the Uniform Commercial Code. In order to answer this question, Friedman poses another: would shorts choose to default if the only penalties for doing so were liquidated damages? In order to calculate these damages, it is necessary to know the competitive price. Conversely, the methodology proposed in this section permits the answering of the question without knowing the competitive price. The criteria established here are therefore implementable.

[120] To see why, assume the opposite. If a price taking owner of a long position faces a futures price of P and a value of the deliverable commodity of V, where P>V, he can increase his wealth by selling the futures contract. Conversely, if V>P, he should take another delivery. A price-taking (that is, competitive) trader cannot be in equilibrium, therefore, unless P=V.

The evidence presented in Indiana Farm Bureau provides a clearcut case of the importance of this fact. Respondent Johnston in that case stated that he preferred to liquidate futures contracts at a price of $3.80 per bushel rather than take delivery at that price because "a minute or two later [that is, after the market closed] the corn would be worth one dollar a bushel less." In re Indiana Farm Bureau at 27,308. Since Johnston took substantial deliveries at prices greater than $2.80 per bushel, this statement is inconsistent with the notion that the Indiana Farm Bureau was acting as a price taker in the July 1973 corn futures contract.

[121] Sometimes (as occurred in the Ferruzzi episode) the large long does not bid in the delivery market, but instead bids in some other market. In this case, it is necessary to calculate the cost of acquiring supplies in the delivery market (the futures price) plus the cost of transporting the delivered commodity to the place where the long is bidding. If this so-called delivery value exceeds the cash bid, one can infer that the futures market is not the cheap source of the cash commodity.

[122] As an example, assume that the futures price at contract expiration equaled 10. This equals the value of a delivery by assumption; that is, taking the trader's justification at face value implies he is willing to pay 10 for a unit of the physical commodity when trading ends. Immediately after it ends, price falls to 9. If the trader's marginal willingness to pay at contract expiration was 10, he should purchase the commodity at the lower price.

[123] Minpeco, S.A. v. ContiCommodity Services et al 673 F. Supp. 684 (S.D.N.Y. 1987). See the Reply Affidavit of Jeffrey Williams at 66-68. The types of manipulation alleged in the Hunt case are somewhat different than those typical of a corner case. It is still worth discussing this possible defense, however, as it could

be employed in a market-power manipulation case in order to rationalize the taking of large numbers of deliveries.

CHAPTER 6
THE EFFICIENT DETERRENCE OF MARKET-POWER MANIPULATION

6.1. Introduction

The previous chapters show that *ex post* deterrence of manipulation has been severely hampered by the poor reasoning in several important cases but that this failure is not inevitable. Armed with a firm understanding of the economics of corners, it is possible to identify market-power manipulation with considerable precision. This allows courts to sanction cornerers and thereby deter market-power manipulation by making it unprofitable.

Despite the attractive features of *ex post* deterrence, it is still possible that the other antimanipulation measures--*ex ante* and contractual deterrence--may be even more efficient than *ex post* deterrence. Therefore, in order to establish the most efficient way to deter corners, it is necessary to conduct a full comparative analysis of the costs and benefits of the alternatives.

Such an analysis (the subject of this chapter) shows that when done properly, *ex post* deterrence holds substantial advantages over alternative methods of reducing the frequency and severity of market-power manipulations. Several factors favor *ex post* deterrence over *ex ante* measures. Better information is available after a manipulation has been attempted than when a corner is in progress. This better information reduces the likelihood that a manipulator will escape unpunished or that an innocent party will be falsely convicted of committing a corner. Since both types of error are costly, superior information economizes on the costs of deterrence. Moreover, more discriminating and powerful sanctions are available *ex post*. Thus, holding the costs of errors arising from mistaken intervention equal across regimes, corners can be deterred more effectively in an *ex post* regime. Furthermore, the types of sanctions available *ex ante* encourage market participants to engage in rent-seeking behavior. That is, traders have an incentive to utilize resources in order to influence decision makers to make favorable decisions. This behavior is costly because (1) real resources are utilized to obtain wealth transfers and (2) influence activities increase the likelihood of mistaken intervention into the market. Finally, *ex post* deterrence requires the expenditure of resources only when a corner occurs, whereas *ex ante* deterrence requires continuous monitoring of a market. As a result, enforcement expenses are likely to be smaller in an *ex post* regime than in an *ex ante* system. Only one factor favors *ex ante* deterrence. Intervention before the completion of a corner can mitigate the price and quantity distortions that would occur if the manipulation is allowed to run its course. It is unlikely, however, that this single advantage to *ex ante* deterrence can overcome the factors favoring *ex post* sanctions.

Ex post deterrence also largely dominates contractual deterrence, although there are certain contractual means that are very valuable supplements to sanctions imposed after the fact. Regulators can rely only on poor information (relative to that available after a corner attempt) when formulating contractual measures such as position limits and entry requirements. These contractual measures also interfere with the essential risk-transfer and price-discovery functions of futures markets and thus impose substantial costs on market users. Furthermore, position limits and contract review entail substantial administrative costs.

One contractual deterrence tool--the inclusion of delivery options in contract terms--offers substantial benefits. This tool is at best a supplement, however, to *ex post* deterrence of manipulation.

In sum, an economic analysis implies that *ex post* deterrence is the most efficient way to deter market-power manipulations. Unfortunately, as demonstrated in Chapter 5, *ex post* deterrence is largely hamstrung in the United States. Moreover, existing regulations rely extensively on position limits and *ex ante* deterrence in order to reduce the frequency of manipulation in American commodity markets. Thus, United States commodity law could be made substantially more efficient by a revitalization of *ex post* deterrence (perhaps through the creation of new antimanipulation laws) combined with the simultaneous elimination of position limits and *ex ante* interventions.

The remainder of this chapter examines the arguments supporting these conclusions. Section 6.2 compares the costs and benefits of ex ante and ex post deterrence. Section 6.3 performs a similar comparison of ex post and contractual deterrence. Section 6.4 examines the issue of whether the government or exchanges should be the primary enforcers of antimanipulation measures. Section 6.5 summarizes the conclusions of the chapter and presents a proposal to reform United States commodity law so as to improve the efficiency of futures markets by deterring manipulation more effectively and at lower cost than is currently the case.

6.2. *Ex Post* Deterrence versus *Ex Ante* Deterrence

6.2.1. Information and Error Costs.

The availability of information is one of the crucial determinants of the effectiveness of a deterrence mechanism. An analysis of the information available to those charged with the *ex ante* and *ex post* deterrence of manipulation reveals that the latter can systematically rely on more complete information and can process it more efficiently. Due to this advantage, fewer errors will occur under properly executed *ex post* deterrence. Since errors are costly, this provides a strong reason to rely on harm-based sanctions to deter corners.

After a manipulation has occurred, fact-finders have access to several sources of information not available prior to the completion of a corner. Most important, an *ex post* fact-finder can determine whether a substantial decline in prices accompanied the completion of an alleged corner. A regulator charged with intervening prior to the completion of a corner cannot observe such a price decline before acting. Since the burying the corpse effect is the most distinctive symptom of a market-power manipulation, an *ex ante* regulator operates under a severe information impediment relative to his *ex post* counterpart. Moreover, an *ex post* fact-finder can examine evidence regarding shipment and receipt patterns following the completion of an alleged manipulation, whereas an *ex ante* regulator cannot. In addition, in order to examine issues of motive and intent, an *ex post* adjudicator can observe an accused manipulator's behavior after the completion of a suspected corner. Again, an *ex ante* regulator cannot obtain such information. All of these factors favor the use of harm-based sanctions to attack manipulation.

Issues of time also favor *ex post* deterrence. This is true for two reasons. First, as demonstrated by the Cargill, Indiana Farm Bureau, and Cox cases, some corners can develop with extraordinary rapidity. In each of these cases, the existence of a manipulation became evident only at the very end of trading of a futures contract. Due to the rapid progression of events, regulators did not possess information alerting them to the existence of a manipulation until it was too late to act. *Ex post* fact-finders operate under no such handicap. Second, even if regulators receive some information revealing the potential for manipulation in time for them to act, the time available to process this information is necessarily limited. This limits their ability to analyze this information thoughtfully and completely. Moreover, the *ex ante* decision makers operate under a strict deadline and enormous external pressure. They must act before the end of trading of the futures contract. Market participants with a vested interest in the outcome have a strong incentive to pressure the regulator for a favorable resolution of the issue. (I discuss this issue in more detail in Section 6.2.3.) Hurried decisions under pressure are frequently wrong. *Ex post* fact-finders do not face the same time constraint as their *ex ante* counterparts. Time, therefore, is on the side of *ex post* deterrence.

In sum, *ex post* fact-finders have access to better information and can process is more effectively than *ex ante* regulators. Due to this superior information, it is possible to construct an *ex post* deterrence system that makes fewer errors than any *ex ante* system. Since erroneous decisions are costly, this implies that error costs should be lower--and perhaps substantially so--in an *ex post* regime.

Decision making errors are of two types, each of which has distinctive costs. The first type of error is mistaken intervention when no manipulation has occurred or is in progress. In the *ex post* regime, this type of error involves the conviction of a trader for manipulation when in fact he has acted competitively. In an *ex ante* regime, this type of error results in the imposition of emergency measures even when all traders are acting competitively. Since (using the methodology of Chapter 5) this type of error is due to the incorrect rejection of the null hypothesis of competition, by analogy with classical hypothesis testing I will hereafter refer to it as *Type I error*.

The second type of error is the failure to intervene when a manipulation has occurred or is in progress. In the *ex post* regime, such an error allows a manipulator to escape unpunished. In an *ex ante* regime, a trader is allowed to complete a corner without interference. Again by analogy with classical hypothesis testing terminology, I refer to this as *Type II error*.

The superiority of information *ex post* implies that for a given probability of making a Type I error in both regimes, the probability of a Type II error will be lower *ex post*. That is, for a given probability of mistaken intervention in the two regimes, fewer manipulators will escape unpunished in the *ex post* regime. Similarly, holding the probability of making a Type II error fixed across regimes, the probability of making a Type I error is lower *ex post.* That is, for a given probability that a manipulator will escape unpunished, there will be fewer mistaken interventions *ex post.* As a result, the *error possibility frontier*--the locus of feasible combinations of Type I and Type II errors--in the *ex post* regime is everywhere inside the error possibility frontier in the *ex ante* regime. Since fewer errors are preferred to more, the relative position of the error possibility frontiers is a decided advantage for *ex post* deterrence.

The value of this advantage depends on the costs of errors. Both types of errors are costly. The costs of a Type I error in the *ex ante* regime depend on the type of intervention employed to stymie a manipulative intent. There are basically two alternative means of emergency intervention available to an *ex ante* regulator. The first method is to force traders to liquidate their positions or a sizable fraction thereof. This method is based on the fact that a successful manipulation requires the cornerer to demand excessive deliveries; by forcing all parties to liquidate most or all of their positions, no one can exercise market power by calling for large numbers of deliveries. By constraining the actions available to traders, this form of intervention affects prices indirectly.

The second method available *ex ante* is to impose a price at which all outstanding positions are closed. This method obviously affects prices in the futures market directly.

Both types of intervention interfere with the free determination of price. If this intervention is mistaken--as is by definition true if a Type I error is committed--this can be very costly. The efficient functioning of a futures market depends on the ability of prices to respond to underlying supply and demand conditions. Indeed, market-power manipulation is objectionable primarily because it represents an artificial interference with the ability of price to reflect market fundamentals. Mistaken *ex ante* intervention to deter manipulation is therefore objectionable on similar grounds. It too is an artificial interference with the free functioning of the price system. This contravenes the proper objective of the regulation of futures markets; perversely, the tool intended to improve the efficiency of futures markets can in fact undermine this efficiency. Thus, Type I error in the *ex ante* regime is potentially very costly.

Of the two methods available to *ex ante* regulators, forced liquidation is likely to dominate the establishment of a settlement price. Under forced liquidation, market participants have some flexibility in setting price. To be sure, their actions are constrained, but as long as some deliveries are allowed (that is, the liquidation order does not require all traders to liquidate 100 per cent of their positions) there will be competition among market participants to buy and sell claims on the deliverable supply. As a result, the parties can still condition their reservation prices (the prices at which they are willing to buy and sell) on their private information concerning supply and demand fundamentals. Since the constraint on the number of deliveries traders can take is imposed by a regulator ignorant of their true valuations of the deliverable commodity, it will sometimes be the case that some are forced to take fewer deliveries than they would as price takers when no constraint is imposed. Similarly, sometimes the number of deliveries allowed by the regulator may be sufficiently large to allow a trader to exercise some market power, although less than would be the case if the regulator imposed no constraint. Thus, the price that results under a forced liquidation may differ from that which would prevail in a perfectly competitive and unconstrained market. Nonetheless, under a forced liquidation, prices can still provide a meaningful signal of private information regarding the relevant market conditions.

Under an imposed price settlement, however, no interplay between buyers and sellers is allowed. They are not allowed to buy or sell based on their private information. Moreover, the regulator setting the liquidation price is extremely unlikely to possess the requisite information to establish the "right" price. That is, since (1) the primary reason why futures markets facilitate price discovery is that market participants have private information about the value of a commodity and (2) the regulator does not have access to this information, the price established by the regulator cannot reflect the relevant information about supply and demand fundamentals. Thus, a price determined under the constraint of a mandatory liquidation should be far more informative than the price established by a regulator. Since the primary cost of a Type I error is the resulting price distortion, this fact favors the use of forced liquidation if *ex ante* deterrence is employed at all.[1]

Type I errors will also impose costs in an *ex post* regime. A trader acting with legitimate intent may act less aggressively if faced with the possibility of paying sanctions for a manipulation that he did not commit. For example, a speculator with information concerning the value of a commodity may liquidate his position at a price less than his estimate of this value rather than stand for delivery in order to force prices to what he considers to be their true level if taking substantial deliveries increases the likelihood of incurring a penalty on a false charge of manipulation.

The nature of *ex post* deterrence helps control these costs, however. If sanctions are chosen correctly and reflect the possibility of a false conviction, marginal cases will result in only marginal penalties. Moreover, in the *ex post* regime all traders can utilize their private information to respond to the possibility of a mistaken conviction. If a trader has private information that a commodity is substantially undervalued, he can take this into account and trade-off the benefits of taking more deliveries on the strength of this information against the costs of a mistaken manipulation conviction.

Ceteris paribus, this ability of traders to choose the best response to a given probability of a Type I error tends to make the costs of this type of error smaller in the *ex post* regime than in the *ex ante* regime. Even if the regulator uses the less restrictive method of *ex ante* deterrence--forced liquidation--traders are constrained in their ability to react to the possibility of a mistaken intervention. Thus, in an *ex post* regime, market participants can mitigate the costs of Type I error in ways that are impossible in an *ex ante* regime. For a given probability of a Type I error, such errors are therefore likely to be less costly and perhaps substantially so, in an *ex post* regime than an *ex ante* one. This is especially true if *ex ante* regulators set settlement prices.

The costs of Type II errors are essentially equal in both regimes. When a Type II error occurs, a manipulation is completed unhindered and unpunished. Thus, a Type II error results in the imposition of the deadweight costs of market-power manipulation on the market.

Taken altogether, this analysis implies that *ex post* deterrence has some strong advantages over *ex ante* deterrence. For a given amount of manipulation deterrence--that is, for a given probability of Type II error--there are fewer mistaken interventions (Type I errors) in the *ex post* regime. Since interference in the pricing process undermines an essential, socially productive purpose of futures markets--price discovery--economizing on Type I errors is very desirable. Moreover, it is likely that Type I errors are less costly in the *ex post* regime because mistaken intervention in this regime imposes fewer constraints on the actions of traders acting with legitimate intentions than is the case than in the *ex ante* regime. Thus, holding the costs of Type II error across regimes constant, Type I error costs are lower, and by a potentially large margin, in the *ex post* regime.

One can make the comparison between regimes another way. Holding the probability of Type I error constant across regimes, (1) Type II errors will occur less frequently in the *ex post* regime and (2) the costs of Type I error will be no larger and perhaps will be substantially smaller in the *ex post* regime. Part (1) of this statement implies that manipulators will escape unpunished less often in the *ex post* regime. Since would-be cornerers can be caught and punished more frequently *ex post*, manipulation can be made less profitable in the *ex post* regime than its *ex ante* counterpart. Reducing the profitability of cornering the market reduces its frequency as well. This reduces the expected costs of Type II error. Thus, it is possible to achieve lower costs attributable to both Type I and Type II errors in the *ex post* regime.

In sum, information advantages provide a very strong reason to favor the reliance on *ex post*, as opposed to *ex ante*, deterrence of market-power manipulation. Analysis of another factor--the differential power of sanctions available in the two regimes--bolsters this conclusion.

6.2.2. Sanctions in Ex Post and Ex Ante Regimes

In an *ex post* regime it is possible to use monetary fines and damages, as well as imprisonment, to punish manipulators. These fines can be chosen to make the expected value of attempted manipulation negative. In contrast, in a pure *ex ante* regime, the regulator can only attempt to impose a competitive outcome on the market when it detects and intervenes such an offense (that is, when it does not commit a Type II error). This difference in feasible punishments confers a further advantage on *ex post* deterrence.

Consider the effects of a forced liquidation on the fortunes of a would-be manipulator. The likely (and intended) effect of this action is to ensure that the futures price at the end of the delivery period is approximately equal to the competitive price. This denies the manipulator any supercompetitive profits. It is always possible, however, to levy a fine or damages that extracts all of the supercompetitive profits from a successful manipulator. Thus, it is always possible to choose penalties in an *ex post* regime that impose an equal cost on a manipulator as would a forced liquidation in the *ex ante* regime. As a result, for a given probability of Type II error, it is possible to choose fines and damages such that the expected profits of manipulation are no higher in the *ex post* regime than in the *ex ante* one.[2]

Moreover, in the *ex ante* regime some manipulators will escape unpunished and earn a positive profit. Since (1) the smallest profit a manipulator earn during the delivery period in an *ex ante* regime that relies on forced liquidation is the competitive profit and (2) the manipulator sometimes earns a supercompetitive profit because the regulator sometimes fails to intervene, the expected profitability of manipulation is necessarily positive in the *ex ante* regime.

Indeed, matters may be even worse if the *ex ante* regulator fixes settlement prices rather than forces liquidations. Given the poor information available prior to the completion of trading, it is possible that the regulator will set a settlement price that exceeds the competitive price.[3] Thus, a manipulator may earn a supercompetitive profit even if the regulator intervenes. Indeed, since the manipulator need not take deliveries--and hence need not bury the corpse--if settlements are forced at a supercompetitive price, he may earn a greater profit due to intervention than if the regulator allows the corner to run its course! This serves to increase the expected profit of manipulation attempts even further.

This is not the case in the *ex post* regime. It is possible to levy fines or damages that exceed the true profits of a manipulation. Since manipulators are almost always firms or individuals with financial resources that substantially exceed the profits they earn in a manipulation (that is, only the wealthy have the resources to attempt a corner), the maximum feasible fine can substantially exceed the profit a trader can earn in a manipulation. By imposing large enough fines and damages, it is therefore possible to make the expected returns to manipulation negative in the *ex post* regime. Thus, for a given probability of Type II error in the two regimes, manipulation can be made less profitable--and therefore less frequent--in the *ex post* system than in the *ex ante* counterpart. This is a decided advantage to harm-based sanctions as opposed to preventative intervention.

Moreover, the flexibility inherent in using monetary sanctions *ex post* affects the trade-offs between Type I and Type II error costs. In general, reducing Type I error requires an increase in the probability of Type II error; the more rigorous the proof needed to sustain an allegation of manipulation, the more likely a cornerer is to escape unpunished. In an *ex ante* regime, this necessarily increases the expected profitability of manipulation and thereby reduces the deterrent effect of early intervention. In the *ex post* regime, in contrast, it is possible to reduce the probability of Type I error without compromising the deterrent effects of antimanipulation laws by increasing the level of damages in conjunction with the increase in the burden of proof. It is well known in the law and economics literature that if the probability of detection and conviction for an offense is less than one, in order to optimize the level of deterrence it is desirable to increase the sanction imposed in the event of conviction to a level that exceeds the actual damage imposed. This is possible in an *ex post* regime. It is not feasible in an *ex ante* regime because the available sanctions are too limited.

This is an extremely important advantage to *ex post* deterrence. In order to limit the substantial costs attributable to an inappropriate intervention, it is desirable to reduce the probability of Type I error. This inevitably increases the probability of Type II error. The effects of this increase are far less harmful in the *ex post* regime, however, because it is possible to offset the resulting effects on deterrence by raising fines and damages. Such a compensating change in punishment is not feasible in the *ex ante* regime. Therefore, a given level of deterrence in the *ex ante* regime necessarily entails a substantially higher probability of Type I error with the associated costs. Put differently, for a given level of Type I error costs, the ability to use monetary sanctions *ex post* allows substantially greater manipulation deterrence.

6.2.3. Rent-Seeking Costs

In addition to the disadvantages arising from poorer information and less powerful sanctions, *ex ante* deterrence is also more vulnerable to rent-seeking behavior. Shorts have a strong incentive to "lobby" a regulator to take actions to reduce prices regardless of whether a corner is in progress or not.[4] Similarly, during a corner, longs have an incentive to pressure the regulator to allow the completion of a corner. These self-interested activities intended to secure profits--called rent-seeking activities in the literature--may well succeed with positive probability.

This is especially true in an *ex ante* regime because, as noted earlier, the regulator possesses relatively poor information about the likelihood of a manipulation. Furthermore, the regulator may have to obtain information from interested sources who have an incentive to provide distorted reports and signals in order to induce the regulator to intervene in their favor. That is, rent-seeking behavior reduces the quality of information available to the regulator.

Moreover, due to the necessarily close and enduring connections between an *ex ante* regulator and the interested parties, these influence activities may well succeed. In addition, regulators subject to legislative oversight (as the CFTC is) are vulnerable to pressure from legislators. Legislators, in turn, respond to the self-interested, rent-seeking importuning of their constituents. In contrast, courts charged with the *ex post* enforcement of anticorner rules are less vulnerable to such lobbying, pressure, and influence activities. Indeed, the court system is designed in large part to insulate judges from rent seekers. Thus, rent-seeking activities are more likely to succeed in an *ex ante* enforcement regime.[5]

Rent-seeking activities are costly for two reasons. First, agents use real resources to exert influence. For example, executives of firms in the futures industry may spend valuable time and effort lobbying regulators instead of finding ways to run their businesses more efficiently. Second, rent-seeking activities increase the likelihood of Type I and Type II errors. A regulator subject to external pressure is more likely to intervene to benefit shorts than one relatively invulnerable to influence. Similarly, such a regulator is more likely to succumb to the blandishments of interested longs to allow a corner to run its course. Thus, the greater susceptibility to rent-seeking activities tends to increase error costs in the *ex ante* regime. This reinforces the effect of information differences on the relative merits of *ex ante* and *ex post* deterrence.

6.2.4. Enforcement Costs

The enforcement costs incurred under the two regimes may also differ substantially. In general, one would expect an *ex post* system to be cheaper to administer than an *ex ante* regime.

In an *ex post* regime, by far the most important component of enforcement costs is the expense of preparing for and conducting a trial. These costs may be quite large. Lawyers and experts for accused and accuser alike must spend valuable hours researching and preparing their cases, negotiating settlement, and perhaps participating in court proceedings. Witnesses for both sides must forego their normal activities to provide testimony. This process is time consuming.

According to Markham, the mean time between accusation and disposition of manipulation charges is five years. Litigation expenses can amount to substantial sums in cases of this duration.

The main enforcement costs in an *ex ante* system are attributable to the necessity of constantly monitoring the activity of futures markets in order to detect impending manipulations. This requires a staff of trained individuals. Moreover, it is necessary to create a data processing infrastructure to collect, process, and analyze the requisite information on a real-time basis. This information includes data on prices, commodity shipments and receipts, cash and futures trading activity, and cash and futures positions. In addition, market participants must make investments to produce and transmit information to the regulator. The decision makers of trading firms must also spend time conferring with the regulator in order to provide other information that is not readily summarized in market reports.

These expenditures are not trivial. The CFTC's most recent budget allocates $5.1 million to market surveillance for the FY1994. Not all of this goes to manipulation prevention, but other CFTC departments (including the Divisions of Enforcement and Economic Analysis, and the Offices of the General Counsel and the Chairman) also expend resources on manipulation-related matters. Thus, $5 million is probably a good estimate of the federal government's annual investment in corner prevention. Moreover, exchanges also spend considerable sums on market surveillance activities designed to detect manipulation attempts. As private organizations, exchanges have declined to provide data on their expenditures to prevent or deter manipulation. Discussions with industry participants suggests, however, that exchange expenses exceed CFTC surveillance costs. Since these costs are incurred on an ongoing basis, they represent a substantial sum.

Given the great differences between the nature of the two systems, it is difficult to evaluate theoretically whether *ex post* or *ex ante* measures are less costly to enforce. An important factor tends to favor *ex post* deterrence, however. Specifically, enforcement expenditures are incurred in the *ex post* regime only when an offense is suspected, whereas in an *ex ante* regime they are incurred on a continuous basis regardless of whether an offense occurs or not. A portion of enforcement activities in the *ex ante* regime are therefore "wasted" in the sense that sometimes no corners would have occurred even if the regulator had not incurred these costs. Moreover, it is possible to reduce the expected expenditures on enforcement in the *ex post* regime by increasing fines and damages. Increasing fines and damages reduces the probability of such an offense and therefore reduces the probability of a trial. This, in turn, reduces expected expenditures on enforcement. The main cost of raising fines in this fashion is attributable to Type I error; given the probability of Type I error, a greater the penalty for a manipulation conviction demoralizes legitimate trader conduct more severely. Since monetary sanctions are not feasible in an *ex ante* regime, however, it is not possible to economize on enforcement expenditures in that regime by altering punishments. Instead, lowering the probability of manipulation requires an increase in enforcement expenditures. That is, in an *ex post* regime monetary fines and damages (and perhaps imprisonment) are a substitute for real resources used to enforce antimanipulation laws. Although monetary sanctions are not costless (as they demoralize legitimate trader activities when errors can occur) they do offer a degree of freedom not available in the *ex ante* regime. This increased flexibility attributable to the feasibility of monetary sanctions again favors *ex post* deterrence.

This conclusion is strengthened further by the fact that it is difficult to adjust *ex ante* deterrence to changing circumstances that affect the profitability of manipulation. *Ceteris paribus, ex ante* enforcement expenditures should rise and fall with the profitability of manipulation; the marginal benefit of deterrence rises (falls), for example, when changes in transport costs increase (reduce) the profitability--and hence the likelihood--of corners. However, adjustment of *ex ante* deterrence efforts require administrative and (perhaps) legislative actions. These actions are time consuming and are the subject of substantial rent-seeking efforts. Due to these adjustment costs, enforcement expenditures are unlikely to vary in a discriminating fashion with the factors that determine the profitability of manipulation.

Furthermore, information about the profitability of manipulation is likely to be very difficult to collect and to articulate. Much of the information is dispersed among millions of market participants and is not in the form of objective data but instead reflects qualitative features of the market that are difficult to communicate effectively.

Due to the high costs of obtaining information about the factors that determine the profitability of manipulation, *ex ante* enforcement efforts are likely to differ quite substantially from the efforts that would be undertaken if the regulator could readily obtain this information.

Sometimes the regulator will spend too much on monitoring and enforcing; sometimes it will spend too little. In any case, given these severe informational problems, there is little reason to believe that the regulator (or its legislative overseer) will undertake the appropriate level of enforcement.

Ex post deterrence is not so dependent on information about the susceptibility of the market to corners. By choosing the appropriate method to calculate damages, if the profitability of manipulation rises due to exogenous changes in the market, penalties will naturally increase without explicit regulatory or congressional intervention. As a result, penalties--and thus the strength of deterrence--adjust automatically and in a discriminating fashion, to changes in market conditions. That is, the profitability of manipulation is observable *ex post* and this information can be used to calibrate penalties that deter manipulation. A trader contemplating a corner can therefore still be deterred by the prospect of sanctions if other conditions change so as to make manipulation more profitable. This implies that in an *ex post* regime it is unnecessary to collect on a continuous basis information about market conditions that determine the profitability of manipulation in order to determine the appropriate enforcement incentives.

This last comparison implies that optimal enforcement in an *ex ante* regime is more dependent on information about market conditions than optimal enforcement in an *ex post* system. The nature of this information and the characteristics of the process required to respond to it, make it very costly to collect and employ. As a result, if *ex ante* regulators collect the information required to make discriminating adjustments of enforcement effort to changes in market conditions, they will incur large direct information costs. If they choose to avoid these direct costs and consequently fail to adjust their enforcement efforts to these changed conditions, they will incur indirect costs in the form of either excessive or insufficient enforcement. An *ex post* deterrence system faces no such Hobson's choice. This further bolsters the case for harm-based sanctions rather than preventative intervention.

6.2.5. The Single Advantage of Ex Ante Deterrence

The foregoing suggests that *ex ante* deterrence suffers from some substantial handicaps. It does offer one advantage. It is doubtful that this is sufficient, however, to overcome the effects of the weaknesses of *ex ante* deterrence.

The advantage of *ex ante* deterrence is that if the regulator makes the correct decision to intervene--that is, if he commits neither a Type I nor a Type II error--he can limit the damage attributable to a manipulation attempt. Early intervention can limit the distortion in prices and in the shipment, consumption, and production patterns that would result if the corner were to be completed. For example, it is possible that a regulator has sufficient confidence that a manipulation is impending to force a liquidation when relative prices have risen 10 percent above what one would expect given the past history of this commodity. If the manipulation were allowed to continue, price would rise 20 percent above this expectation. By intervening early, the regulator halves the price distortion (and presumably reduces the related quantity distortions) that results when someone attempts to exercise market power. In contrast, if a trader attempts a corner in an *ex post* regime, the manipulation will run its course with all of the attendant price and quantity distortions. Thus, in an *ex ante* regime it is possible to mitigate the damage associated with attempted manipulation.

It should be noted, however, that there is a trade-off between savings associated with mitigation and Type I and Type II error costs. If, in order to economize on the costs of Type I error, the regulator does not intervene unless the signs of manipulation are nearly unmistakable, the benefits of mitigation are limited. In this case, intervention will occur only when the price and quantity distortions are nearly full-blown. There will be little difference, therefore, between the price and quantity distortion that triggers the intervention and the distortions that would occur if the manipulation were allowed to continue unhindered.

In contrast, if in order to mitigate manipulative distortions, the regulator intervenes when there is the slightest suggestion of manipulation, he is likely to commit Type I error with great frequency. Given that such intervention into the market can wreak havoc on the integrity of the pricing process and the informational efficiency of prices, mitigation at damages due to manipulation through early intervention may carry a very high price.

Another complication strengthens these conclusions. The market prices on which a regulator must rely in order to determine whether an intervention is justified depend in large part on how market participants *expect* the regulator to behave. This expectational feedback can both raise the probability of making errors and reduce the efficacy of mitigation.

As an extreme example, assume that market participants believe that the regulator will always intervene to ensure that the market is competitive during the delivery period. Based on this belief, the equilibrium futures price will equal the competitive price until very late in the delivery period even when the conditions are ripe for a market-power manipulation. If no price distortions are manifest, however, the regulator will have little evidence to support an intervention in the market despite the threat of manipulation. When the end of trading nears, shorts may frantically bid up the futures price in order to avoid incurring the costs of making delivery. By then, however, it is too late for the regulator to intervene.

This is admittedly an extreme example. It illustrates an important point, however. Namely, the effectiveness of *ex ante* deterrence depends crucially on the beliefs of market participants about how the regulator will behave. A regulator that builds a reputation for intervening aggressively when there is evidence of a corner can lull market participants into a false sense of security. This, in turn, affects the pricing process in a way that reduces the amount of information available to a regulator. This reduction in information impairs the ability of the regulator to intervene effectively in order to mitigate the damages of manipulation and increases the likelihood of erroneous interventions. Thus, the expectational feedback in the "game" played by market participants and regulators introduces a degree of indeterminacy that further undermines the effectiveness of *ex ante* intervention.

Free riding exacerbates this problem. Any trader who bids up the price because of the threat of a corner provides information to the regulator that improves the quality of his decisions. However, this information is a public good because all shorts (and others harmed by manipulation) benefit from more efficient emergency intervention. Thus, an individual trader has too weak an incentive to bid up prices.

Similar problems do not plague *ex post* deterrence. Timely (that is, real-time) access to information is not crucial in the *ex post* regime. If a corner occurs, the evidence will exist after the end of the delivery period.

6.2.6. Summary and Conclusions: The Superiority of Ex Post Enforcement

This analysis suggests that *ex post* deterrence offers several crucial advantages over *ex ante* deterrence.

First, enforcers have far better information and can process it more efficiently, *ex post* than *ex ante*. This information advantage reduces the probability of errors. As a result, for a given amount of manipulation deterrence, there are fewer mistaken interventions *ex post*. Since mistaken interventions interfere with the futures pricing mechanism and such interference is very costly, this is a decided advantage. Alternatively, holding the costs attributable to mistaken intervention constant across regimes, fewer manipulations will succeed in a properly structured *ex post* regime. This reduces the deadweight costs attributable to monopoly power in futures markets.

Second, sanctions are more powerful and flexible *ex post* than *ex ante*. It is always possible to choose penalties that make the expected profitability of manipulation negative in an *ex post* regime; this is not possible in the *ex ante* system. Moreover, the ability to levy monetary penalties *ex post* makes it possible to reduce the costs attributable to mistaken intervention and enforcement while maintaining a strong deterrent against corners. This option is unavailable *ex ante*. Again, therefore, it is possible to have both less manipulation and fewer mistaken interventions in the *ex post* regime.

Third, rent-seeking costs are almost certainly lower in the *ex post* regime.

Fourth, it is likely that the optimal amount of manipulation in an *ex post* regime is substantially smaller than the optimal amount in the *ex ante* regime (due to the information and sanction advantages of the former). As a result, a smaller number of completed manipulations may impose fewer costs on society than a larger number of partially completed ones.

The primary advantage of *ex ante* deterrence is that early intervention can mitigate the costs attributable to price and quantity distortions incurred when a trader attempts to manipulate the market. The practical importance of this advantage is problematic at best, however. Effective and substantial mitigation requires intervention on the basis of limited evidence of distortions. Intervention based on such slim evidence is often mistaken and therefore interferes with the pricing process. Moreover, a regulator committed to such a strategy is likely to be subjected to continuous influence activities by rent-seeking shorts. In contrast, if in order to avoid the costs of mistaken intervention the regulator intervenes if and only if substantial distortions are evident, little mitigation occurs. Given the very high costs of disrupting the market through mistaken intervention, the costs of mitigation are likely to be very high. Thus, it is unlikely that a regulator properly weighing the costs and benefits of intervention will substantially mitigate the damages attributable to manipulation.

In conclusion, it is almost certain that a properly structured system of *ex post* deterrence dominates *ex ante* deterrence. Harm-based sanctions intended to deter manipulation by making it unprofitable offer several crucial advantages over interventions designed to prevent it. Although *ex ante* deterrence offers one benefit that *ex post* deterrence does not, it is unlikely that this benefit is sufficient to offset the other advantages the latter offers. Indeed, a market-power manipulation exhibits all of the features that law and economics scholars have identified as favoring harm-based sanctions over prevention.[6] Specifically, as the analysis of the earlier chapters shows, a corner has distinctive effects on price and quantity that make it easy to detect. As a result, the probability of detecting and punishing this offense is can be made very high and the probability of incorrectly convicting an innocent trader is small. Moreover, the perpetrators of manipulation are typically wealthy and therefore are vulnerable to substantial monetary penalties. The law and economics literature demonstrates that when these conditions hold, the imposition of *ex post*, harm-based monetary sanctions can substantially reduce the frequency of an offense. This reduced frequency economizes on the deadweight costs attributable to the offense and on the expenses required to deter it.

Thus, there are compelling reasons to rely on *ex post* deterrence of manipulation. As a result, the existing regulatory structure in the United States, which (1) relies extensively on *ex ante* intervention and (2) has effectively gutted the *ex post* penalties on cornerers, is almost exactly the reverse of the structure which an analysis grounded in law and economics implies is appropriate. This conclusion concerning the inadequacies of the existing regulatory framework in the United States is bolstered when one considers the costs attributable to the other leg of the existing deterrence triad--contractual deterrence.

6.3. *Ex Post* Deterrence vs. Contractual Deterrence

6.3.1. Position Limits

As discussed in Chapter 4, congressional suspicion of all large speculative activities--not simply speculative market-power manipulations--motivated the enactment of position limits in the 1930s. Market-power manipulation deterrence remains, however, a primary justification for their existence.

It is clear that the existing position limits are far broader than necessary to deter corners and squeezes. Most important, deterrence of corners and squeezes would require limits on longs only during the delivery period. (If short market-power manipulation like that analyzed in Chapter 2 were a sufficiently grave danger, position limits on shorts during the delivery period would reduce the likelihood of this form of activity.) Existing position limits are imposed on all speculative positions and not just on long positions during the delivery month. This expanded scope of limits does not provide any additional deterrence of manipulation over and above delivery-month-only limits.

Moreover, the broad limits impair the operation of futures markets in important ways. Specifically, they constrain the risk-shifting capacity of futures markets. Futures markets allow the transfer of risk from very risk-averse hedgers to individuals that are very risk-tolerant (that is, either risk-loving or not very risk-averse) or futures funds that can bear risk at low cost because they facilitate investor diversification. This transfer of risk from parties that incur a high cost to bear it to those that incur a low cost to do so increases the welfare of market participants. Position limits prevent some risk-tolerant individuals and funds from taking positions that would minimize risk-bearing costs. In turn, this constraint on the ability of speculative traders to bear risk can actually produce results that are exactly contrary to the stated purpose behind position limits. In particular, position limits can increase price volatility because when hedging demand increases it is necessary to attract more risk-averse (less risk-tolerant) speculators to the market in order to absorb the risk that hedgers wish to lay off than is the case without position limits. These more risk-averse speculators are willing to absorb the additional risk only if they receive a favorable price. Thus, in a world with position limits, a given change in hedging demand leads to a larger change in price than would occur in the absence of the limits. Put another way, position limits constrain the supply of risk-bearing services and therefore make this supply more inelastic. It is well known that given the volatility of demand for risk-bearing services, a reduction in the elasticity of supply thereof increases the volatility of the price of risk-bearing services. In futures markets, this increase in the volatility of the price of risk-bearing services translates directly into an increase in price volatility.

In addition, position limits may reduce the informational efficiency of futures prices. Position limits sometimes force traders with private information about the value of a commodity to take smaller positions than they would in the absence of such limits. As a result, the realized supply and demand for futures contracts does not fully reflect this private information. Futures prices are less informative as a result. Since the information embedded in futures prices is an important output of futures trading, this is a potentially serious effect of position limits. (It should be noted that constraining informed trading may have some offsetting benefits. In particular, asymmetrically informed trading reduces market liquidity and thereby increases the costs of hedging. Position limits that reduced informed trading could therefore increase market liquidity. However, there is no evidence that this benefit of position limits outweighs the costs attributable to less efficient risk-bearing and reduced price efficiency.)

In sum, broad position limits provide no marginal benefit (relative to delivery-month-only limits) in the form of reduced manipulation and may impose large costs.[7] There is therefore little merit in retaining these limits as a means of deterring market power in futures markets. Delivery-month-only limits are not as costly as the broader limits, however. They could also serve to reduce the frequency of manipulation. Moreover, some writers on futures markets have advocated a reliance on such limits in order to deter manipulation. Some of these proposals actually place an upper bound on the number of deliveries traders can take but this is economically equivalent to a position limit. Therefore, in order to determine the most efficient way to deter the exercise of market power in futures, it is necessary to compare the costs and benefits of delivery-month-only position limits with those pertaining to *ex post* deterrence. (Only *ex post* deterrence is considered because of its superiority to *ex ante* deterrence.)

An analysis of this issue reveals that even delivery-month-only position limits face one severe problem. (For the remainder of this section I will refer to delivery-month-only limits as simply position limits.) Namely, they are necessarily based on less information than is available after the end of trading of a particular futures contract.

The optimal position limit should be determined by trading off the benefits of a smaller limit against the costs of such limits. The benefits of limits stem mainly from a reduction in market power; the costs arise from the fact that position limits can constrain legitimate, competitive speculative activity and thereby impair risk-bearing, price efficiency, and the efficient transfer of commodity ownership via the delivery process. Unfortunately, the fundamental factors that determine these costs and benefits are almost certainly unknown to the regulator charged with setting position limits. For example, the susceptibility of a market to a monopoly power manipulation depends crucially on the spatial distribution of commodity supplies, transport costs, and the reservation prices of competitive producers and consumers of the commodity. (These reservation prices determine the supply and demand curves for the commodity; the model in Chapter 2 reveals the importance of demand elasticity in determining the marginal cost of delivery.) A regulator almost certainly possesses only vague information about these conditions. This is particularly true inasmuch as these conditions can change dramatically and unpredictably over time. Most of the necessary information is scattered among myriad individuals and firms. The information regarding the costs of position limits is similarly inaccessible to the regulator. The effects of position limits on risk-bearing requires information about the supply and demand of risk-bearing services, which in turn depends on individual preferences and the correlations between the prices of the commodity of interest and other asset prices in the economy. Again, such information is largely private and highly dynamic. The effects of limits on price efficiency are impossible to quantify. Finally, the costs of restrictions on the number of deliveries that firms can take depend on the reservation prices of market participants, which are also private information.

There are other complications to setting the "right" limits as well. The Cournot analysis of Chapter 2.4 implies that the susceptibility of a market to manipulation depends on the sizes of all positions in the market. For example, a trader holding a 1 million bushel long position may not be able to exercise market power if 20 other traders are long 5,000 bushels each. However, the trader long the 1 million bushels may be able to exercise substantial market power if two other traders are long 500,000 bushels each. That is, the market power potential of any individual trader depends on the positions held by other traders in the market. Position limits of the kind currently employed do not reflect this complementarity between individual positions in determining the vulnerability of a market to manipulation. Since they do not vary in a discriminating fashion with market concentration, sometimes position limits will be too large and sometimes too small.

In sum, the regulator that establishes position limits necessarily possesses very little information about their costs and benefits. As a result, the regulator will sometimes choose position limits that are too stringent and sometimes will choose limits that are too lax. Such errors can impose substantial costs on market participants in the form of incomplete risk-shifting, inefficient transfer of commodity ownership, and manipulation (which will occur if limits are too small given prevailing market conditions).

It is also necessary to recognize that position limits impose substantial administrative costs. It is necessary to collect information about trader activities on a continuous basis and to monitor the accuracy of this information. Moreover, it is possible for traders to circumvent limits through collusion. Several ostensibly independent traders can agree to act in concert. Each buys the maximum amount allowed under the position limit but by acting together at contract expiration can effectively control a position far larger than allowed by the limit. Although position limits can be constructed to proscribe such collusion, it is costly to enforce such proscriptions. Thus, the necessity of policing collusion in order to make position limits effective inflates the costs of using such limits to deter manipulation.

Despite these costs, delivery-month-only position limits could still be desirable unless there is some more efficient means of manipulation deterrence. Given the attractive features of *ex post* deterrence of manipulation, however, it is highly unlikely that position limits are the most efficient way to curb corners. As noted earlier, *ex post* deterrence can rely on far better information than is available before the expiration of a futures contract. Indeed, in this regard, even *ex ante* deterrence offers advantages over position limits, as the *ex ante* regulator can rely on information embedded in market prices and quantities to reach his decisions. Moreover, *ex post* deterrence offers administrative cost advantages over position limits because harm-based sanctions impose enforcement costs only in the (unlikely) event of a bad act, whereas position limits require continuous expenditures for data collection and policing. Furthermore, position limits offer no appreciable advantages over *ex post* deterrence to offset these handicaps. Therefore, even delivery-month-only position limits--which are less costly than the existing position limits--are almost certainly a less efficient means of deterring corners than properly executed *ex post* deterrence.

6.3.2. Restrictions on Entry

Another form of contractual deterrence used in the United States is the contract designation process, which prevents the trading of futures contracts that are deemed too susceptible to manipulation. This method also suffers from severe defects.

As is the case with position limits and *ex ante* deterrence, a major disadvantage of entry requirements relates to the poor information possessed by the regulator at the time of a contract's introduction. The analysis in Chapters 2 and 3 implies that a contract's susceptibility to information depends on the factors that determine the marginal cost of delivery (such as, transport costs, the spatial distribution of consumption and production and demand elasticities) as well as the level and variability of trading volume. Much of the information about these factors is private and therefore very costly for the regulator to obtain, if he can obtain it at all. Even if the regulator can obtain good information concerning the marginal cost of delivery at the time a contract is introduced, these factors can change dramatically and unpredictably over time. Thus, prior review may do little to prevent manipulation in the future, or may turn out to be too restrictive. Moreover, other information that determines a contract's manipulability--especially concerning its trading volume and the variability of this volume--cannot be observed at all before trading begins. As was seen before, this poor information makes it highly likely that prior review will not reliably deter manipulation in a cost-efficient fashion.

Other considerations also inflate the costs of using entry restrictions to prevent manipulation. Most important, if a contract is traded despite the fact that it is manipulated often, it is necessarily the case that the private benefits of trading exceed the private costs. That is, the net private benefit of an actively traded contract is positive regardless of the frequency with which it is manipulated. Barring or delaying the trading of this contract because it is too susceptible to manipulation destroys this private benefit. This is costly. Therefore, entry restrictions (or an outright ban of a contract) can create a positive net social benefit if and only if the harmful externalities caused by manipulation exceed the sum of (1) the net private benefit earned by those who trade the contract and (2) the positive externalities resulting from the introduction of a new contract.

It is highly unlikely that this condition could ever hold in practice. The primary positive externality that results from the introduction of a new contract is the value of the information summarized in the futures price. The futures price communicates dispersed private information about supply and demand conditions to producers and consumers. This information allows these agents to make better decisions about production, storage and consumption. The primary negative externality that results from manipulation is that it reduces the informativeness of the futures price. Manipulation reduces price informativeness for two reasons. First, manipulations cause the futures and spot prices at contract expiration to diverge substantially and unpredictably from the competitive price. This divergence reflects the artificial stimulus of the demand for deliveries due to the exercise of market power and therefore obscures the effect of underlying supply and demand fundamentals on prices. Second, as noted in Chapter 3, the mere possibility of manipulation causes futures prices to vary unpredictably with uninformative shocks to noise trader (that is, hedging and speculative) order flow.

Even though manipulation reduces the informativeness of futures prices, it is exceedingly implausible that there is less information available to producers and consumers if an oft-manipulated contract is allowed to trade than if no trading in the contract is permitted. To the extent that the futures price is uninformative due to manipulation-induced noise, market participants always have the option to ignore the futures price altogether and simply rely on the information that they would possess if the futures contract did not exist. That is, the existence of an uninformative futures price does not destroy the information that market participants already possess. Moreover, the price of even an oft-manipulated contract may transmit substantial information about fundamentals. Therefore, delaying entry of a futures contract or banning it altogether cannot eliminate harmful externalities that are more costly than the private net benefits and positive externalities that would be realized if the contract were traded. (Moreover, even if the condition could hold as a theoretical possibility, a regulator would not possess the information required to verify the condition's relevance with any accuracy. As a result, the decision making process would be error riddled; consequently, the regulator would allow some contracts where the condition did hold to trade anyway and would delay or ban some contracts where the condition did not hold.)

In sum, the net benefit of entry regulation is almost certainly negative. Delaying the entry of a contract or banning one altogether, destroys wealth even if it reduces the frequency of manipulation. Moreover, the review of contracts prior to designation is costly for both the government regulator and for the exchange that creates a new contract. Indeed, these costs can be quite large. According to the staff members of several major United States exchanges, the direct costs of obtaining regulatory approval on an innovative contract can run into the millions of dollars. Moreover, exchanges and would-be traders incur substantial opportunity costs as well. The contract review process can last up to three to four years for an innovative contract. The benefits of trading during this period are forever foregone. Moreover, the regulatory delays in the United States can present a competitive advantage to overseas exchanges that are not subject to similar lags in listing contracts. These expenses exacerbate the costs of entry restrictions. Therefore, the contract designation process is a perverse way to prevent market-power manipulation.

6.3.3. Delivery Options

As demonstrated in Chapter 2, delivery options reduce the profitability of manipulation by increasing the elasticity of the marginal cost of delivery function. In contrast to the other means of contractual deterrence, there is no compelling evidence that this benefit comes at the expense of substantial costs. Indeed, theory suggests that adding delivery options may improve hedging effectiveness for a variety of hedgers for spatial commodities as well as reduce the frequency of manipulation. Moreover, there is empirical evidence to support this theoretical prediction. Therefore, of all the forms of contractual deterrence, the expansion of shorts' contractual rights is the most attractive.

Some analysts argue that delivery options are a costly manipulation deterrent because they reduce the hedging effectiveness of futures contracts.[8] Their reasoning is that adding delivery options reduces the correlation between the futures price and the cash price in the original deliverable commodity (that is, the sole commodity that was deliverable prior to the addition of delivery options). Since the hedging effectiveness of a contract is greater, the greater the correlation between the futures price and the good to be hedged, it is certainly true that the reduction of the correlation between the futures price and the price of the original deliverable harms those hedging this particular commodity.

This fact is not sufficient to imply, however, that the provision of delivery options makes *all* hedgers worse off. Not all hedgers want to reduce the risk of transacting in the original deliverable. Some hedgers want to manage the risk of holding inventories at locations away from the original delivery point. For example, a mill operator may use the Kansas City Board of Trade wheat futures contract to hedge his inventories of wheat held in South Dakota. Some traders want to hedge the risk of transacting in grades that differ from the original deliverable. For instance, a consumer of durum wheat may use the hard spring wheat futures contract traded on the Minneapolis Grain Exchange. Thus, for spatial commodities or commodities which vary extensively in quality, most hedges are so-called *cross-hedges* where there is a mismatch in the location or grade of the hedge and the location or grade deliverable against any futures contract. Indeed, the contracts most susceptible to manipulation--spatial commodities like grains, for instance--are widely used by cross-hedgers. For such commodities, it is therefore a non sequitur to assert that a decline in hedging effectiveness for the original deliverable caused by the addition of delivery options uniformly impairs hedging effectiveness. Instead, it is necessary to determine how such an expansion in delivery points or grades affect hedging effectiveness for cross-hedgers as well as hedgers of the original deliverable.

Along with Roger Kormendi and Philip Meguire, I have examined this issue in detail. This analysis demonstrates that expanding delivery options can improve the effectiveness of cross-hedges for three reasons. First, in a spatial market, the futures price of a contract requiring delivery at a single location and of a single grade varies with idiosyncratic shocks to supply and demand for that grade at that location. For example, an increase (decrease) in demand for corn in Chicago raises (lowers) the price there by a larger amount than at locations away from Chicago. Therefore, if demand and supply shocks are imperfectly correlated across locations and grades, relative prices will vary randomly. These relative price variations imply that cross-hedges are imperfect.

It is well known that one way to reduce the risk attributable to idiosyncratic shocks is to construct a diversified portfolio. In effect, a futures contract with multiple deliverable grades or locations is a diversified portfolio. For example, the theory of delivery option pricing implies that the price of a futures contract permitting delivery of corn in Chicago, Toledo, St. Louis, and Kansas City behaves like a portfolio consisting of corn inventories held in each of the four cities. (The weights in this portfolio depend on (1) the relative prices at the four locations and (2) any exchange-established delivery price premia or discounts.) Like the price of any portfolio, the futures price of the contract allowing delivery options is less affected by idiosyncratic supply and demand shocks at any one of the four locations than is a contract requiring delivery at only one point. As a result, diversification reduces the location-specific "noise" in the futures price. This tends to increase its effectiveness as a cross-hedging tool.

A formal analysis demonstrates this point clearly. Consider a futures contract that allows shorts to deliver at n different locations. The cash forward prices at these locations are distributed lognormally and trading in the futures and cash markets is continuous and costless. The theory of delivery options implies that the futures price at time t with τ years to contract expiration equals

$$F(t) = \sum_{i=1}^{n} P_i(t) w_i(t) \tag{6.1}$$

where $P_i(t)$ is the forward price at location i at time t, and $w_i(t)$ is a weight that is less than one and where the sum of the weights on the n cash prices is also less than one. The weights are functions of the prices of all the deliverable cash prices and time to contract expiration. In general, the weight at location i increases as the price at that location falls relative to the prices at other delivery points.[9]

It is possible to demonstrate that the instantaneous correlation between the percentage change in the futures price (as given by the foregoing expression) and the percentage change in price at any location z (which may or may not be a delivery point) equals

$$\rho_{Fz}(t) = \sum_{i=1}^{n} \frac{\rho_{iz}\sigma_i}{\sigma_F(t)} w_i(t) \qquad (6.2)$$

where ρ_{iz} is the correlation between the percentage change in the forward prices at point z and delivery location i; σ_i is the standard deviation in the percentage change in the forward price at location i; and the standard deviation in the futures price is

$$\sigma_F(t) = \sqrt{\sum_{i=1}^{n}\sum_{j=1}^{n} w_i(t) w_j(t) \rho_{ij} \sigma_i \sigma_j} \qquad (6.3)$$

Given these formulae, a somewhat extreme example shows how expanding the number of delivery points can reduce the variance of the futures price. Assume $\sigma_i = \sigma_j = \sigma$ and $\rho_{ij} = \rho_{iz} = \rho_{jz} = \rho < 1$ for all $i \neq z$ and $j \neq z$. Then

$$\sigma_F(t) = \sigma \sqrt{\sum_{i=1}^{n} w_i^2(t) + \sum_{i=1}^{n}\sum_{j=1}^{n} w_i(t) w_j(t) \rho^2} \qquad (6.4)$$

Note that since (1) $w_i(t) < 1$ for all i and (2) the weights at each location approach 0 as n becomes large the first summation term approaches 0 for large n. Thus, for a large number of delivery points

$$\sigma_F(t) = \sigma\rho \sqrt{\sum_{i=1}^{n} w_i(t) \sum_{j \neq i}^{n} w_j(t)} \approx \sigma\rho \qquad (6.5)$$

The second approximation follows from the fact that the sum of the weights is approximately equal to one when the number of delivery points is large. Moreover, under these assumptions, for large n the numerator in (6.2) is also equal to $\sigma\rho$. Thus, for a large number of delivery points, $\rho_{Fz}(t) \approx 1$ even though $\rho_{Fz}(t) < 1$.

This result shows that increasing the number of delivery points can reduce the variance in a hedgers wealth in the same way as an increase in the number of securities held in a portfolio can reduce the variance of an investor's wealth. namely, diversification reduces idiosyncratic variance. Although the formal analysis makes simplifying assumptions and assumes a large number of delivery points, simulation results (described shortly) demonstrate that diversification of location-specific noise can also substantially improve hedging effectiveness under more realistic assumptions and for a smaller number of delivery points.

Adding delivery points can improve hedging effectiveness for another reason. Specifically, the analysis of Chapters 2 and 3 implies that manipulation reduces cross-hedging effectiveness because it causes unpredictable variations in relative prices both before and during the delivery period. That is, a corner causes an increase in the price in the delivery market relative to the price in other markets. This harms (benefits) short (long) hedgers in those other markets. Since manipulation is unpredictable, moreover, these relative price shocks are stochastic. This increased relative price risk reduces hedging effectiveness. In addition, recall from Chapter 3 that the mere possibility of manipulation causes the basis between the delivery market and other markets to vary randomly with order flow shocks. This basis risk further impairs hedging effectiveness. To the extent that the addition of delivery options reduces the frequency of manipulation--and thus reduces the frequency and severity of these relative price shocks--cross-hedgers benefit.

Moreover, even if hedgers of the original deliverable suffer reductions in hedging effectiveness due to the addition of new delivery points and grades, hedgers of the new deliverable(s) may enjoy an improvement in hedging effectiveness.

In order to determine the importance of these effects, Pirrong, Kormendi and Meguire (PKM) conduct a simulation analysis calibrated to corn and soybean prices from the 1984 through 1989 period.[10] This analysis shows that expanding delivery options can increase substantially the hedging effectiveness of futures contracts. Specifically, PKM simulate how adding St. Louis and Toledo as delivery points at price differentials that reflect the typical price differences between markets to Chicago Board of Trade corn and soybean futures contracts affects their hedging effectiveness at several important grain producing, processing or exporting locations. These locations include Central Illinois, Central Iowa, Kansas City, Minneapolis, and the Gulf of Mexico. In virtually all simulations, the correlations between cash price changes in these locations and the change in the price of the broad contract are higher than the corresponding correlations between the cash price changes and the change in the price of a contract allowing delivery at Chicago only.

Obviously, the broader contact provides a poorer hedge in Chicago than the single delivery point contract but this is of little importance given the fact that Chicago is currently far less important as a cash grain center than the other locations studied. Thus, contrary to the claims cited earlier, a futures contract including delivery options to deter manipulation need not reduce its value as a hedging instrument. Indeed, expanding the number of delivery options can dramatically improve hedging performance for a majority of hedgers. Therefore, this is a potentially attractive way to reduce the profitability of market manipulation.

Adding delivery options can have other desirable effects. Most important, delivery point-specific demand and supply conditions play a smaller role in determining the futures price with a broad futures contract. For example, the price a broad grain contract allowing shorts to deliver at Chicago, Toledo, St. Louis, and Kansas City reflects supply and demand conditions in each of these locations. Idiosyncratic conditions at any one location exert little influence on price. As a result, systemic supply and demand conditions (such as, an export boom, or a nationwide drought) are the primary determinant of the futures price. In contrast, the price for a contract calling for delivery in Chicago depends more on technical conditions in that city and less on systemic conditions than the broad contract. Thus, a broad futures contract can provide a more accurate measure of systemic demand and supply fundamentals. This enhances the value of the futures contract as a price-discovery tool for individuals and firms located away from the delivery point. Moreover, a futures contract including numerous delivery options is similar to a market basket security. Individuals with private information about supply and demand conditions at a particular location (such as, Chicago) find trading on this information less profitable if the futures contract calls for delivery at several points (such as, St. Louis, Toledo, and Chicago) than if it calls for delivery in Chicago alone. Therefore, a broadening of the delivery terms of a futures contract attenuates the adverse selection problem that arises from the existence of private, location-specific information. This improves contract liquidity, which further benefits hedgers.

The main disadvantage of a contract with multiple delivery points or grades is that it is a less effective means of transferring ownership of the physical commodity. Longs may receive delivery of the commodity at an unsatisfactory location. For example, a corn miller in Chicago may receive delivery in St. Louis if the corn futures contract allows delivery in both locations. This may require the miller to acquire corn on the cash market rather than via the delivery process. This may be costlier to the miller than taking delivery on a contract that allows delivery in Chicago only.

Although the futures delivery process does serve as a merchandising tool for all physical commodities, this is a secondary function of futures markets. Even using a grossly upward biased measure of deliveries and a grossly downward biased measure of the number of hedges during the 1984 through 1989 period, delivery occurred on only about 11.6 percent of wheat hedges, 2.7 percent of corn hedges, and 8.8 percent of soybean hedges. Given the substantial bias in the data available to make this calculation, it is evident that few hedges are closed by delivery.[11] Thus, the merchandising function of grain futures contracts is secondary to the hedging and speculative functions. Similarly biased measures of the importance of delivery on the crude oil, heating oil and gasoline contracts produce the same result. From the beginning of trading of each contract through 1992, the upward-biased delivery-to-hedge ratio has averaged .69 percent for crude oil, 2.77 percent for heating oil, and 4.80 percent for gasoline. In sum, data from the two most important groups of physical commodity futures contracts--grains and energy--demonstrate that delivery for merchandising purposes is unimportant to use of the contracts for hedging purposes.

Given minor role of futures contracts as a means of transferring ownership of physical commodities, the addition of some delivery options to a futures contract is unlikely to impose substantial costs on market users. Since the addition of delivery options can offer substantial benefits in the form of less manipulation, superior hedging effectiveness, better price discovery, and enhanced liquidity, there are compelling reasons to use this form of contractual deterrence.

In sum, the benefits of allowing delivery at a variety of points (or of a variety of grades) may well exceed the costs. This does not imply, however, that delivery options are more than a supplement to *ex post* deterrence. Manipulation can still occur even if shorts have delivery options. Moreover, it is necessary to consider whether exchanges or the government will have the appropriate incentives to chose the right delivery mechanism. Again, information considerations are paramount here. Moreover, exchanges may have very weak incentives to reduce the frequency of manipulation. This is true for two reasons. First, most of the costs of manipulation may well be external to exchange members. Second, the political nature of exchange governance may make collective action to add delivery points very costly. In addition to affecting the probability of manipulation, changes in delivery specification can also affect the distribution of wealth among exchange members. Conflicts over these rents may make it difficult, if not impossible, for the exchange to adopt the efficient set of rules.[12]

Historical experience suggests that these considerations may be important. The New York Cotton Exchange refused to add delivery points in the South even though its contracts (which allowed delivery only in New York, a dying cotton port) were frequently manipulated. Similarly, during the nineteenth and early twentieth centuries the Chicago Board of Trade often refused to extend delivery options to shorts even during acute corners despite the fact that it was well understood that the existing narrow delivery specifications encouraged manipulation. In addition, the exchange members voted down a rule permitting delivery in railcars even during a period in which regular warehouse space was declining substantially, thereby facilitating squeezes. Although the exchange passed the rule in 1914, it revoked it eighteen years later. In more recent times, the CBT added delivery points in the aftermath of the Ferruzzi squeeze of 1989 only under immense pressure from the government and important cash market interests.

Since (1) exchanges may not have the appropriate incentive to devise a delivery system that efficiently deters manipulation and (2) government regulators may not have the requisite information or incentive, it is unwise to eschew *ex post* deterrence measures and rely exclusively on delivery options to control manipulation.

The incentives of exchange members to deter manipulation and the costs they incur doing so, raises another, more general issue: Who should bear the primary responsibility for deterring and preventing manipulation, exchanges or the government? Current United States law relies heavily on the former. The following section analyzes this issue in detail.

6.4. Who Should Regulate: Exchanges or the Government?

The foregoing analysis strongly supports the view that *ex post* deterrence is the most cost-effective way to reduce the frequency of market-power manipulation. There is also reason to believe that the expansion of delivery options also represent an economical way to deter manipulation. These conclusions do not complete an analysis of efficient manipulation deterrence, however. It is also necessary to determine the identity of the optimal enforcer.

Current United States law designates two enforcers: a government agency (the CFTC) supplemented by the courts and the futures exchanges themselves. That is, ever since the passage of the Futures Trading Act of 1921, United States commodity law has relied heavily on exchange self-regulation to deter manipulation.

This reliance on self-regulation is problematic, at best. This is especially true for *ex post* deterrence. Exchanges do not possess police power to enforce sanctions. As private organizations, exchanges do not possess the same power to levy sanctions as the state. An exchange can revoke a manipulator's trading privileges but does not have the same power to fine and impose damages as the state. This limits its ability to deter manipulation. Moreover, even if this problem could be overcome, the nature of commodity exchanges and exchange governance makes them less effective fact-finders and adjudicators than independent bodies like the courts or the commissioners of an independent agency accountable to the executive and legislative branches of government. Exchanges are membership organizations. *Ex post* adjudication by exchanges requires members to judge and perhaps sanction other members. These members expect to trade with one another in the future. Even if a decision maker does not have a personal stake in his decision, he expects to deal in the future with those that do. This repeated interaction between parties facilitates cooperation between those accused of manipulation, those judging them, and other exchange members that have a vested interest in the issue. This may permit rent-seeking longs or shorts to influence decisions. Such influence activities increase the probability of Type I and Type II errors.

There are strong reasons to believe that self-regulation may be an ineffective way to implement *ex ante* and contractual deterrents as well. I have analyzed this issue in excruciating detail in earlier work, so in the interest of brevity I will simply review the broad outlines of the argument here; the interested reader is invited to consult my longer analysis.[13] Put simply, exchanges may have very weak incentives to impose these measures. Moreover, they may incur very large costs to intervene in the market or alter the contractual rights and duties of market participants. I consider these issues in turn.

Exchange members may receive few benefits from preventing manipulation for a variety of reasons. First, the benefits exchange members receive when they reduce the frequency and profitability of manipulation depend on how manipulation affects the marginal demanders of exchange services. These marginal demanders determine the price and quantity of services exchange members sell. However, the social costs of manipulation also depend on how the exercise of market power affects inframarginal demanders of exchange services. Since the harm imposed by corners on these inframarginal demanders has no impact on the price or quantity of services exchange members sell, they have no incentive to take these harms into account. This tends to lead the exchange to take too little effort to prevent manipulation. This is especially the case if manipulation increases the demand for exchange member services at the margin even as it imposes substantial costs on inframarginal demanders. This may be true for two reasons. First, manipulators trade in massive quantities, which offsets in whole or in part any loss in business from hedgers and speculators that results from manipulation. Second, speculators may be attracted to a market by the increased price volatility that results from manipulation.

A positive relation between exchange member wealth and manipulation is not merely a theoretical possibility. Historical experience suggests that corners excited intense speculative interest in futures trading and that exchange volume increased as a result. At the Chicago Board of Trade, brokerage clerks frequently struck for higher wages during squeezes because their services were vital during the hectic trading that accompanied them and brokerage firms frequently earned very large commissions during corners.[14] On the New York Cotton Exchange, brokers gave the manipulator Sully a "cotton boll parade" in which they showered him with cotton fluff because they were grateful for the volume his corner caused. Most tellingly, during the huge Patten cotton corner of 1910, the price of an NYCE seat rose 150 percent due to higher trading volume.[15] During Patten's trial on antitrust charges, he argued--and the Circuit Court and Supreme Court agreed--that corners actually increase trading volume.[16] Given these facts, it is not surprising that some futures markets participants have stated that corners can increase exchange business. For example, an ex-president of the CBT stated that "to be frank about it, I think these occasional congestions add to the attractiveness of the market to the public. Like the congestion we had in 1921, I think it stimulated trade, not discouraged it." [17] This evidence that manipulation and high volume go hand in hand (or that at the very least exchange members believe it does) implies that exchange members may have little incentive to deter corners.

Second, corners reduce the informativeness of futures prices but this cost is largely external to exchange members. Informative prices are valuable to society because they allow producers and consumers to allocate resources more efficiently. There is only a tenuous tie--if there is any tie at all--between this value and the demand to trade futures contracts. Therefore, a substantial decline in price informativeness may impose only a trivial cost on exchange members. This further dulls their incentive to deter manipulation.

Third, competition does not discipline exchanges that fail to deter manipulation. The nature of futures trading makes a futures contract on a given commodity--such as corn--a natural monopoly. A contract's liquidity is maximized if all trading is concentrated on a single exchange. Since a liquid contract is cheaper to trade, this is a strong force to centralize trading in a particular commodity in a single market. Moreover, an exchange's natural monopoly is not perfectly contestable. That is, potential entrants into the market for corn futures contracts (for instance) incur higher costs than the incumbent exchange. This is true because a new entrant must coordinate the simultaneous defection of all of the traders using the contract traded at the incumbent exchange in order to achieve the same liquidity as offered by the incumbent's contract. Such coordination is costly. Therefore, even if a competing exchange offers a contract or rules that make manipulation less likely than is the case for the existing contract, traders may continue to trade the existing instrument because it is more liquid. Furthermore, the externalities discussed in the previous paragraphs are likely to plague both the incumbent exchange and any potential entrant. If so, the potential entrant cannot credibly threaten to deter manipulation more effectively than the initial entrant. As a result, competition will not induce the incumbent exchange to take better measures to deter manipulation.

Two factors inflate the costs exchanges incur to employ *ex ante* or contractual deterrents. First, an exchange that employs *ex ante* deterrence measures intervenes in the contracting process. These interventions redistribute wealth among buyers and sellers of futures contracts. This redistribution potential creates incentives for traders to engage in rent-seeking. During a manipulation, longs will attempt to influence exchange decision makers to allow the completion of a corner; shorts will attempt to do the opposite. If longs are successful in convincing an exchange's decision makers from intervening during a corner, a Type II error will occur. Since during a corner, longs are concentrated and have a large *per capita* stake in ensuring the success of a manipulation, they have very strong incentives to exert influence. As a result, they may frequently succeed in their object.

Rent-seeking also raises the probability of a Type I error. Even when no manipulation occurs, shorts have an incentive to induce exchange decision makers to take actions that would reduce futures prices. By alleging the existence of a corner (even when one does not exist), shorts may be able to persuade exchange decision makers to force a settlement at a price favorable to shorts. These Type I errors are very costly to an exchange and undermine the fundamental purpose of futures exchanges--the enforcement of contractual obligations assumed voluntarily in competitive conditions. That is, the enforcement of antimanipulation rules clashes with the primary function exchanges serve. Therefore, the enforcement of these rules may be very costly and exchanges may be extremely reluctant to do so.

The second reason that exchanges may incur high costs to use *ex ante* measures is that the enforcement of rules is effectively a nonexcludable public good. Any benefits resulting from a reduction in manipulation accrue to all exchange members, although in varying amounts. In these circumstances, an individual exchange member therefore has an incentive to free ride off of the enforcement efforts of other members. Indeed, the literature on the private provision of public goods implies that if the number of exchange members is large, this free-rider problem induces an exchange to spend far less on the enforcement of anticorner rules than the amount that would maximize the wealth of exchange members. Thus, even if exchange members internalize a large portion of the costs of manipulation, they may have little incentive to deter it because of the public good nature of enforcement.

In sum, theory suggests that exchange members may incur very high costs and receive very few benefits from the deterrence of manipulation. This would induce them to take few *ex ante* or contractual measures to prevent it. An examination of the historical record bears out this prediction. In the era prior to the passage of laws requiring exchanges to self-regulate in order to prevent manipulation, exchanges largely failed to do so. The Chicago Board of Trade adopted rules against manipulation on three separate occasions in the 1868-1921 period but twice repealed them. Even when the rules were in force, the Board did not use them to punish manipulators. The CBT also steadfastly refused to liberalize contract delivery terms for most of the period between 1868 and 1915.[18]

The reasons for both the repeal of the rules and the failure to enforce them are consistent with the theoretical analysis just presented. Specifically, the attempted enforcement of anticorner rules sparked intense rent-seeking contests that undermined the ability of the exchange to enforce futures contracts. Moreover, business on the exchange frequently boomed during corners. Finally, exchange members expressed little concern for the effect of corners on hedgers (who were likely inframarginal consumers of exchange services).[19]

Other prominent exchanges, such as the New York and New Orleans Cotton Exchanges, the New York Produce Exchange, the New York Petroleum Exchange, the Oil City Oil Exchange, the Titusville Oil Exchange, the New York Stock Exchange, and the New York Gold Exchange--also failed to adopt anticorner rules or to revise contractual terms to reduce the profitability of manipulation. The case of the New York Cotton Exchange is particularly instructive. Despite the fact that the Federal Trade Commission found that the exchange's contract was so "frequently cornered" that it was "a truism to state that for some years past the New York futures market has failed to perform satisfactorily . . . [as] as safe hedge for cotton merchants"[20] the exchange took no actions to reduce the frequency or severity of corners. Unlike the Chicago Board of Trade, the exchange did not pass rules banning corners. Moreover, despite the fact that the New York cash cotton market declined dramatically in importance during the last quarter of the nineteenth century, the exchange refused point-blank to add delivery points in Southern cities located along the primary cotton transport routes. In part, this inaction was due to the fact that exchange business increased dramatically during corners as was noted earlier.

In sum, both theory and history strongly suggest that self-regulation of manipulation is a very ineffective form of manipulation deterrence. This analysis raises the question: If self-regulation is so problematic, why does United States commodity law rely so heavily on it? A reading of the legislative history of the FTA suggests that the mutual interests of Congress and the exchanges--especially the Chicago Board of Trade--made self-regulation a convenient legislative solution.

Exchange members were violently opposed to any government intervention into their affairs. Their imaginations heated by fresh images of the Russian Revolution, some futures traders considered any regulation of their industry a "Bolshevist" outrage.[21] In all fairness, some of the rhetoric directed against futures trading by witnesses before the House and Senate committees and by the congressmen themselves was extremely tendentious and highly misleading.[22] Moreover, exchange enemies within and without the Congress periodically floated radical proposals to reduce futures trading or to eliminate it altogether. Thus, exchange members were rightly concerned about ham-handed intervention. Exchange members saw in self-regulation a means of avoiding more direct government control of the market.

In arguing against the Futures Trading Act, exchange representatives testifying before Congress consistently argued that government regulation was unnecessary because exchanges could deter manipulation. For example, Julius Barnes, a grain merchant and former President of the government's United States Grain Corporation during WWI, asserted that:

> Exchanges clearly have made some progress in eliminating these things [that is, corners]. . . . The same objectives [as government regulation] can be attained through the action of exchanges themselves, without risking the unnecessary disturbance which follows the injection of government regulation unnecessarily into business.[23]

Similarly, Chairman Moore of the Duluth Board of Trade argued that "manipulation is so infrequent and usually so obvious when it is in progress that the exchange can easily check it."[24]

For its part, Congress was willing to rely mainly on self-regulation because it wanted to deter manipulation but was at a loss on how to achieve this end directly. The statement of the Chairman of the Senate Agriculture Committee--Senator Norris from Minnesota--during hearings on the Futures Trading Act is revealing in this regard:

> The difficulty, as I understand it, is that these things [that is, what constitutes manipulation] are various and perhaps impossible of direct definition. I do not know how we could draw a definition to bring it home to the individual.[25] At least it

is the theory of the bill, as I understand it . . . that the board of trade itself could bring about these reforms, and they [that is, the House and the Senate] are trying to hold the board of trade responsible.[26]

This inability of Congress to deter manipulation through the imposition of sanctions on individual manipulators is rooted in its confusion over what kinds of futures trading is manipulative. As noted in Chapter 4, it is clear that although the supporters of futures regulation considered the exercise of market power manipulative, they also strongly believed that other kinds of conduct were manipulative as well. Indeed, the sponsors of the bill--Senator Capper and Representative Tincher, both of Kansas--were far more interested in preventing short manipulation than stopping corners. They could neither define nor enumerate, however, these other forms of manipulation with sufficient precision to permit the creation of an antimanipulation statute that courts or a government agency could effectively enforce. Instead, Congress dumped the problem into the hands of the exchanges.[27] The exchanges were not enamored with the method that the FTA and GFA utilized to incent them to prevent manipulation--the ability of the Secretary of Agriculture to suspend trading of a futures contract--but they grudgingly preferred self-regulation to more direct government intervention into the markets.[28]

In sum, the statutory reliance on self-regulation of manipulation was in large part the product of congressional confusion. If Congress had limited its attempts to regulate manipulation to the deterrence of those forms of manipulation that were more clearly understood in the grain markets and the courts--corners and squeezes--it would have been possible to create a legal mechanism to sanction individual manipulators; in Senator Norris' words, to "bring it [punishment for manipulation] home to the individual." Note that in the decision in the antitrust case of United States v. Patten, the Supreme Court had already demonstrated that it was possible to identify and punish cornerers *ex post*; moreover, the Court's decision in the case establishing the constitutionality of federal commodities regulation would soon give more evidence of the ability of courts to recognize corners. Instead of relying on courts to punish individual manipulators *ex post*, however, Congress chose to enact a broad proscription that it did not know how to enforce and "passed the buck" to the exchanges.

A law clearly focused on deterring market-power manipulation alone would avoid the sorts of difficulties that the existing broad and vague law creates. The enactment of a properly constructed *ex post* deterrent of corners and squeezes enforced by the courts or by the CFTC could free exchanges from an activity in which they do not have a comparative advantage--the prevention of manipulation. This would allow exchanges to engage in those activities in which they do have a strong comparative advantage: the development of institutions to control credit risk and the creation of new types of contingent claims.

6.5. A Proposal to Reform United States Manipulation Law

Two conclusions follow from the preceding analysis:

- *Ex post*, harm-based sanctions are the most efficient way to deter market-power manipulations.

- Government, rather than exchanges, are best suited to impose *ex post* sanctions.

The first conclusion flows from the analysis of the optimal methods of law enforcement contained in the law and economics literature. This literature implies that four factors affect the optimal form of enforcement. *Ex post*, harm-based sanctions are preferable to preventative measures for an offense with the following characteristics:

- The probability that the offense is detected is high.

- The malfeasor has the financial capacity to pay damages or fines equal to the magnitude of the harm done.

- The malfeasor knows that he is committing an offense.

- The administrative costs of imposing harm-based sanctions or small.

Each condition obtains for a market-power manipulation. As demonstrated in Chapters 5 and 6, manipulation has distinctive effects on prices and quantities that are readily measured. This allows the detection of corners, especially the acute corners that are most important to deter. Successful manipulators can be forced to disgorge their winnings; unsuccessful manipulators pay damages imposed by the marketplace. In addition, a would-be manipulator requires substantial financial resources in order to complete a corner. He therefore possesses the financial capacity to pay punitive damages. Furthermore, one cannot corner a market by accident. The execution of a market-power manipulation requires the perpetrator to take positive, conscious actions that have effects on prices--and thus the manipulator's wealth--that are impossible to miss. Since a cornerer acts with full knowledge of his actions, he can be deterred by the prospect of paying substantial sanctions. Finally, administrative expenses are incurred in an *ex post* regime only in the event a manipulation occurs. Since the reliable imposition of penalties ensured by conditions 1-3 sharply reduces the profitability of manipulation, corners will seldom occur. This implies that administrative expenses will be small as well. In sum, all of the conditions that favor *ex post* deterrence hold in the case of market-power manipulation.

The second conclusion flows from an analysis of the incentives exchanges face to deter corners. Theory suggests that most of the benefits of manipulation deterrence are external to the exchange. Moreover, its members may incur very high costs to prevent corners because of rent-seeking and free-rider problems. The historical record of self-regulation suggests that left to their own devices, exchanges will take very few measures to reduce the frequency and severity of manipulation. Therefore, government regulation is preferable to pure self-regulation if the reduction in the cost of manipulation (net of enforcement cost) that results from regulation is positive. Since (1) the characteristics of market-power manipulation make it perfectly suited to deterrence through the use of harm-based sanctions and (2) courts are better suited to impose these sanctions than exchanges, it is almost certainly the case that a reliance on court enforced *ex post* deterrence is more efficient than pure self-regulation.

Unfortunately, the contrast between existing antimanipulation law in the United States and the efficient structure implied by economic analysis could not be more stark. A series of recent court and regulatory decisions have neutered *ex post* deterrence of corners. Instead, *ex ante* emergency measures and objectionable forms of contractual deterrence including broad position limits and entry barriers are currently the most important bulwarks against corners. Moreover, current federal commodity law relies heavily on exchange self-regulation.

The costs of this maladapted regulation are probably quite large. This is true because each of the measures employed to prevent manipulation constrain the ability of futures markets to perform their essential functions. *Ex ante* emergency measures can interfere with the competitive pricing mechanism. Position limits impede the efficient transfer of risk to those who bear it at a low cost (including both individual speculators and funds with numerous investors). Entry barriers raise the costs of creating new contracts. This reduces the number of futures contracts introduced. Moreover, regulatory delays deny market participants the opportunity to trade those contracts that are introduced for some period of time, thereby causing them to forego the benefits of hedging and speculation during this interval.

Due to the excessive costs of deterring manipulation inherent in existing United States commodity law, the public interest would be well served by a complete revision of the relevant statutes. The revised statute should focus explicitly and exclusively on the exercise of market power during the delivery period. The existing overbroad prohibition of "manipulation," which is predicated on a belief that much speculative activity--especially short selling--is harmful, has created much confusion and has motivated much bad policy. In order to achieve this objective, the language of the revised statute could be patterned on Section 1 of the Sherman Anti-Trust Act, which makes it a crime to "monopolize or attempt to monopolize or combine or conspire with any other persons to monopolize" a market. For example, it could read

> Any person or firm who during the delivery period of any commodity traded for future delivery shall exercise market (or monopoly) power or attempt to exercise market (or monopoly) power in that commodity or restrain or attempt to restrain the trade of that commodity, shall be guilty of a felony.

Moreover, the revised antimanipulation section(s) should specify the sort of evidence that courts can rely on to determine whether a trader has exercised market power. In particular, the law should prescribe, endorse, recommend, or explicitly allow the use of econometric and statistical evidence to determine whether a trader has exercised market power. Price and quantity patterns that can provide evidence of market power should include large declines in cash market prices absolutely, relative to deferred futures prices and relative to prices at other locations when a futures contract is liquidated; large spreads between the prices of expiring and deferred futures contracts, especially if there are large stocks in the delivery market; large spreads between the expiring futures price and the prices of the same commodity at other locations; uneconomic flows of the commodity to the delivery market prior to contract expiration; abnormally large shipments of the commodity from the delivery market after contract expiration; and abnormally small shipments from the delivery market before contract expiration.

Any other activities considered manipulative should be spelled out in detail rather than left to the imaginations of interested parties and adjudicators. As one example, spreading false rumors in order to influence price could be banned. The list of these other activities should be short. Other than market-power manipulation and perhaps the spreading of false rumors, most of the actions sometimes described as manipulative are of minor practical importance, impose little or no harm on market users, and are very costly to deter or prevent because they are very difficult to detect.

Finally, the law should allow courts to impose sanctions that are sufficiently powerful to make market-power manipulation an unprofitable activity. Courts should be allowed to consider the profitability of a manipulation and evidence on the deadweight losses attributable to a corner (due, for example, to consumption and transportation distortions) when setting monetary penalties for market manipulation. The allowable fine should also be high enough to permit a court to impose penalties in excess of the amount of damages resulting from a manipulation. As noted earlier, punitive sanctions of this sort permit more efficient deterrence.

The advantages of the alternative system are clear. It imposes severe penalties with high probability on those that abuse the integrity of futures markets by exercising market power. Moreover, it does so without demoralizing legitimate uses of futures markets, as existing regulations do all too frequently. Thus, the adoption of this alternative means of manipulation deterrence should improve substantially the efficiency of United States futures markets. This would clearly redound to the benefits of market users, including commodity merchants and processors and the managers of investment portfolios and futures funds. It would also benefit the myriad customers of these users. In brief, manipulation deterrence is worthwhile but it should be done efficiently as possible. The existing system is unnecessarily costly and its replacement by a harm-based, *ex post* deterrence mechanism firmly grounded in an understanding of the economics of market power would benefit many, including many who are completely unaware of how their lives are affected by the seeming (but deceptive) chaos of the trading pits in Chicago and New York.

Endnotes

[1] Another disadvantage of establishing a settlement price is that the regulator may sometimes impose too high a price, i.e., a supercompetitive price. This allows a would-be manipulator to earn a supercompetitive profit. Indeed, it is possible that a trader can earn a higher profit under a forced settlement than if he is allowed to complete his corner unhindered. I discuss this possibility in Section 6.2.4 infra.

[2] It may be possible to impose losses on a would be manipulator in the *ex ante* regime by forcing a settlement price that is below the competitive price. This is not a very desirable solution, however, as it distorts prices. It is by no means clear that a manipulation attempt that leads to the imposition of an artificially low price is any less costly than an attempt that leads to an artificially high price. This form of intervention is inconsistent with the fundamental objective of manipulation deterrence: namely, to preserve the integrity of the pricing process. In any event, it is always possible to level fines or damages *ex post* that impose the same cost as a subcompetitive settlement price. Therefore, harm-based sanctions can impose the same penalty at smaller social cost than setting a settlement price.

[3] This is not a mere theoretical possibility. In May 1979 the CFTC forced settlement of the maturing wheat futures contract at the CBT because manipulation was suspected. The CFTC imposed a settlement price equal to the price that prevailed in the pit before the intervention. Note, however, that the CFTC intervened in part because there was evidence that this price was artificially high. See Jerry Markham, Manipulation of Commodity Futures Prices: the Unprosecutable Crime, 8 Yale J. on Reg. 339-342 (1991). Thus, if its suspicion about the possibility of manipulation was correct, the agency imposed settlement at a supercompetitive price that already reflected traders' anticipation of a squeeze. Although this price was probably lower than what would have been reached in the absence of intervention, it still allowed longs to earn a supercompetitive return.

[4] The regulator could be an exchange, or a government body.

[5] Shorts may have an incentive to engage in rent seeking activity in an *ex post* regime if they can collect monetary damages from a long found guilty of manipulation. This may induce them to expend resources in legal efforts to extract settlements from innocent traders. The practical importance of this sort of rent seeking is minor, however. Exploiting the legal system for private gain by bringing a manipulation case is profitable only to the extent that mistaken convictions—That is, Type I errors--are likely. Since the probability of Type I error is likely to be small in the *ex post* regime, opportunistic shorts face the prospect of receiving little in return for their legal expenses. Moreover, even if this problem is potentially serious, it is readily corrected by relying only on criminal fines to deter corners and eschewing civil damages or reparations.

[6] Steven Shavell, The Optimal Structure of Law Enforcement, 36 J. of Law & Econ. 255 (1993).

[7] In theory, broad position limits on both short and long positions prior to the delivery period could reduce the frequency and severity of manipulation by reducing the variability of order flow. Position limits should reduce volume overall. According to the analysis in note 10 of Chapter 3, the order imbalances become less variable when volume declines. This reduction in the volatility of the net order flow would in turn tend to make manipulation more difficult and therefore less likely.

This means of reducing manipulation is extremely indirect and, as noted in the text, constrains the ability of futures markets to perform their essential functions. Position limits that bind only in the delivery month would reduce the frequency and severity of manipulation directly and with less deleterious effects on risk bearing and price discovery. Therefore, narrow position limits dominate broad position limits.

[8] See, for instance, Kenneth Garbade and William Silber, Futures Contracts with Multiple Varieties: An Analysis of Premiums and Discounts, 56 J. of Bus. 249 (1984); Linda Edwards and Franklin Edwards, A Legal and Economic Analysis of Manipulation, 4 J. of Futures Markets 237 (1984); and Daniel Fischel and David Ross, Should the Law Prohibit "Manipulation" in Financial Markets?, 105 Harvard L. Rev. 503 (1991).

[9] Herb Johnson, Options on the Maximum of Minimum of Several Assets, 22 J. of Fin. & Quant. Anal. 277 (1984), derives this expression and provides the formula for the weights.

[10] Stephen Craig Pirrong, Roger Kormendi, and Philip Meguire, Multiple Delivery Points, Pricing Dynamics, and Hedging Effectiveness in Futures Markets for Spatial Commodities, 14 J. of Futures Markets (1994), and Grain Futures Markets: An Economic Appraisal, ch. 5 (1993).

[11] The data are biased for two reasons. First, a given warehouse receipt for grain can be delivered several times during the delivery month. Over the 1984 through 1989 period, the ratio of deliveries to registered warehouse stocks in Chicago was larger than 2 for corn, soybeans, and wheat. Thus, the numerator in the ratio is biased by a factor of approximately 2. Second, the measure of hedging positions outstanding used is the number of recorded exchange for physical transactions. Since EFPs represent only a fraction of the number of hedges outstanding, the denominator of the ratio of deliveries to hedges is biased downward by a substantial amount. Together, these biases imply that only a small fraction of hedges are closed by delivery.

[12] Gary Libecap, Contracting for Property Rights (1992), shows how distributive conflicts can prevent the creation of efficient property rights.

[13] Stephen Craig Pirrong, The Self-Regulation of Commodity Exchanges: The Case of Market Manipulation, 38 J. of Law & Econ. 141 (1995).

[14] Charles Taylor, 2 A History of the Chicago Board of Trade 623-624 (1917).

[15] Robert W. Bouilly, The Development of American Cotton Exchanges, 1870-1916 406,436 (Ph.D. dissertation, University of Missouri, 1975).

[16] 187 U.S. 664 and 226 U.S. 525.

[17] 2 Report of the Federal Trade Commission on the Methods and Operations of Grain Exporters 16 (1922). *Congestion* is a euphemism often employed in lieu of *corner* or *squeeze* or *manipulation.*

[18] Pirrong, supra note 13.

[19] Id.

[20] 1 Federal Trade Commission, The Cotton Trade 20 (Senate Doc. 100, 68th Cong., 1st Sess., 1924).

[21] In January 1923, the President of the CBT, John J. Stream, stated that "It [i.e., manipulation] is a problem which the national government has seen fit to regulate by the creation of an un-American system of bureaus and commissions for business inquisition and control. Our neglect to correct the abuses that have entered into our trade has brought on us the Capper-Tincher law, with its destruction of our individual freedom of action." Federal Trade Commission, 2 Report of the Federal Trade Commission on the Methods and Operations of Grain Exporters 18 (1922).

[22] Two Chicago reporters who covered the 1989 fraud cases at the CBT and CME and who are by no means shills for the exchanges, write that these congressional inquiries "rivaled the Salem witch hunts for objectivity." David Greising and Laurie Morse, Brokers, Bagmen, and Moles 55 (1991).

[23] Senate Hearings on the Futures Trading Act, at 79, 84. Ironically, a large "May squeeze" executed by a grain exporter named Field rocked the Chicago Board of Trade on the very day that Barnes testified before the Senate. The price of May wheat on the CBT rose $.17 per bushel (almost 10 percent) on the last day of trading in May 1921 and the price of cash wheat fell $.20 per bushel (12 percent) on June 1, 1921. This squeeze annoyed Barnes and he vented great bitterness at the exchange in private correspondence with his business partner. He wrote "nothing has embarrassed, in recent years, like the gyrations in Chicago May on the last day--the very day we were arguing before the Senate Committee that the governors of these exchanges were making some progress themselves in eliminating manipulation." 2 Federal Trade Commission, supra note 17, at 23. It is of great

interest to note how the attitudes of CBT witnesses changed as a result of this episode. In his testimony on the FTA before the House committee on April 28, 1921 (one month before the Field squeeze), the President of the exchange--Mr. Griffen--asserted confidently (and almost scornfully) that the exchange could effectively prevent manipulation without any government oversight. On the very day of the squeeze, Barnes also argued strongly (although more courteously than Griffen) that self-regulation was sufficient. After the squeeze, however, the exchange's representative was much less confident. Interestingly, Griffen did not testify personally. Instead, in June, 1921 he sent another exchange member, former president L. F. Gates, to appear in his place. (Perhaps Griffen was reluctant to appear due to embarrassment over his previous strong statements in light of the Field episode.) In a clear contrast to Griffen's attitude in April, Gates was much less confident of the exchange's ability to deter manipulation single-handedly. He stated, "The trade recognizes the manipulator as an enemy of the whole organization. We dislike him as much of any of you gentlemen do, and if we could find any way of shutting him out absolutely, we would do so. *Maybe you can help us on some of these problems*" (emphasis added). Senate Hearings on the Future Trading Act, at 328.

[24] Id. at 96.

[25] By this, Senator Norris meant that Congress was unable to devise sanctions that could be applied directly to individual manipulators, as numerous witnesses had suggested.

[26] Senate Hearings on the Futures Trading Act, at 335.

[27] President B. L. Hargis of the Kansas City Board of Trade argued that the anti-manipulation clause of the FTA "passes the buck back to the board." Senate Hearings on the Futures Trading Act, at 274.

[28] President Hargis believed that the task of preventing manipulation or face the closure of their market by the government imposed an "appalling" burden on an exchange's decision makers. Id.